*I*n *Managing Telework*, Jack Nilles illustrates that telework is undeniably the corporate wave of the future on a global level. Telework, or telecommuting, a term coined originally by Nilles, means basically moving the work to the worker instead of the other way around. Although there are both risks and opportunities involved in managing a virtual workforce, the opportunities usually far outweigh the risks. As Nilles explains, the key to a successful virtual workforce is making the best use of those opportunities through proper planning and the development of an appropriate management style. Management philosophy, style, and technique constitute the foundation of this indispensable resource.

Managing Telework provides crucial information on every part of the telecommuting process. Nilles first explores the issues of selecting the right type of telecommuter—candidates who are likely to be effective workers without the structured environment of the office—and how to find or make proper workplaces for an eff program. He then goes on to often unspoken managerial ing: the threat of losing con  that leaders, not administrators, are the key players in successful telecommuting, and that leadership can be taught. There must also be a basis of trust between the worker and the manager, and constant, open communication.

(continued on back flap)

MANAGING
Telework

Upside Books examines events in business and management through the lens of technology. *Upside Magazine* is the preeminent magazine for executives and managers eager to understand the business of high-tech.

PUBLISHED:

High Tech, High Hope: Turning Your Vision of Technology into Business Success, Paul Franson

Risky Business: Protect Your Business from Being Stalked, Conned, or Blackmailed on the Web, Daniel S. Janal

Web Commerce: Building a Digital Business, Kate Maddox

Managing Telework: Strategies for Managing the Virtual Workforce, Jack M. Nilles

FORTHCOMING:

Silicon Gold Rush: The Next Generation of High-Tech Stars Rewrite the Rules of Business, Karen Southwick

PEOPLE · TECHNOLOGY · CAPITAL
UPSIDE
WWW.UPSIDE.COM

MANAGING
Telework

Strategies for Managing the Virtual Workforce

JACK M. NILLES

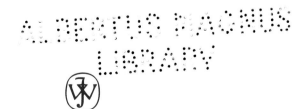

John Wiley & Sons, Inc.

New York · Chichester · Weinheim · Brisbane · Singapore · Toronto

Illustrations by Christine Suddick Neiburger

This book is printed on acid-free paper. ∞

This publication is designed to provide accurate and authoritative information in regard to the subject matter covered. It is sold with the understanding that the publisher is not engaged in rendering professional services. If professional advice or other expert assistance is required, the services of a competent professional person should be sought.

Library of Congress Cataloging-in-Publication Data:

Nilles, Jack M.
    Managing telework : strategies for managing the virtual workforce
  / Jack M. Nilles.
      p.   cm.
    Includes index.
    ISBN 0-471-29316-4 (cloth : alk. paper)
    1. Telecommuting centers—Management. I. Title.
HD2336.3.N55 1998
658.3—dc21   98-13509
                                                CIP

Printed in the United States of America.

10 9 8 7 6 5 4 3 2 1

To Laila

Preface

This book is the result of more than twenty-five years of thinking about and testing teleworking. After almost two decades of being a "rocket scientist" designing various types of spacecraft for the U.S. government and managing a number of research and development programs, I began to think about ways by which all of that technology could be applied to "the real world." In my education as a physicist and engineer with a liberal arts background, as well as my subsequent management assignments, I learned to continually question the fundamentals: *Why are we doing things this way? Why can't we use technology to do things better?* Two series of events changed the direction of my thinking.

The first was an assignment in 1970 to brief James Fletcher, the incoming Director of NASA on the potential civilian applications of space in the 1980s, a twenty-year forecast for NASA's planning purposes. Many of the interesting applications we postulated had to do with communications satellites. One of them revolved around sending medical information via satellite from the U.S. to Africa in order to help cope with a natural disaster. The satellite was used because it wasn't possible to send the doctors there in time. The experiences with the famine in Ethiopia, the Sudan and Somalia more than twenty years later were an eerie reminder of that scenario.

The second series of events was a set of visits I paid to city planners in 1971. A recurring item in our discussions was the problem of reducing the commuting that was polluting the landscape. Again, the questions kept circulating: Why are we doing things this way? Why not use our technology to make things better? We got around to the possible uses of telecommunications and computers to do the job. The proverbial light bulb went on in my head. An epiphany. This was an incredibly simple and powerful idea. One that could change the world. Why do we all have to GO to work when technology allows most of us to work at or near home at least some of the time?

I spent a good part of that year and the next trying to talk my company and the National Science Foundation into supporting some research on what I called the telecommunications-transportation tradeoff. My point was, no matter how brilliant the idea, it had to be reduced to practice—and shown to make good economic sense—in order to be widely accepted. In order to test the concept, my company would have to hire economists, lawyers and psychologists, among others, to make sure that it really worked. No soap. The company wanted to stick strictly to engineering problems, not fool with that fuzzy sociological stuff.

In frustration, I complained one day to one of my colleagues, Dr. Jack Munushian, who had left my company to develop (among other things) an interactive instructional television system at the University of Southern California. At his suggestion I, too, moved to USC in 1972. In 1973 I headed an interdisciplinary research team that received a grant from the National Science Foundation (where the idea apparently had been percolating for a year or two). The objective of the grant was to study federal policy issues on the telecommunications-transportation tradeoff, using a real live company as a test bed.

However, *Development of Policy on the Telecommunications-Transportation Tradeoff,* the grant's title, does not come trippingly off the tongue, so I had to think of a term for this concept that was more direct and intuitive. *Telecommuting* was the result, followed shortly by *teleworking* to describe broader applications. The project went swimmingly. In 1974 we published the final report, followed by a book, *The Telecommunications-Transportation Tradeoff: Options for Tomorrow,* that was published in 1976 in the U.S. and in 1977 in Japan.

In the midst of the project, early in 1974, I had an experience that I have often used to illustrate the motivation for telecommuting. I was driving (alone, like most of my freewaymates) from home to the university one morning. As usual, the traffic was start and stop, mostly stop, on the Santa Monica "Free"way. The freeway has a series of large electric signboards located at intervals along its median strip. The purpose of the signboards is to flash traffic advisories to the freeway occupants. That morning there I was, completely stopped, staring at a seemingly endless string of glowing red brakelights ahead of me. I glanced up at the electric signboard ahead. It said: MAINTAIN YOUR SPEED. My speed was zero! And the clock was ticking. I was convinced that telecommuting had a future.

Having demonstrated that telecommuting was economically effective, our team thought that the world would then follow the better mousetrap (or field of dreams) scenario. For several years I tried to encourage various federal agencies to launch further demonstration projects, if only to see whether our 1973–74 project was a fluke. None would. The general excuse was: it's not our mission. It was not the mission of the U.S. Department of Transportation because its task was to improve roads, freeways, and mass transit systems, not reduce demand for them. It was not the mission of the U.S. Department of Energy because its job was to increase automobile engine efficiency, not reduce automobile use. It was not the mission of the Environmental Protection Agency, because its job was to reduce automobile pollution, not reduce the number of polluters, and so on. Bureaucratic ring around the rosy.

By 1980 I had given up on the feds. The government of the state of California turned out to be more responsive and, in 1983, the California Energy Commission sponsored my study of the energy impacts of teleworking. That study expanded on the work we had done in 1974 and particularized it to California. Again, the results looked promising but, I felt, needed further testing to see if telecommuting really would work as promised for large numbers of people.

Also, during the late 1970s and early 1980s, a number of companies in the U.S. and Europe tried telecommuting on a small scale. Often, the projects failed, usually because the originators had not thought out and prepared for the management issues. The most important of the management issues was the reluctance of managers to change their methods of management. Some of the projects that were successful died later because the intrapreneur who sparked them was promoted out of the program before they had reached critical mass. The continuing successes tended to go underground; the companies wouldn't talk about them. Their shyness was easily explained: why tell your competitors that you have a method of increasing productivity by more than 10%—while actually reducing costs—that doesn't require much of an investment?

This situation convinced me that telecommuting needed some more demonstration projects that were both public, in that the results would be made available, and quantitative; they had to show the bottom-line impacts.

In the mid-1980s, I was able to assemble a group of Fortune 100 companies, to support and participate in a project at the Center for Futures Research at USC, that would make another extended test of telecommuting. The results were similar to those of a decade earlier. Telecommuting still worked and the primary barriers to it were still the attitudes and training of managers. Technology was not a particular problem.

The 1983 Energy Commission project instigated a request by the state of California to plan a telecommuting demonstration project. We completed that in 1985, with a number of state agencies participating in the plan development. In 1987, the state decided to go ahead with a multi-agency, multi-year demonstration project involving more than 230 telecommuters. By 1990 it, too, was a success. The governor established telecommuting as a mandatory option to be considered by every state agency, both as a means of travel reduction and for disaster preparedness. The Loma Prieta earthquake of 1989 may have had an influence on that decision; several telecommuters in our project, from the California Public Utilities Commission, were able to keep right on working from home, even though the Commission's office building in downtown San Francisco was closed for post-quake cleanup and repairs.

During all this period, the global forces toward telecommuting were strengthening: the population was growing; air pollution and the daily commute were getting worse; young families were being forced to move farther away from their employers in order to find affordable housing; political instability in the Middle East continued; energy conservation was still an issue; the other ways of reducing car use for commuting—ride sharing and increased mass transit use—weren't having enough impact.

And the word was getting around. Millions of U.S. information workers were becoming *teleguerillas,* inventing telecommuting for themselves and somehow convincing their supervisors to let them work at home part of the time. The Southern California Association of Governments ran a small internal test of telecommuting. California's South Coast Air Quality Management District issued Regulation XV: a requirement that employers with at least 100 employees reporting to a specific site in the area require ride sharing, telecommuting or some other way of reducing the number of cars coming into the parking lot—or pay a stiff fine. The Telecommuting Advisory Council was formed in Los Angeles to spread the word about telecommuting. The Washington State Energy Office initiated a public-private-sector multi-year demonstration of telecommuting in the Puget Sound area. Both the city and county of Los Angeles began telecommuting programs for their employees; the county's as an operational reality, the city's as a demonstration program. The Federal Government began its

Flexiplace program. In 1992 the European-Community-sponsored European Community Telework Forum began a continuing series of seminars around Europe to inform government and business of the advantages of teleworking. In 1993, the EC funded an initiative to demonstrate telecommuting in four major European cities. The state of California started its Telecenters program to establish a set of neighborhood telework centers throughout the state. On January 17, 1994, a major earthquake in the Los Angeles area—and its destruction of major sections of freeways—caused a massive reawakening to the potential of telecommuting at all levels of government and business.

Ever since we formalized our telecommuting training manuals in the mid-1980s we have been asked to release them to the public. With all of the growing interest in telecommuting, it is clear that there is a need for basic how-to instruction. The first version of this effort was *Making Telecommuting Happen,* a compilation and expansion of those manuals. Published in 1994, shortly after the earthquake, it quickly became known as "the Bible of telecommuting." It comprised two parts: the largest one designed for telemanagers, and a shorter section for telecommuters.

Since 1994 a number of important events and trends have been developing. First, the growth of the Internet has altered the scope of potential management options. Technology, particularly of computers and telecommunications, has continued its rapid growth, to the extent that most office desks in the developed world have microcomputers on or near them. Telework, in its broader sense, has become more important for many types of organizations. Therefore an expansion of *Making Telecommuting Happen* was in order. In particular, there is a need for a comprehensive volume on telework that concentrates and expands on the management issues, including future global trends.

That is the intent of this book.

JACK M. NILLES

Los Angeles
August 1998

Acknowledgments

An enormous number of people contributed to this book in one way or another. Among the first were the regional planners who goaded me into rethinking the problems of transportation congestion; Zohrab Kaprielian and Jack Munushian of USC, who talked me into jumping from outer space to the earth's surface; and my colleagues at The Aerospace Corporation whom I was able to infect with enthusiasm about this crazy idea in 1970. The research faculty team at USC, particularly Paul Gray, Rick Carlson and Gerry Hanneman, were major contributors to that first proof-of-concept project in 1973. Paul Gray has continued his contributions to telecommuting since then, lately at Claremont Graduate University. Rich Harkness of Boeing, Peter Goldmark of CBS Laboratories, Alex Reid of University College in London, Joe Coates of the National Science Foundation, Quincy Jones (the architect) and Murray Turoff of the New Jersey Institute of Technology also helped crystallize my thinking in those early days.

Burt Nanus and Sel Enzer of USC's Center for Futures Research, and Warren Bennis of the Graduate School of Business Administration at USC have given me moral support and contributed their special insights for years. Monty Mohrman and Omar El Sawy of USC were instrumental in honing some evaluation concepts for telecommuting. Rick Higgins of Pacific Bell, Frank Miller of IBM, Dennis Acebo of GTE, and Donna Stubbs of Honeywell were important players in making telecommuting happen in the mid 1980s. Those projects helped prompt my development of telecommuting training manuals.

As the instigator and manager of the California Telecommuting Project, beginning in 1984, David Fleming was a major force in making telecommuting happen in California government. He and his collaborator, Lis, also contributed their senses of humor at stressful points—it isn't always easy to make telecommuting happen. David continued his dedication to telecommuting in the

California Neighborhood Telecenters Program and again within state government and his own Web site. Susan Herman and Wally Siembab served in similar roles for the city of Los Angeles project. Wally has continued to contribute his insights since the official end of that project in 1993. He has added further anecdotes from his role in the Telecommunications for Clean Air program and the Blue Line TeleVillage, as well as our own urban tele-development project for the City of Modesto, California. Susan was instrumental in the development of the Southern California Telecommuting Partnership. Gil Gordon has offered his humor and cogent observations since the mid-1980s.

Hundreds of telecommuters and telemanagers have been given previous versions of much of this material over the past decade. They are the people who ultimately had to make telecommuting happen in the real world. They have done a great job of it. Their comments have instigated a number of additions and revisions to the various versions of the manuals and to *Making Telecommuting Happen.*

Christine Suddick Neiburger has added her inimitable sense of humor—sharpened by personal telecommuting experience—to help humanize what could easily become a very dry topic. A cogent validation of her skill was when one of our telecommuter trainees pointed to the cartoon that now caps Chapter 11 and said: *"That's me!"* Her cartoons are the most often requested excerpts from *Making Telecommuting Happen.* Kristin Kirkpatrick, our associate for the California Neighborhood TeleCenters marketing program, was and is a down-to-earth source of knowledge and inspiration (including Chapter 12).

The editorial staff at Wiley did a masterful job. Special thanks to Jeanne Glasser and Debra Alphers for their quick response times and excellent advice.

A constant source of inspiration and motivation for at least two score years has been my wife and partner, Laila (the LA of JALA). Without her help, understanding, participation and encouragement, this book (as well as all of my others) might not have been written.

A major problem with writing acknowledgments is that someone is always left out in the heat of final delivery deadlines. For that I apologize in advance.

J.M.N.

Contents

Introduction
and Overview

> **Teleworking:** ANY form of substitution of information technologies (such as telecommunications and computers) for work-related travel; moving the work to the workers instead of moving the workers to work.
>
> **Telecommuting:**[1] Periodic work out of the principal office, one or more days per week either at home, a client's site, or in a telework center.

This is a guide to what seems to many to be a new kind of work situation: teleworking. As with most new situations, it presents both opportunities and risks. The term telework refers to a growing array of alternative work styles that involve substituting telecommunications for what was formerly done via travel—or was not possible at all. Telecommuting, as defined above, emphasizes that major portion of telework that acts to reduce or eliminate that stressful daily commute to work for employees (or owners) of an organization. Our tests over the past (almost three) decades have shown that, for most organizations, managers and teleworkers, the opportunities of teleworking far outweigh the risks. The key to making the best use of these opportunities is proper planning and the development of an appropriate management style. Management philosophy, style, and technique are the main subjects of this book.

---

[1] More formally, the partial or total substitution of telecommunications technologies, possibly with the aid of computers, for the commute to work.

1

The book is designed to be a ready reference to you as—and after—you embark upon a rewarding experience as a manager of teleworkers, or a teleworker yourself.

There are 13 chapters and 5 appendices. Chapter 1 describes telecommuting, the arguments for and against it, and its various options. Chapters 2 and 3 explore the issues of selecting people who are likely to be good telecommuters and finding or making the proper workplaces for effective telecommuting. Chapters 1 and 2 are mostly review material if you already have been selected as a telemanager.

Chapter 4 explores both today's and future technology needs as telecommuting grows. Its fundamental message is that contemporary, readily available levels of technology are perfectly adequate for large quantities of telecommuting. Chapter 5 gets at that central, often unspoken managerial fear of telecommuting: the threat of losing control. If you don't read anything else in this book, read Chapter 5. It contains a revolutionary central theme: *leaders, not administrators, are what make telecommuting work well.* Leadership *can* be taught. A good leader of telecommuters is a good manager in general. Poor leadership and telecommuting disasters seem to be inseparable. Aside from those philosophical issues, Chapter 5 treats the key procedures for successfully managing telecommuters.

Chapter 6 discusses some of the formalities of telecommuting, rules and regulations, both from the management point of view and the externally imposed ones, such as union rules and zoning laws. This is the chapter that usually gets reworked by the corporate legal staff and/or union representatives. It is very important to study this chapter, discuss it with senior management—and the legal staff—and make any necessary revisions, *before* formal telecommuting begins. Chapter 9 continues that line of thought, concentrating on training workers to cope in different telecommuting situations.

Chapter 7 gets down to the all-important bottom line. Regardless of how warm and fuzzy telecommuting makes everyone feel, we live in a world where economic competitiveness and survival are real and daily issues. Chapter 7 reviews these matters from all sides: the employer, the telecommuter, and the community. However, the emphasis is on the employer's point of view because that's who makes the critical decision to allow or encourage telecommuting.

Chapter 8 focuses on telework from the point of view of the teleworker, although every telecommuter should also read Chapters 3 and 6. Chapter 8 concentrates on the details of setting up a home office. It also reviews the practical aspects of peaceful coexistence with the other members of the teleworkers household, neighbors, boss, and colleagues.

Related to the issues of management control is that of the design of organizations. Telework and its underlying technologies can enable new ways of addressing organizational design problems. With telework, entirely new organizational forms become practical on a global scale. These are reviewed in Chapter 10.

While each of the 10 initial chapters focuses on one aspect of telework, Chapter 11 ties it all together with a prose checklist of the steps needed to mount a successful telework demonstration program. Use this as a review of your own program plans in order to make sure that you haven't left anything out.

If you are also developing a telework center, particularly if it is to attract multiple clients, be sure to read Chapter 12. It covers both the philosophy and the practical details of getting your message to your potential occupants.

And then there is the big picture. Telework and telecommuting are not confined to the United States. Although the U.S. is currently the world leader, many other countries are testing various forms of telework. In fact, the European Commission has a program involving multi-tens of millions of ECU's (soon to become Euros) to support telework research and implementation programs. Chapter 13 takes a peek into telework's future around the world, as well as some of its implications.

Finally, there is a set of appendices that provide sample forms for various aspects of the mutual employer-employee agreement on the terms of telecommuting. Your legal staff, too, should scour this, before formal telecommuting begins. The appendices end with a brief primer on futures research, to help you plan the impacts of telework in your own company.

This book is a variant and major expansion of the one we have been using since the mid-1980s for Fortune 100 companies and large government and/or public sector organizations. Although I often use the term *company* in what follows, please take that to mean your own organization, of whatever size and type.

The book is written under the presumption that your company will want to test (we prefer *demonstrate)* telecommuting with a selected sample of the staff before making it generally available to all eligible employees. Therefore, in many places the book discusses telecommuting in terms of the "Company Demonstration

Project." After a demonstration project of suitable duration (say, at least one year) is complete, then more permanent rules can be written that apply to your firm, based on that experience.

One other point: although the terms *teleworking* and *telecommuting* may seem to be used interchangeably in this book, I have tried to use *teleworking* when the topic being discussed applies to *all* forms of telework. I use *telecommuting* when the topic is most relevant to that local aspect of telework. Please note that most—at least 80%—of contemporary teleworking is telecommuting, although the future holds much promise for the more general forms.

Concepts of Teleworking

■ PRINCIPLES OF DECENTRALIZATION

Teleworking is a form of *distributed* or *decentralized* work. Since the industrial revolution started early in the 19th century the trend in industrializing countries has been to *centralize* workplaces. The reason is simple: industries, factories and assembly plants, needed centralization. To run efficiently, they needed to be located near sources of materials, supplies, and production workers: cities and their transportation hubs. As industries grew, so did the cities in which they were located. As new forms of transportation developed it was possible to make ever bigger cities, with ever bigger industries hiring ever bigger and more concentrated workforces. Everything was at hand to the industrial manager: the raw materials brought by train or truck, the processing machines, and the industrial workers. This model of the world pervades our society, even in businesses and government organizations that have nothing to do with manufacturing.

We don't think twice about it. In order to work you must *GO* to work. Just like all the other factory workers.

But the immense success of the industrial revolution has brought with it a number of serious problems. The industrial model of the world doesn't work nearly as well anymore. To paraphrase Fagin in the musical comedy *Oliver,* I think we'll have to think it out again.

■ WHY DECENTRALIZE?

Since the mid-1950s manufacturing has been steadily declining as a source of employment in the developed world. In 1990 only about 1 in 4 U.S. workers were in manufacturing or repair trades; fewer than 1 in 54 U.S. workers were on farms, according to the Bureau of the Census. On the other hand, **57%** or more of the U.S. workforce comprises information or knowledge workers whose jobs derive from their creation, collation, manipulation, transformation, and/or dissemination of information or from their operation of information machines, such as typewriters and computers. Figure 1.1 tells the story: most work now and in the foreseeable future will be information work.

Increasingly these information workers are using telephones, computers, or telecommunications-connected computers to do their work. They are moving their work around, instead of themselves.

Here are some situations where the traditional ways of doing things—centralized work in the information factory—is not only old hat but is counterproductive. Score your own organization on these.

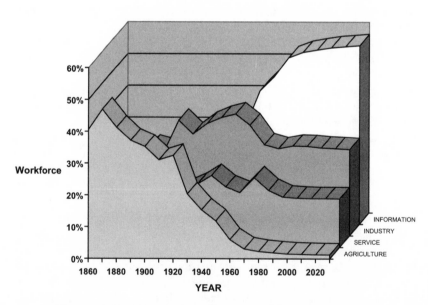

Figure 1.1 Historical and future workforce composition.

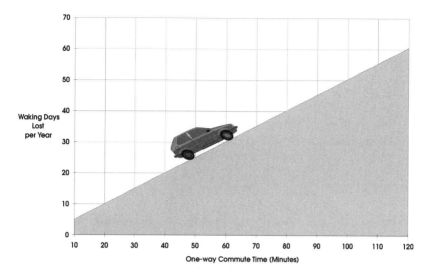

Figure 1.2 Commuting as a time waster.

➤ The commute to (and from) work is more than normally dangerous and/or takes more than **forty** minutes a day **round trip** (for at least half your employees), and during that commute you and/or your employees are not doing something either pleasurable or useful. See Figure 1.2 for a view of what commuting costs you in terms of waking days per year (that is, sixteen-hour days—I assume that you sleep about eight hours per day, but not while you're commuting). Multiply that by every one of your commuters. This one is worth 20 points.

➤ The perils of commuting chronically create late arrivals and early departures among your employees, with adjustment to- or from-work periods immediately adjacent thereto. Minor complaints, problems with the kids and routine dental or medical appointments turn into sick days off. Productivity is sliding. This, too, gets 20 points.

➤ There are too many meetings that are insufficiently focused and wander off into time-wasting, irrelevant topics. Time management is a growing problem.[1] At least 15

---

[1] Scott Adams, the creator of Dilbert, has built a career on his cartoons of situations like this.

points for this. You get 25 points if you attend more than ten meetings per week.

➤ The working environment produces high levels of stress and productivity loss because of those crucial *Three I's:* interruptions, interruptions, and interruptions. This nets 15 points. Minimum.

➤ You are running out of office space—or rental costs have gotten out of hand. Overcrowding is having serious effects on morale and productivity. Another 15 points here; more if you're the facilities manager.

➤ You're having trouble attracting or retaining *skilled* employees. 15 points for this; make it 20 points if your annual turnover rate for skilled workers is higher than 10%, and 40 points if it's higher than 20%. To put it another way, it costs at least six months salary, in terms of lost productivity, search and training costs, to replace a skilled worker.

➤ Air pollution in your area is getting worse. A good part of it is because of all those commuter cars on the roads. Another 15 points for this, 25 points if you're in an area that has strict regional air pollution regulations.

➤ You're increasingly finding that the teams you need for project development require people from distant and diverse locations. Your regional, national, or global expansion plans are severely affected by the supply of competent people. Another 20 points here.

This is by no means an exhaustive list, but it delivers the message: physical centralization brings a variety of problems in urban environments. Big cities, in particular, impose growing costs on everyone who works within them. Further, if the scope of your organization extends beyond your immediate locality, several of the performance issues are magnified. If your score on this list was above 75, centralization is seriously eroding your organization's performance. A score between 50 and 75 shows significant damage and even 15 points or more should cause you to consider whether there might not be a better way than what most organizations have been doing for the past twenty years. Please note that some of the situations just described (such as meetingitis) are not confined to centralized organizations, but sometimes decentralization helps. Also note that centralization can be just as bad—even worse—in the suburbs as in central cities. Just because your company relocated to the boonies, it doesn't get you off the hook. You may also want to change the weighting of some or all of the questions to better suit your organization's priorities. Do so, then test the situation again.

■ HAVING YOUR CAKE AND EATING IT TOO

The industrial motive for centralization—efficient geographic concentration of resources—was vital for effective industrial development. That concentration of resources, that accessibility to the raw materials and tools you need to do the job is equally vital in information work. If you are an information worker you need to have the information necessary for your job; you need to have that information when *you* need it and in the form best suited for your requirements—or at least moldable by your information tools. You and your employees need to be the foci of information flows. Well, of course. That stands to reason. No doubt about it. *[Add your own favorite cliché here.]* Everybody needs centralization!

But suppose you and your employees could get all of this information *without* commuting more than forty minutes (round trip) per day, eroding working time, failing to meet scheduling challenges, getting stressed out, losing key people, violating air quality regulations, and otherwise debilitating the organization. Suppose that you could keep that form of *logical* centralization—continuous access to the information you need to do the job—without the *physical* centralization characteristic of an industrial society.

Well, it's possible. You can keep connected *logically* while decentralizing *physically*. You *can* keep many of your means of production accessible without clumping them together in the same place. You *can* keep your heads together without having to keep your bodies together. You *can* move the work to the worker instead of moving the worker to the work. You and/or your employees *can* telework.

■ HOW IS IT POSSIBLE?

The reason you can telework is that information technology has developed to the point where the necessary information can get to us no matter where or when we are. Our jobs, for some of us, have become *location-independent*. The number of people who fit this category is increasing daily. You probably already have a number of telecommuters in your organization, covert though they may be. There's more on this in Chapter 4 but here is an overview.

➤ Telecommunications

In the last few years telecommunications technology has made significant advances. Electronic switching and fiber optics have multiplied both the speed and volume of telephone circuits where they have been installed. Fiber optic networks have become so capable that they are replacing satellite circuits for many long-distance communication paths.

The telephone network is going digital all over the world. This means that it is becoming easier and more reliable for computers to talk to each other over the phone lines. This digital switching and communications technology also allows a number of new services to be provided to business and residential customers. Call forwarding, call waiting, caller identification, call blocking, auto dialing, voice mail, electronic banking, telephone-, computer-, and video-teleconferencing, and more are becoming ubiquitous. Cellular telephones add mobility as well as versatility for the individual telecommunications user. LANs, WANs, ISDN, XDSL, and ATM are the acronyms of instant electronic togetherness.[2] The Internet burst into public view in 1993 with the appearance of browsers and the World Wide Web, so that even the smallest companies can have a virtual global presence.

Many kinds of information work may need only one or a few telecommunications services to make teleworking viable. But each new technology addition—and each new reduction in cost for the existing technology—opens the way for more teleworking and more telecommuters.

➤ Computers

Computers, particularly personal computers, add an entirely new range and intensity of colors to the teleworking palette. Personal

---

[2] Local Area Networks, Wide Area Networks, Integrated Services Digital Networks, and Asynchronous Transfer Modes are methods of sending information around the building or the world in digital—computer understandable—form. Although LANs aren't strictly telephone-based, they are often connected to the telephone system.

computers suitable for most routine business functions: text and document processing, spreadsheets, graphics, data banks, and the like, are available for less than what an electric typewriter used to cost a few years ago. Most office desks in the U.S. have computers on or very close to them. Most of those computers will be connected (ultimately, if not at first) to some form of telecommunications, probably a telephone line or a local area network (which in turn will be connected to one or more telephone lines or satellite circuits). Furthermore, the capabilities of the computers, per dollar invested in new hardware, are increasing every year; by a factor of ten about every seven years.

At present it is quite feasible to have a home-based office that has greater information processing capability than the "Principal" (that is, main/headquarters) office, if the principal office has not kept up with technological advances. More than one-third of U.S. households own at least one personal computer. This book was produced in a home-based office. As you see it. A product of teleworking.

■ FORMS OF TELECOMMUTING

There is much more on the technology later. For now, rest assured that there are few technological barriers today for effective teleworking. The biggest barriers are right behind our eyes. But before we look at those, let's examine the different flavors of telecommuting, since that constitutes the primary urban-centric mode of telework—and exemplifies the other modes of telework as well. There are two main variants: home-based and telework center telecommuting. And then there are variants of those variants, to suit your needs.

➤ Chocolate—Home-Based Telecommuting

Everyone loves chocolate. The press particularly love home-based telecommuting. It's such a startling departure from *Work As We Know It*. It immediately captures the imagination: work in idyllic surroundings at home instead of some miserable, stuffy, noisy old office. Work at your own pace, neither pushed nor impeded by your fellow workers. Fit your work life into your family life instead of *vice versa*. Design your own job. Dramatically increase your productivity—and your job opportunities.

Sounds too good to be true, doesn't it?

For some people it *is* true *all* of the time. For many, many others, *some* of it is true *all* of the time. For still more, *some* of it is true *some* of the time. For still others, none of it is true. Part of what we do in the next chapter is to sort these options out.

The basic idea of home-based telecommuting is this:

Home can be an effective base for telecommuting by:

➤ Allowing significant cost reductions for both employer and employee

➤ Allowing employees access to jobs that otherwise might not be available

➤ Allowing employers access to people who otherwise would not be available

➤ Providing significant productivity gains and a host of indirect benefits to society (energy conservation, pollution reduction, etc.)

The air pollution reduction aspect of this is a major incentive for many organizations to be involved in telecommuting, generally in response to increasingly strict environmental regulations. For others, the facilities reduction impacts are the primary incentives.

For most employees, home-based telecommuting works only as a part-time option.

Home-based telecommuters should have a well-defined area that is treated as office space within their homes. Within that space is all the equipment and supplies that are needed for their job.

In 1997, most U.S. telecommuters were home-based, telecommuting only part of the time, according to our own estimates and those of a number of other sources. Estimates of the number of U.S. telecommuters in 1997 ranged from about 15 million (our estimate) to more than 20 million (an estimate presumably including *all* work-at-home people, most of whom are not telecommuters, although many may be teleworkers). About 1,000,000 telecommuters were in Southern California alone.

➤ Vanilla—Satellite Telework Centers

A satellite telework center may seem much less glamorous than home-based telecommuting. A satellite telework center is an office building, or part of a building, that is wholly owned (or leased) by an organization, to which its employees regularly report for work. It looks much like any other set of offices—with some individual cubicles of various sizes, desks, computers, telephones, conference rooms, and so on—although the mixture of these may be different from a more conventional office.

There is one important difference between a satellite office and a traditional office: *all of the center's employees work there because they live closer to that facility than to their regular or principal office, regardless of what their jobs are.* That is, for an organization with several satellite telework centers (or field/branch offices), its telecommuting accountants may be scattered physically among a few or all of the satellites, rather than at a single location to which they all report. The interconnectedness of the Accounting Department comes through telecommunications, not through collocation. Of course, as in home-based telecommuting many, if not most, satellite office telecommuters also telecommute only part-time.

Satellite telework centers can save significant amounts of commuting while still providing environments like those of traditional offices. They also can take advantage of lower costs per square foot of the office space they do use, because of their suburban, small town, or redeveloping central city locations. The main disadvantage of satellite centers is that they require a certain amount of facilities planning and administration to operate effectively. Further, if employees mostly still drive their cars to the centers, the air pollution improvements may be diminished significantly.[3]

➤ Chocolate Chip—Local Telework Centers

A local telework center is almost the same as a satellite center. The difference here is that the building may house employees from several different organizations. Otherwise, each organization's set of offices is arranged as if it were a satellite center.

---

[3] For example, the South Coast Air Quality Management District in Southern California does not count telecommuting to a telework center as the equivalent of eliminating a commute to work unless the one-way commute has been reduced by at least 20 miles.

Some of the additional advantages of local telework centers are: the ability to share services (telecommunications, large computers, cafeterias, environmental control, etc.); the ability to have smaller, distributed offices; relief from building ownership worries. Disadvantages, compared with satellite telework centers, seem to concentrate on less control over office space, including physical security.

Some local telework centers are *very* local, serving a neighborhood. Naturally enough, they are called *neighborhood* telework centers. As you might expect, neighborhood centers tend to support only a few telecommuters, generally fewer than 20. The emphasis in neighborhood centers is to eliminate car use in getting to and from the center. Telecommuters either walk there from home, bicycle or take mass transit. In 1994 the State of California, in its TeleCenters project, began testing several different versions of neighborhood centers scattered throughout the state. The U.S. federal government, in its Flexiplace Program, has established a number of telework centers for federal employees throughout the country. Often, particularly in Europe, the telecenters are located in rural areas, towns, and villages, and combined with other types of businesses, such as retail stores and business services, in the same building.

➤ Tutti Frutti—Combinations

These four (three-and-a-half, really) flavors of telecommuting can be combined and mixed as appropriate for any given organization. For example, most home-based telecommuters will work part-time at home, the rest of the time in their principal office, a satellite, or a local telework center. A few home telecommuters will still go to the office most days, but will telecommute at both ends of the workday, going to and from the office during off-peak traffic hours. (This is OK for cutting commuting time but doesn't have much of an impact on reducing air pollution.) Satellite and local centers in well-designed operations are likely to have both permanent office space for their full-time employees and temporary spaces both for their home or occasional telecommuters and for employees from other cities who need temporary space during a trip.

The central criterion for telecommuting is the same for all of these:

> If a job, or major portions of it, does not intrinsically depend on the location of the worker, then it is teleworkable.

The issue then becomes one of who, when, where, and how, not whether.

The issue of who and when comes in the next chapter.

■ BUT DOES IT PAY?

Unquestionably. Our own experience and that of others shows a number of benefits of successful teleworking, benefits for employers, employees and the community at large. These benefits include:

➤ Significantly increased productivity
➤ Reduced turnover rates (and related new employee recruitment and training costs)
➤ Reduced office space requirements
➤ Lowered real estate costs
➤ Better management
➤ Increased organizational flexibility
➤ Faster response times
➤ Increased employee morale
➤ A cleaner environment
➤ Reduced energy consumption and diminished dependence on fossil fuels
➤ Greater participation by teleworkers in local civic activities

This is what you can expect to get from *successful* teleworking. Our experience has been that new teleworking programs, even including all the costs of planning, design, organization, technology change, training and management innovation, will pay for themselves in a year or less.

Unfortunately, as in so many other areas of life, it is distinctly possible to have *unsuccessful* teleworking. There are many ways to do it wrong, several of which have already been tried and proven by large organizations. In an unsuccessful teleworking program the reverse of the list above can occur.

Which is why this book exists. There are a few key principles to making teleworking work. None of these principles is particularly difficult or revolutionary; they are simply good management practices. But they are more important, perhaps, in teleworking than in ordinary management situations. Here they are:

➤ Pick your teleworkers carefully;

➤ Set up the proper working environments and technology and telecommunications support;

➤ Jointly establish performance-oriented evaluation procedures;

➤ Train the teleworkers, their co-workers, and (as appropriate) their families;

➤ Get frequent feedback on how well you're doing; and

➤ Alter your procedures and rules, as appropriate, in response to the feedback.

■ TELECOMMUTING VERSUS TELEWORKING

Much of the preceding discussion—and of this book—concentrates on telecommuting, the substitution of information technology for the commute to and from work, as defined in the Introduction and Overview. But most of the material in this book also applies to teleworking as well. The two are related as shown in Figure 1.3.

Telecommuting is a form of teleworking. In fact, if you stretch the commute distance to a few hundred miles, or whatever distance precludes frequent commuting, you have teleworking. Teleworking also includes your everyday travel substitution that occurs while you're in your principal office—after you have commuted to work. Almost everyone is a teleworker at least some of the time.

In Europe, the situation is somewhat more confusing. Several European languages have no word for commuting,[4] so telecommuting is lumped together with other forms of telesubstitution under teleworking. Whatever you call it, the operating principles are the same.

The importance of teleworking and telecommuting is a question of degree. A little telecommuting/teleworking may not make an enormous difference to you, your company or your country. But as the amount of telesubstitution increases, so do the options for organizational design and effectiveness, life-style, family and other social relationships, even the shape and nature of villages,

---

[4] In 1992 the French coined a term for telecommuting: *télépendulaire*. Loosely translated, it means going back and forth, pendulum-like, at a distance. The Swedish and Spanish versions are similar (*telependla* and *telependlando*, respectively). As of this writing, there appears to be no comparable term in German, or any of the Finno-Ugric languages.

Figure 1.3 The relationship between telecommuting and teleworking.

towns and cities. Teleworking and its telecommuting components provide tools for change that, properly used, can have positive effects on all of these.

The following chapters address the nature and uses of those tools. By following them, you can enhance your chances of developing and maintaining an effective telecommuting or teleworking operation.

Chapter 2

Selecting Teleworkers

Over the years we have developed a feel for what it takes to make teleworking work. A feel backed up by almost three decades of empirical data. It is possible, we believe, to estimate, before the fact, the likely success of a potential teleworking situation. The first step is picking the teleworkers themselves. This is done in two stages. The first stage relates to the nature of the job that is to be done. Some jobs are simply not good candidates for one or the other—or any—forms of teleworking. Some jobs are ideal for teleworking. Similarly, some job incumbents are perfectly suited for teleworking, others would be unhappy in some or all teleworking situations.

Thus there are two parts to the teleworker selection process. The first part consists of an examination of the content of a potential teleworker's job. The second part, of most importance to home teleworkers, is an evaluation of the psychological/behavioral aspects of the job and of the potential teleworkers, their colleagues, and their supervisors.

■ DISSECTING JOBS

It is easy to see that some jobs are perfect for teleworking and others are terrible candidates. An author is likely to be a good teleworker, a bus driver wouldn't work out at all as a teleworker. But what about those thousands of jobs that are in the middle somewhere? The way to decide whether a job can be teleworked is to analyze its work locational requirements.

➤ Jobs as Collections of Tasks

Each job, yours, mine, everyone else's, can be viewed as a collection of tasks that must be performed. Tasks are such things as writing reports, analyzing figures, collecting information, providing information, developing plans, coordinating activities of others, digging ditches, painting the house, making coffee. Any job can be analyzed this way. Table 2.1 shows three different, if nameless, information jobs broken down into tasks to be performed.

To test this, try it on your own job. Make a list, not too detailed, of the tasks you have to perform to satisfy the requirements of your job. A dozen or so tasks should cover most of what you do. Table 2.2 provides some space to try it on.

Make sure that you consider your job over a period of time such as a week, or even several weeks or months, to take into account the fact that most jobs vary their structure and work demands from day to day. The task of preparing a report, for example, may take several straight days at a time, but averaged over a period of a few months, report preparation may be only 5% of the total work time.

If you don't like to think in percentages, try fractions. The point here is that we want to get an estimate that is quantitative enough so that you'll have a good idea of the job structure. *Do not use hours as a measure*; what's important here are the proportions of total time spent for each major task type.

Table 2.1 Task Breakdowns for Some Information Jobs

Jobs as Collections of Tasks			
Tasks for Job:	A	B	C
Preparing reports	5%	10%	
Analyzing figures	15%	5%	10%
Collating information	5%		10%
Providing information	5%	5%	10%
Developing plans	20%	5%	
Interacting with the public	10%	20%	10%
Coordinating information	5%	15%	
Presenting information	10%	15%	
Composing letters and memos	5%	10%	25%
Copying information	5%		15%
Retrieving information	10%		20%
Supervising employees	5%	15%	

Table 2.2 Task Breakdown Worksheet

Jobs as Collections of Tasks			
Tasks for:	My Job	_____'s Job	_____'s Job
Total	100%	100%	100%

➤ The Simplified Selection Version

Now do the same thing for some of your employees. Just one or two of them for now, to get an idea of how the pieces of each job fit together: preparing reports, communicating with the public, clients, or co-workers, getting information, performing analyses, whatever.

The main question is: how well can you (or they) do some or all of these tasks from home (assuming that the necessary equipment and files are there to do it) and how much of the job needs to be done in the (or an) office? Chances are that there's some of each; that you or they might be able to work at home part of the time, but there's also a need to be in the office part of the time, too. Estimate how much of the time you and each of these employees *don't* have to be in the office to do each task.

You can rate each job with the assistance of Table 2.3. Here's the procedure.

1. First, let's concentrate on the *Importance to Job* column in Table 2.3. Think about how much time you or your prospective teleworkers spend communicating with other people. The first three items deal with the amount of time spent communicating personally with others, either face-to-face

Table 2.3 General Job Task Analysis

Nature of Tasks	Importance to Job	Suitability for Work at:			
		Traditional Office Only	Telework Center	Part-Time Home	Full-Time Home
High level of face-to-face daily interaction with others	_____	Best solution	Depends on location of others	Poor	No
Large amount of face-to-face interaction but may be clumped in time	_____	Excellent	Excellent	Good to excellent	Fair to poor
High level of interpersonal contact but performed via telecommunications	_____	Excellent	Excellent	Excellent	Good to excellent
Fragmented tasks, many "fire drills" requiring coordination	_____	Good to excellent	Good to excellent	Fair to good	Fair to poor
Fragmented tasks, but often requiring high concentration	_____	Poor	Good to fair	Good to excellent	Good to excellent
Requiring extended concentration, medium to long duration	_____	Poor	Poor to good	Excellent	Excellent
Need physical access to special, fixed resources	_____	Excellent	Excellent (possibly)	Good if access can be clumped	Poor
Involves sensitive information requiring physical security	_____	Excellent	Good to excellent	Good to poor	Poor
Involves sensitive information that can be protected readily (e.g., by encryption)	_____	Excellent	Excellent	Excellent to good	Excellent to good
Totals	_____	_____	_____	_____	_____

or otherwise (over the telephone, by fax, e-mail, etc.). Note that we are concerned with what is *necessary* for the job. This may not be the way it is done today. For example, the first item deals with the *need* for daily face-to-face contact. You may have a job in which you ordinarily have daily face-to-face contact with others most of the time but there are many occasions when you could substitute telephone calls, faxes, voice- or e-mail, or videoconferencing for some, if not all, of the contacts.

Here's where it gets a little complicated. *The total of your answers for the importance of these first three items should equal one-tenth of the portion of your time that you spend in such communication.*

For example, let's say you spend 16 hours[1] communicating during an average 40-hour week; that's 40% of your time (16/40ths of the week), so the first 3 entries under Importance to Job should add up to 4 (or one-tenth of 40%). If all of that time is spent in meetings or other face-to-face conversation, then the first two entries should add up to 4 and the third entry should be 0. If, on the other hand, all your communicating time is on the phone, then the first two entries should be 0 and the third should be 4. Most people have a number in each of the spaces. The trick for maximum teleworking is to arrange life so as to get a 0 in the first entry: zero daily face-to-face meetings. (After this an IRS Form 1040 should be easy!) Don't forget that we're asking about the way that you spend your time over a long period; weeks or months. So average these activities over that kind of period.

2. Next, take each of the remaining items in the *Importance to Job* column; and decide how well it describes the *average requirements* of your (or your employee's) job, on a scale from 0 to 10, where *0* means it *does not apply* to your job and *10* means it applies completely, *all* of the time.

3. Then, look at each of the rows in the table in turn, and add up the points for each column under *Suitability for Work At.* Our ratings are given for each item under *Suitability for Work At:* for the traditional office, telework office, etc. Score 5 points for each Excellent (or Best Solution), 4 for Very Good, 3 for Good (or OK), 2 for Fair, 1 for Poor, and 0 for No. Multiply each rating by your assessment of the requirement level of the job (the number in the *Importance to Job* column, then add all nine ratings to get the column total.

For example, to continue the face-to-face case, a job importance rating of 2 would work out to a score of 10 for the traditional office (Best Solution, or 5×2); some number between 10 (5×2) and 0 (0×2) for the telework center (10 if

---

[1] On average, telecommuters spend about 14 hours per week communicating.

you could still have all the meetings at the center, 0 if you couldn't have any); 2 for part-time home teleworking (Poor, or 1×2); and 0 for full-time home teleworking. Do this scoring for each row and each of the Suitability columns. Now add up all the columns to get a preliminary total score.

And the answer is—whichever column has the highest number of points is the one most suited for that job. For some jobs it's still the traditional office only. For many jobs another column will rate higher. Please note that there is no absolute answer; most jobs can be fitted into several categories with acceptable results.

Now there's one other thing to keep in mind. For this table, make sure you think *only* of the work and communication requirements of the job. Try to divorce those from the personalities involved in your real job, or those of your employees, as if you were filling out a job description for someone else in a different department.

➤ A Slightly More Complicated Version

If you want to explore these issues in more detail, try the following. Use Table 2.4 as an example. If you're into computers, set up the list of tasks as column A of a spreadsheet. Head the column "Tasks for the job of < a job title for a prospective teleworker >." Try it with your job first, in order to get a feel for the method. If computers are not an intimate part of your life, make the list on a piece of paper.

Down the left-hand column (Column A in the spreadsheet), write out a list of the tasks that fulfill the requirements of the listed job. Table 2.4 gives some typical examples. If those don't match your job, enter ones that do. Make sure that everything you are required to do in your job is covered by one of the task items. Keep in mind that these are generic kinds of tasks, analyzing figures, for example, that describe certain kinds of activity.

Label the next column (Column B in the spreadsheet): "Percent of Job." As in the previous analysis, think about how you spend your time over a period of several days to several months; in any case, long enough so that you have spent time doing all of the tasks listed in the first column. If you keep a desk calendar or online scheduler, maybe it would help to refer to it. Now, estimate what percent of that total time you spend doing each of the listed tasks. For example, in Table 2.4 the holder of Job B spends 15% of her time coordinating information and 0% collating information.

Table 2.4 Analysis of Job B

Task	% of the Job	Location Dependent % of Task	Location Dependence as % of Job	Location Independence
Preparing reports	10	10	1	9
Analyzing figures	5	0	0	5
Collating information	0	0	0	0
Providing information	5	60	3	2
Developing plans	5	20	1	4
Interacting with clients or public	20	40	8	12
Coordinating information	15	20	3	12
Presenting information	15	100	15	0
Composing letters and/or memos	10	0	0	10
Copying information	0	0	0	0
Retrieving information	0	0	0	0
Supervising others	10	20	2	8
Keeping current	5	0	0	5
TOTAL LOCATION INDEPENDENCE				67
REALITY FACTOR (average in-office days/week)				3
AVERAGE PRACTICAL INDEPENDENCE* (potential home teleworking days/wk)				2

* Assuming a five-day week. For compressed or other modified work schedules, subtract the number after Reality Factor from the average total work days per week to the final answer.

You might want to ask some of your colleagues or people who work for you to complete a similar analysis. Just one or two of them for now, to get an idea of how the pieces of each job fit together.

Now comes an important part. Make another column (Column C in the spreadsheet). Label it "Location-Dependent Percent of Task."

What we're looking for here is a number that summarizes the fraction of time that specifically depends on the location of the person who performs the task. This number is composed of three elements. To keep Table 2.4 less daunting, we show only the one column; but think of each entry as composed of three elements:

➤ The face-to-face requirement

➤ Dependencies on specific, fixed locations

➤ Dependencies on alternate or variable locations

➤ Separating Face-to-Face and Other Location-Dependent Tasks from the Rest

Face-to-Face Tasks

First, for each task, decide how much of its successful performance *requires* that there be *face-to-face* interaction between the performer of the task and other people. The *requires* part of this is important. If interpersonal interaction is needed to do the task, but that interaction can be accomplished over the telephone or by electronic mail or teleconferencing, or even interoffice memo, then face-to-face interaction is not required for the task.

For some parts of your task list, this is a simple problem. If you need to write a report, but only need written reference materials to do it, you have those materials at hand and you're doing the writing on a personal computer, then it is likely that you can put 0% as the percentage of face-to-face interaction required for that task. If the task depends entirely on interacting with others face-to-face, such as checking out groceries in a supermarket, put 100% in that slot.

Maybe it's more complex than that. If you need a secretary to handle the text production for the report, estimate the fraction of time that you must interact face-to-face with your secretary to get the job done. Note that the *fraction of time* is the critical part here. Of the total time you spend (or someone else spends) performing this task, how much has to be face-to-face. If you can do it conveniently over the phone, or by telegram, pony express, smoke signals, or other non-face-to-face medium it doesn't count in the face-to-face race.

Notice that the face-to-face requirement may be dependent on the sophistication of the technology available to you. If you don't even have a telephone, you may need a lot of face-to-face interaction. If you have a switchable, full-motion video teleconferencing system on your desktop, then the need for face-to-face interaction on a daily basis may dwindle into insignificance.

If you're uncertain about how much face-to-face interaction is required, try keeping a short log the next time you have to perform that task. Note how long it took to do that task overall and how much of the time you needed to have face-to-face interaction. If you are analyzing one of your employee's tasks, have him/her keep the log.

Don't get carried away by all of this. We are not searching for Ultimate Truth here, just a first estimate of what goes on in particular jobs.

Other Location Dependence

Now think of the other two of the three location-dependence elements. There are basically two types of necessary location dependence. Type 1, the first of these, encompasses those situations in which specialized or immovable resources are needed for the job, where there are physical security considerations, or where there is something special about a *specific geographic location* that is important.

Type 2 location dependence comprises the circumstances in which it is important to be in *some* location, but the details of where that location is either are not critical or may change from time to time.

Examples of Type 1 dependence are a central file repository (not computerized), a nuclear particle accelerator facility, a major hospital, an airport, a jail,[2] a concert hall or a museum, and a large computer center, the latter only being location-dependent for the operators of the computers. Examples of Type 2 are a branch bank, Social Security, or utilities payment office where people from the neighborhood come to transact business, a conference center, a client's offices, and a shopping center. Even in those installations it is quite likely that not all of the people who are there today *need*

---

[2] Many police detectives are telecommuters. The paper work is done at home but the perpetrators still have to be locked up in person although they can be arraigned via videoconference.

to be there all of their working time. As in the case of the face-to-face requirement, think of the percent of time people *must* be in a specific location.

Where the tasks involve operations using transportable records, such as paper forms whose contents are to be entered into computer files, it is possible to have delivery and pickup arrangements to homes or telework centers in order to allow telecommuting or longer distance teleworking. For example, a "distribution pool" could be arranged so that one worker could distribute the day's/week's forms to the telecommuters. Or workers living nearby might carry materials back and forth in a "paper pool." Or the materials could be sent to one of the organization's facilities that is a short distance from the employee's home—or to a teleworker in another city. In some instances the telecommuter will come on site as necessary to pick up and/or deliver materials and confer with a supervisor and/or co-workers.

➤ Job Design Possibilities

Don't forget some work flow and job design considerations here. For example, let's say that a set of home teleworkers is doing nothing but primary text entry from dictation, while the regular office workers are reduced to correcting the errors of the teleworkers. That is, both groups are given only portions of the overall task, with little means of interaction. This is almost guaranteed to cause scheduling and morale problems. This doesn't mean that teleworking is inapplicable, only that it takes thoughtfulness in the final application. Those assignments should be reevaluated so that the work flow is uninterrupted and neither group feels thwarted.

Here's an example of what can go wrong if you don't consider such things, quoted from *The Wall Street Journal*:[3]

> *TELECOMMUTING: Is it fair to those who still must go in to the office?*
>
> Some 27% of the telecommuters' office colleagues say the innovation has increased their workload, reports the Washington State Energy Office. Among the complaints, having to answer phones and deal with walk-ins for the absent

---

[3] From the Labor Letter column, Tuesday, May 18, 1993. The article goes on to say: "Hewlett-Packard has a different problem: Its telecommuters get too far ahead of their office colleagues on independent work teams." Why is this considered to be a problem? What should be done about it?

telecommuters. Workers at Apple Computer complained that managers tend to overlook telecommuters when it comes to assigning tasks. *Phone mail, better scheduling and training* [italics added] have helped alleviate such problems.

Back at the spreadsheet, put 100% opposite a task if it *must* be performed in a particular place, either because it needs face-to-face interaction or either type of other location dependency. In the example for Job B, the only 100% dependency is because of the face-to-face requirement for presenting information (the company doesn't have a videoconferencing system).

Put 0% opposite tasks like "Analyzing figures" and "Composing letters and memos" unless there is only one place where these tasks are relevant. One can analyze figures and compose letters and memos anywhere, in principle. On the other hand, if you need some equipment to do those things— and the equipment is only in the main office or a telework center—then enter the percentage of the time you need to use the equipment. Put 100%'s opposite tasks like "Piloting the Plane to Tulsa," "Reading Top Secret documents," or "Briefing the Board of Directors" (if you don't have a color videoconferencing system in your organization) although the task of *preparing* the briefing might have a 0%.

The chances are that many, if not all, of the tasks you have just reviewed have *a portion* of their content that is both face-to-face and location independent. These are necessary conditions for home-based teleworking. Telework center teleworking requirements are less rigorous; Type 2 location dependence may not hinder establishment of either of these. On the contrary, it may enhance it.

HINT: In working with a variety of different organizations, most of which do not have high- or mid-tech options like video teleconferencing or electronic mail available to them, we have found a fairly common set of responses to the location independence question. Managers tend to respond that their own location independence is in the range[4] from 10% to 80%, and averages 40%. Prospective telecommuters' estimates of their own location independence ranges from 20% to 90%, averaging 60%. Thus, the average manager could be somewhere else two of five days per week, while the average telecommuting prospect could be away from a traditional office three out of five days per week, in their estimations.

➤ Getting to the Bottom Line

It's time for the last two columns in your spreadsheet. Label the first one (spreadsheet column D) "Location *Dependence* as % of JOB." Label the second (spreadsheet column E) "Location *Independence*" The rest is simple arithmetic. To get the number in the "Location *Dependence* as % of Job" column (Column D), simply multiply the number in the % of the JOB Column (Column B) by the number in the next column (Column C) and divide by 100. For example, in Table 2.4, for the "Preparing reports" task has Location *Dependence* as % of JOB as (10 × 10/100) or 1. The Dependence Fraction column shows how much of the time you, or your employees, have to be at a certain place.

"The Independence Fraction," the last column, is simply the number in Column B minus the number in Column D; in the case of "Preparing reports" in Table 2.4, that works out to 10–1 or 9, which is simply 100% minus the Dependence Fraction. Add all the numbers in the Independence column and you get the theoretical fraction of your (or someone else's job) that is teleworkable. In the case of our example, the number is 67%; two-thirds of the time.

➤ The Reality Factor

It is important to remember that, even though a worker may have a substantial requirement for face-to-face interaction, it may be possible to clump these interactions such that they all occur in one or two days per week, for example. This is easiest to arrange when the required face-to-face interaction is at weekly staff meetings or other regular events. This is most difficult to arrange when the interaction is irregular and/or depends on coordinating schedules of several other people. In the latter case, the proviso must

---

[4]The ranges quoted here include 90% of the responses; the lower and upper 5% of managers' and prospective telecommuters' responses go to 0 and 100%, respectively.

be repeated: *must* meetings really be face-to-face or could some telecommunications-mediated technique, such as telephone conferencing or electronic mail, serve as an effective substitute for some of the meetings?

It may not be feasible in some offices for the workers to telecommute if they are needed to respond to in-person public or customer inquiries.[5] On the other hand, it is quite feasible with call forwarding, for example, to have teleworkers handle phone inquiries. Further, it may be possible, with cross-training, to rotate those in-person activities among the staff members so that everyone gets a chance to telecommute and no one feels put upon.

One of the main features of teleworking (particularly home teleworking when no one else is at home) is that it allows workers to devote relatively long periods to work tasks without the interruptions or fragmentation common in traditional offices. Where a person's job has a relatively high number of these long-duration tasks, or where such tasks as there are can be grouped into one or two days per week, telecommuting might be particularly appropriate.

This question is most crucial for home-based teleworkers: can these location-dependent portions of all the tasks be arranged so that they clump into one, two, three, or four days per week, on average?

Be careful with this one! There is a great difference between *can* and *will*. At this point the main question is, is it possible, in principle, to arrange your own (or your employees') schedule(s) so that *all* the required face-to-face meetings occur on two (or fewer) days per week? So that all the other location-dependent activities occur on the same two days? On one day? On three days? Put the number of days per week that you *must* devote to these tasks in the last column after the title *Reality Factor*. Don't forget that this is an *average* estimate that we need here, where the average may be taken over several months. Some weeks may have more, some fewer such days.

All of the jobs for which the bottom line number of groupable days is less than five are potentially teleworkable from home on a regular basis. Even jobs that have an average number of groupable days per week that is between 4 and 5 are teleworkable from home some of the time and, possibly, from a telework center a significant part of the time. Those jobs for which the answer is 5 (or

---

[5] I recently had occasion to ask for advice about a software problem and found that the technical support person, who answered my Los Angeles-office phone call, was in Scotland—a telework center teleworker.

greater) are not suitable for home-based teleworking. Those people simply have to be in an office somewhere—again, the office could be in a telework center.

For those jobs where there is a *daily Type 1* location dependence, teleworking of any sort is not a possibility. We estimate that category encompassed about 60% of the total U.S. work force in 1987, shrinking to less than 50% by 1993. That leaves about half of the work force (about 60 million people) whose jobs are candidates for some form of teleworking, some or all of the time. We also expect that the fraction of teleworkable jobs will increase over the next few decades, because of technological changes.

Output Quality Issues

In some cases of teleworking, the nature of the output changes. This may be relatively minor, such as the use of laser printers instead of typewriters (the quality differences are small in many moderately priced printers now on the market). A similar possibility is that remote secretarial services, in which dictation is being transcribed for printing elsewhere, may have difficulties in switching paper forms between individual documents. A solution to this is to adopt common message and letter forms for all of the participating organizational units or, barring that, to include letterhead printing (for example) as a routine accessory in the finished product. Our experience has been that the acceptance of general (or computer-stored-format) forms is rapidly increasing, as personal computers and intra-company networks become common.

In other cases the product is different, such as sending informal reports via electronic or voice mail instead of via interoffice memos. These may not be in accordance with established tradition and may cause acceptance problems.

An Incomplete List of Teleworkable Jobs

None of the issues in this section is a fundamental barrier to teleworking. Their fundamental nature notwithstanding, one or more of them have caused disruption of other organizations' teleworking in the past because of their alteration of the organization's culture/quality criteria. Hence these issues should be considered in establishing the final selection.

I am frequently asked about what types of jobs are suitable for teleworking. To give you an idea, Table 2.5 provides a list of

Table 2.5 Some Teleworkable Jobs

Job Title	Full-Time Home-Based	Part-Time Home-Based	Full-Time Satellite or Local Center	Part-Time Satellite or Local Center
Accountant		☺	☺	☺
Actuary	☺ maybe	☺	☺	☺
Advertising Executive	☺ maybe	☺	☺	☺
Applications Programmer	☺	☺	☺	☺
Architect	☺	☺	☺	☺
Auditor		☺	☺	☺
Author	☺	☺	☺	☺
Bookkeeper		☺	☺	☺
CAD/CAM Engineer		☺	☺	☺
Central Files Clerk			☺ maybe	
Civil Engineer	☺	☺	☺	☺
Clerk-Typist	☺ maybe	☺	☺	☺
Clinical Psychologist		☺	☺	☺
Computer Scientist		☺	☺	☺
Counter Clerk			☺	
Data Entry Clerk	☺	☺	☺	☺
Data Search Specialist	☺	☺	☺	☺
Department General Manager		☺	☺ maybe	☺
Design Engineer		☺	☺	☺
Economist	☺ maybe	☺	☺	☺
Financial Analyst	☺	☺	☺	☺
General Secretary		☺	☺	☺
Graphic Artist	☺	☺	☺	☺
Industrial Engineer		☺	☺	☺
Journalist	☺	☺	☺	☺
Laboratory Director		☺	☺ maybe	☺
Laboratory Scientist			☺ maybe	☺ maybe
Lawyer	☺ maybe	☺	☺	☺
Mail Clerk			☺	☺
Mainframe Operator			☺ maybe	
Maintenance Technician		☺	☺	☺

Table 2.5 (Continued)

Job Title	Full-Time Home-Based	Part-Time Home-Based	Full-Time Satellite or Local Center	Part-Time Satellite or Local Center
Manager of Managers		☺	☺	☺
Manager of People		☺	☺	☺
Manager, Machine Systems	☺ maybe	☺	☺	☺
Market Analyst	☺	☺	☺	☺
Marketing Manager		☺	☺	☺
Natural Scientist		☺	☺	☺
Office Machine Operator			☺	☺
Personnel Manager		☺	☺	☺
Purchasing Manager	☺ maybe	☺	☺	☺
Radio Newscaster	☺	☺	☺	☺
Realtor	☺	☺	☺	☺
Receptionist			☺	☺
Risk Analyst	☺	☺	☺	☺
School Administrator		☺	☺	☺
Software Engineer	☺	☺	☺	☺
Statistician	☺ maybe	☺	☺	☺
Stock Analyst	☺	☺	☺	☺
Stock Broker	☺	☺	☺	☺
Supervisor	☺ maybe	☺	☺	☺
Systems Engineer		☺	☺	☺
Systems Programmer		☺	☺	☺
Technical Writer	☺	☺	☺	☺
Telemarketer	☺	☺	☺	☺
Telephone Operator	☺	☺	☺	☺
Theoretical Physicist	☺	☺	☺	☺
Traveling Salesperson		☺	☺	☺
University Professor		☺	☺	☺
Word Processing Secretary	☺	☺	☺	☺

Key: ☺ = OK;
☺ maybe = For some people;
Blank space = Not likely.

possibilities. Because the Federal list of job titles has thousands of entries, this is necessarily just a rough sketch. For example, our list of teleworkable jobs for government employees of the city of Los Angeles includes more than 400 job classifications, covering almost 16,000 positions.

■ IS THERE A TELEWORKER PERSONALITY?

Aside from the characteristics of a person's job, some people will work out better than others as teleworkers. In teleworking, as in many job situations there seem to be ideal types of people, particularly for home-based teleworking. This section concentrates on the psychological factors that are important in successful teleworking, with emphasis on the home-based teleworker, since that's the hardest.

➤ Teleworker Traits

The ideal home-based teleworker is a person who is strongly self-motivated and self-disciplined, who has all the required skills for his or her job, who has a home environment all set up for teleworking and who is enthusiastic about the prospects. Since it is possible that not all of your employees fall immediately into this category, here are some of the key characteristics to consider.

Self-Motivation

THE WEIRD PART IS I DON'T EVEN LIKE CARROTS ...

Since home-based teleworkers do not have the visual and aural cues of the traditional office to keep them motivated—and may have distractions that are not in the traditional office—the more internal drive they have to get the job done the easier it is to adjust to teleworking. With some workers this motivation is apparent. With others it may be latent, appearing in strength when they are given the chance. Motivation can still be supplied externally, as discussed in later sections on technology and management techniques, but the self-starter characteristic is an important one.

Self-Discipline

Of comparable importance is self-discipline. Even if a worker is highly motivated it can all come to nothing if self-discipline is lacking. Since a home-based teleworking environment is not amenable to constant monitoring[6] it is much better to have workers who do not need it. As in the case above it often happens that people who may need frequent urging in the traditional office can adapt readily to a home teleworking environment. The key derives from the fact that they can work at their own pace and in their own style, and they have new feelings of responsibility.

Job Skills and Experience

The smoothest transition to home-based teleworking is with a person who already has the skills and experience to do the job. In some cases the skills part can be addressed by some additional training, but this should be assessed *before* active teleworking begins. The need for specific job experience is less certain. We have found that individuals with comparable experience, but who may be new to a particular job—or even to the organization—can function effectively as home-based teleworkers. An efficient electronic mail system might help greatly in this respect, once they have passed the initial familiarization stages. However, for teleworkers who will depend on computer and network technology for work, it is crucial that they be given sufficient training for their needs.

Flexibility and Innovativeness

Teleworking is a new way of working. Employees who generally have difficulty adjusting to new situations may also have difficulty in a teleworking environment. Employees who are innovative and flexible in their attitudes will likely have little or no difficulty adapting.

---

[6] Actually, it *is* technologically possible to monitor home teleworkers continuously. We strongly recommend against it for reasons of good management practice, not to mention invasion of privacy issues.

Socialization

Home-based teleworking—and to a lesser extent, satellite and local center teleworking—places restrictions on the amount and scope of face-to-face socializing that can be contained within a job. To some extent this can be replaced, or even surpassed, by electronic forms of communication, but it is clearly a different situation than the traditional office environment. The office is a social arena in addition to its nominal function as a place for business to occur. Frequently the informal communication that occurs during office socializing is as important as formal office communication. On the other hand, some people do much better without the socializing that ordinarily goes on in an office. The key here is to facilitate necessary social exchange while paying less attention to unnecessary interaction. There are also the factors of introversion and extroversion to be considered. People who are very extroverted are not likely to make good frequent home teleworkers. Most people fall in a middle range, desiring some time to be left alone, at other times wanting to be with other people.

The policy of selecting volunteers for teleworking generally eliminates those people who strongly desire always to be with others and who are very other-directed. Part-time home teleworking takes care of most of the intermediate situations. Therefore, these criteria should be used primarily to indicate *relative* needs for face-to-face interaction that is in addition to task-related communications. Often, informal after-work group meetings can meet additional social needs.

Life Cycle Stage

In addition to characteristic personality traits, many successful home teleworkers are at stages in their lives when working at home has positive tradeoffs. As a counterexample, young singles, who often depend on peer contact to meet and form social relationships, may want to be on site around the coffee machine or in the hallways or cafeteria with access to a pool of potential leisure, as well as work friends.

At other times in their lives these same workers may enjoy being able to work in their homes where they can spend "break" times with their children, a retired spouse, an infirm parent, or neighborhood friends. This may be a particularly good way to attract valued retirees who still want to spend part-time working.

The Family

Home teleworkers should not be considered in isolation from their families (however you may wish to interpret "family"). The family environment while a teleworker is working at home becomes the surrogate for the office environment. If work disruptions from the family become intrusive, productivity and morale can fall. If the family environment is supportive, productivity and morale can soar.

The primary issue here is whether the worker can come to a satisfactory working relationship with his or her family at home. The best approach to this at the screening stage is to point out some of the problems of family interaction, such as interruptions for non-work activities, leisure-work conflicts, schedule or space conflicts with family members, and "break-in time" expectations. As a key example, home teleworking is **not** a satisfactory substitute for childcare, particularly with very young children. A home teleworker with a young child either will require someone available to take care of the child while he or she is working or will have to adjust his or her work schedule around the child's active periods (say, between midnight and 2:00 A.M.?).

Compulsions

Some home teleworkers have found themselves affected by various compulsions that they were able to forestall or avoid in their previous office environments. They find themselves giving way to these drives when in an isolated environment such as home. These compulsions include overeating, drug abuse, and workaholism. For most people there are countervailing pressures at home, or they develop new self-disciplines to fight them. However, some teleworkers may succumb. As in the case of family-related issues, the screening process should consist primarily of cautions about the possibilities rather than questions about workers' possibly compulsive habits.

Physical Environment for Home Teleworking

Although this is not strictly a socio-psychological issue, it is important to require at least some location in the teleworker's home that is suitable for an office during working hours. It is preferable, but not mandatory, that this be a permanent location, not requiring daily set-up and takedown. If there is no place that can be isolated during working hours (whatever those may be), then the likelihood of successful long-term teleworking is very small.

➤ These May Be Better Off in the Office

From the list above, a pattern appears for people who would be better off in a formal/traditional office environment. This can often be in a satellite or local center, so it doesn't necessarily preclude people from teleworking. But clearly people who need direct physical supervision, for reasons of motivation or discipline, should not be assigned home-based teleworking jobs (but then, why were they hired in the first place?).

People who are great socializers, who need face-to-face interaction with others to function well, should stick to the office. People who are inflexible in their work habits, the stereotypical bureaucrats, may have difficulty working at home. Singles who also use the office or its environs as a mate-meeting opportunity similarly may prefer the office to home. Substance abusers, assuming their sources of supply are equally available, may get worse if they are home-based teleworkers. (They may also get better if the office figured as one of the irritants motivating them to their abuse. In any case they should get treatment!) One of the substances most abused by home-based teleworkers once was thought to be food. Our evidence is that few teleworkers experience any significant weight gain or loss.

As you consider these factors, also remember that most home-based telecommuters will only be part-time at home. The rest of the time they will be in an office in which many of the needs just mentioned will be satisfied.

➤ Try Some and See

None of the factors just discussed is an absolute predictor of potential teleworking performance. It is possible, if unlikely, that apparently ideal teleworkers won't work out. It is also possible, or maybe less unlikely, that people who you might think wouldn't work out as teleworkers will do just fine. We suggest that your implementation strategy go as follows:

➤ Pick some of your best candidates for teleworking to start as your seed team. If you have a satellite facility, start there.[7]

➤ Then, as you develop experience managing them, have some work at home and add some of your less-teleworkable employees. You will pick up your own clues as to what does and does not work for you as you go along.

➤ Keep adding teleworkers until you feel you have reached a reasonable limit—or until you have run out of employees. We keep being surprised at the variety of people who are successful home-based teleworkers.

■ THE SELECTION PROCEDURE

A formal selection procedure consists of identifying potential participating organizational units and volunteers within those units. The basis for individual selection is the series of considerations just outlined. Here are some schedule and administrative details.

➤ Volunteers Only!

I suggest that you first identify the potential participating organizational units, then select individual participants, using the screening criteria described below, rather than ask for volunteers in general and then reject some. In any case the criteria described here are intended to enhance the likelihood of success of the project, not to provide a comprehensive survey of all the possible cases where teleworking may, or may not, work well. You are likely to find that the number of volunteers grows after your first group has been teleworking for a while. Those of your employees who were initially against it, or were uncertain, may well change their minds as the risks they imagined fail to appear.

➤ Evaluating Jobs and Work Groups

Start by identifying the organizational units that have the largest number of potential teleworkers by virtue of the willingness of

---

[7] By the way, *don't* try to acclimate them by locking them in a conference room in the office for a few days. It's been tried and it is counterproductive.

their managers to participate, the job characteristics of the members of the units, and the economic leverage teleworking might provide, in that order. If you have only one unit, your own, that part is easy. Go through the job characteristics in some detail. JALA International has developed a computerized screening service, called *TelePicker,* that automates the process on an individual basis.[8]

➤ Details

The following describes in more detail the selection procedure that was outlined earlier.

Jobs

First, the jobs. Here it is important to wrench your mind away from thinking about the process details of how each job is done today. Think about the *content* of each of your employees' jobs. What really has to happen to make that job work? What sort of results does the job produce? Can you recognize the results easily—typed memos, reports, lines of debugged software code, engineering drawings? What is it, exactly, that you use to evaluate the employee's work today? How often are these discernible products produced? What sorts of skills are required to produce the products? What sorts of resources are needed to get the job done? With whom—or what—must the worker communicate to get or send the information necessary for good performance? How frequently must that communication occur? How "rich" does the communication have to be?

Think of each person as a community, or a factory if you're mechanically minded. Each one requires inputs of materials and information at regular intervals, sometimes continuously, other times sporadically. Each one contains a number of different actors, agents, or doers. Each of those is busy some of the time, not so at others. So what we see is great burst of visible activity at times, while at other times everything seems to be dormant—resting, ruminating, developing, re-energizing. No job, unless it's incredibly boring, is the same thing all the time. What we're after is to get a

---

[8] The original plan was to have the TelePicker program available as a stand-alone package, but the level of customization required for most companies was too high. Hence it is only available as a service at present.

feel for the relative concentrations of activities that can be done alone—or alone with telecommunications, versus the ones that have to be done someplace in particular, with someone else. If you think the alone-with-phone jobs can be lumped into whole days at a time, you have identified a home-teleworkable job. Make a list of the candidates.

The criteria for satellite center teleworking are much less exacting. Most jobs can probably be done at a properly equipped satellite center, with the exception of those with distinct physical security or specialized equipment restrictions, *provided* that they also do not require relatively constant face-to-face interaction among specific people in specific locations.

Make a list like that in Table 2.6 for the jobs in your group. In Column 1 are the jobs that must be done in the **principal office all of the time.** In Column 2 are the jobs that must be done in the **principal office some of the time.** In Column 3 are the jobs that must be done in **some office all of the time.** In Column 4 are the jobs that must be done in **some office some of the time. Some** here means at least one day per week. If there are any jobs left in your group list, they could belong to full-time home teleworkers in Column 5. Remember, at this point we're talking about **jobs,** not **people.** If all your jobs are in Column 1, stop. You need go no further; there is no possibility for teleworking in your group (assuming you listed your own job as well). For the other columns there are increasing possibilities for home teleworking.

Now, some of those jobs may still require that there be regular face-to-face communication between specific other jobs. That is, there may still be groups of jobs that are geographically inseparable. Move them into Columns 1 or 2 even if they started out in 3, 4, or 5. That should complete your list of dispersible jobs.

People

Next, put the real live people in the jobs. How well do you think they would function away from the principal office? *How often do*

Table 2.6   Job Location Requirement Examples

Full-Time at Principal Office	Part-Time at Principal Office	Full-Time at Some Office	Part-Time at Some Office	No Significant Office Requirement
Counter Clerk; Mainframe Operator	Accountant; Most Managers	Field Engineer; Most Information Workers	Many Professionals; Administrative Assistant	Super-Specialists; Sales Reps

they need your personal supervision? How often do you need to see them to do your job?

If your thoughts in this line make you tend to move some more people to Column 1, **stop.** Is that because they need more training, are difficult to communicate with, are unreliable, are unmotivated, or what? Is the problem unapproachable or can it be improved by a new job or changes in the details of the job? If it seems insoluble, move the job/person toward Column 1. Otherwise, this may be a good opportunity to improve that person's situation. Also consider the option that you might have a group of first teleworkers that you can add to as time passes and your and their experiences develop.

After all of this soul-searching you have a list as follows: Column 1 includes those who simply must be in the principal office almost all of the time. Column 2 has the people who must be in the principal office some of the time but could be part-time telecommuters from a satellite office or from home (you might want to have columns 2a and 2b to decide which). Column 3 contains the satellite office telecommuters. Column 4 has those that might share time between satellite office and home, and Column 5, if any, has the potential full-time home teleworkers—or those who might be *really* far away, such as in a distant city. For all of these the term *all of the time* should be interpreted liberally. For practical purposes, *all of the time* means an average of four days per week (or slightly more), not *forever*, unless videoconferencing will suffice.

➤ Discussing the Options

Most of the above can not be done unilaterally. It is important to discuss the possibilities of teleworking with all of those people who are likely to be directly involved, whether or not they will all be teleworkers. The first step may be a briefing to all of the potential managers of teleworkers, followed by a similar one to prospective teleworkers themselves. Each of these briefings should contain at least the following topics:

- ➤ What teleworking is as it applies to us from home, from a telework center (if applicable)
- ➤ The criteria for teleworkers, for example: discuss the screening quiz
- ➤ The volunteer nature of teleworking

➤ Advantages and disadvantages of teleworking, both at home and at satellite centers; myths and realities

➤ Responsibilities of home teleworkers

➤ The practical realities, equipment, working environment

Don't go overboard at this stage. This is just a briefing to acquaint people with teleworking in a realistic way. The training briefings for the actual teleworkers come later, as does a comprehensive plan for telework program development. *It is important at this stage to stress that teleworking is neither a privilege nor a penalty for those involved—just a different way of working.*

➤ Final Selection

Now for the decision-making. We suggest that you give a formal screening test[9] to all the volunteers that you—and their supervisors—have identified. The test will provide an evaluation of the likely success of each individual as either a home or satellite telecommuter. The formal evaluation is not the final word. It is merely one input for your own decision. Is this person a good candidate for teleworking? There will be some clear yes's, possibly some equally clear negatives, and likely some borderline cases. Generally, fewer than 15% of the potential teleworkers get a "no telecommuting" recommendation from such tests, but those may be important *no*es.

We suggest that you keep in mind our earlier advice: try some of the borderline people as well as the definite winners. Sometimes the feeling of added responsibility will convert them into your star performers.

---

[9] You may want to invent your own, based on the material discussed here. Otherwise, JALA International, Inc. has a standard screening test service that has been used for thousands of telemanagers, teleworkers, and their colleagues.

Site Location

There are basically two types of fixed locations from which one can telework: one's home or a more formal office somewhere. This chapter discusses the general management issues of deciding the mix of locations that is appropriate for your organization.

In 1989 we surveyed about one thousand information workers who were employed by a large California organization. One of the survey's purposes was to develop a feel for the likely distribution of telecommuting sites for that employer. That is, about how many could work at home, how many from a telework center, and how many would be required to keep commuting daily to their principal office. The survey questions were taken from a questionnaire we use routinely to assess the likely telecommutability of individuals. The questions considered only the job content, not the behavioral issues of telecommuting. None of the individuals questioned had received any prior information about telecommuting.

We found that about 20% of the respondents to that general survey would be able to telecommute at least part-time from home; 50% would be able to telecommute from a telework center; and the remaining 30% might have to remain at the principal office. A careful review of the answers of that last 30% leads me to believe that at least half of them could work effectively at a telework center.

That conclusion also matches the results from our usual screening surveys of pre-briefed telecommuting candidates: about 15% would still have to work full-time at the principal office, while 30% could telecommute from home some of the time. Note that none of these surveys assumed a technology level greater than that of the late 1980s in a middle- to low-tech, although large, organization.

So, the chances are that, in your company, somewhere between 70% and 85% of the information workers could be teleworkers, based on their reported location independence. The practical split between home and telework center depends on the details of management practices and the physical characteristics of the respective sites. However, in the U.S. the preponderance of telework sites are teleworkers homes.

■ HOMES

In most work situations, the condition, size, and location of an employee's home are unrelated to whatever goes on at work; as a manager you probably never even think about it. Further, there is a generally accepted view (in the U.S., at least) that employers should not interfere with employees' home lives.

➤ Who Decides?

But whether a prospective teleworker's home is suitable for telecommuting has to be a critical decision in the site selection process. Is it an equally or more suitable environment (as compared to the principal office) for performing useful work? Or is it likely to be a place with distractions that are more powerful than at the principal office? How can you know?

The obvious way to find out is to inspect the premises. The obvious policy question is whether you, as an employer, even want to inspect the homes of all of your current or prospective home-based teleworkers. Some employers insist on it, as part of their plan for minimizing liability risk. Most simply reserve the right to inspect a teleworker's home, after giving appropriate notice, and require that each telecommuter agrees to keep his or her home in a condition no more hazardous than that in the principal office. That is, you explain the requirements to the telecommuters and trust them to adhere to them.

As an aid to making that decision, here is a general overview of home office standards. Chapter 8 has more on the details of home office design.

Home telecommuting is both the easiest and the hardest form of telecommuting in terms of selecting the site. It's the easiest because the location is automatically chosen when the home-based teleworker is selected; no problems of finding the right address. It's the hardest form of teleworking because homes are definitely not offices. It may take some straining and shoving to get them to be suitable work places. In some parts of the world—such as in most countries other than the United States[1]—no amount of shoving and straining will work; most homes are simply too small to contain a permanent office environment in addition to the rest of the household furnishings and necessary living space.

If an employee has sufficient determination, it is possible for that person to telework from almost any home situation where there is a reasonable amount of space, even if it is only temporary. But it is more desirable to modify the household space layout in order to provide a workspace with control over noise, interruptions, work equipment, and materials. What follows are some general parameters for setting up a wide variety of home offices, including criteria for screening[2] domestic environments to anticipate their suitability for business. As a telemanager, you should be aware of these issues, especially the ones that might have legal implications.

➤ Standards for the Physical Setting

Homes are definitely not designed to be offices, although many homes have space designated as office-like—the library or den. The management problem is to increase the likelihood that home-based teleworkers will maximize these attributes, either in the home proper or in outlying buildings:

- ➤ Adequate work space; at least as much as in the principal office
- ➤ Access to telephone or electrical outlets, if needed
- ➤ Security and safety of work materials
- ➤ Sound control
- ➤ Separation from on-going domestic activities
- ➤ Temperature and light control

Almost any place in the home is being successfully used for teleworking now: the basement, attic, the dining room table, a

---

[1] In the U.S., our average home-based telecommuter lives in a home with about 180 square meters. In Japan and Europe, homes typically have less than 100 square meters of floor space. The typical office space for a mid-level information worker is about 15 square meters.

[2] If "screening" sounds too intrusive, then consider this material as information to be communicated to your telecommuters.

spare bedroom, an outbuilding, and even the kitchen of a mother-in-law who lives next door. What makes the use successful, however, is that during the period of work, the space meets the criteria above.

People who would have chronically conflicting uses of residential space should probably not be accepted as home teleworkers. Even part-time teleworkers should have a permanent space for their work if they share their space with other people. Otherwise they may have significant problems in integrating work with the other household activities—with a resulting loss in productivity and an increase in stress.

However, this caution does not preclude the use of convertible facilities, where the work area may be used for other household purposes during non-working hours. For example, the teleworker may have a piece of furniture that encloses the computer, monitor, and printer, opening up for work and folding away into a compact, out-of-the-way module at other times.

Many professionals whose work is task-oriented can work at home for the duration of a given project. For those workers it may be enough to continue such present informal practices as taking a notebook computer home, preparing the work on the dining table, and transmitting data from the kitchen where the household telephone is located. *Intermittent home teleworkers should not be disqualified from teleworking, particularly at the demonstration project stage, since they form a precedent-setting group important in the implementation of formalized teleworking.*[3]

However, in departments where the periods to be spent teleworking can be anticipated and found to justify the expense of employer-provided telephone lines and other office equipment, encourage the teleworker to upgrade the home work space to facilitate uninterrupted work.[4] In many cases, in our experience, the teleworkers are willing to bear the expense of many or all of these additions. Nevertheless, company policy should be explicit on who bears the costs. It also may be useful to publish a list of home office

---

[3] Most companies still require an average of one telecommuting day per week as a condition of participation in their initial demonstration project. However, someone who telecommutes from home four or five straight days in a month still qualifies under this rule even though he or she is an intermittent telecommuter in this sense.
[4] This move also brings up a legal question: who owns the changes and/or additional equipment? What happens if the teleworker quits the company—or just quits teleworking? Most companies simply write off the installation expense, provided that it is fairly modest. Nevertheless, this is a point that should be considered by the legal staff *before* teleworking begins.

requirements for prospective telecommuters—or have them read this chapter and Chapter 8.

➤ Who Pays?

In general employers of teleworkers do not provide employer-owned furniture or equipment for home office installation for teleworking, although some may provide allowances or purchase discounts for teleworking employees—and some do outfit home offices with at least the basic furniture and equipment elements. The office at home, as at work, should be equipped with furniture and lighting appropriate to the tasks performed. You can't expect high levels of productivity from a worker stressed by aching arms and back, strained eyes and ears, or other discomforts. Special attention must be given to employees working in home offices at computer monitors because poor positioning of the keyboard and screen relative to the worker's body can cause extreme fatigue.

➤ Some Details on Setting Up a Home Office

A key item on the selection and training agendas is ensuring the adequacy of the physical space where the teleworker is going to work. If he is already a multimillionaire, or otherwise has a 25,000 square foot cottage with detached office complex, this may not be an important consideration. Otherwise, here are some rules of thumb for finding that ideal location at home for teleworking. For more information about the architectural details, you might want to consult a book on the topic.[5] These points should be used in discussions with prospective teleworkers, preferably before they begin teleworking.

Locating the Workspace

The Best Choice. If the teleworker already has an office or den in a detached building, such as a converted garage or guest house with enough electrical power and environmental control (windows and/or air conditioning and adequate lighting) to make working life comfortable, and if no one else in the family has the least desire to use that same space, then the search is over.

---

[5]One example is *Home Offices & Workspaces,* by the editors of Sunset Books and Sunset Magazine. Lane Publishing Company, Menlo Park, CA., 1986.

If there is a den, basement, attic, or spare bedroom of sufficient size that is not being used by anyone else, then the teleworker is in almost as good shape as the outside facilities owner. "Sufficient size" means at least as much space as the teleworker has in her present office away from home. If a personal computer or other technology is needed as part of her work, it's important to make sure that there is room for it and all of its or her accessories (printer, plotter, filing cabinet(s), reference works, books, fax machine, photocopier, answering machine, etc.). Figure at least 100 square feet for a permanent installation, more if there are already other things in the space that can't be displaced. If she is going to use a computer or other electrical gadgets make sure that there is adequate electrical power. In this high tech age of multiple electronic devices there may be much need for large amounts of power but it's nice to have several electrical outlets conveniently located.

Next Best. If there is no place at home that is sacrosanct, then there are two considerations to make. First, is there a location in the house where a permanent office layout can be set up, even though the room may also be used by others in the family? If so, this may work well, particularly if the other users of the space aren't there when the teleworker is.

Ask the prospective teleworker to take a careful look around his home. There may be little used closets, alcoves or other nooks that, with a little ingenuity, can be turned into effective and permanent office space. There are two key selection criteria:

➤ The office should be out of the daily traffic flow of the rest of the family; that is, relatively out of sight

➤ It should be relatively quiet, at least free from unwanted disturbances[6]

If the space available just isn't large enough—even for a notebook computer and desk space, then it is possible to resort to the

---

[6]"Wanted" disturbances include such things as the doorbell and cries of distress from the kids.

use of fold up or stow-away furniture to compress the home office at times when the teleworker is not using it. There are a number of commercially available desks geared for computer use that collapse into inscrutable small cabinets during leisure hours. In either case, space is still needed around the working teleworker. He may have to move the grand piano or the billiard table from the family room in order to do this, but it will be worth it in the long run.

Worst. Suggest that teleworkers avoid using the kitchen, dining room table, bedroom or bathroom as a work place unless they're going to quit using it for its original purpose. Avoid temporary work places of all sorts, unless they plan to be only very sporadic telecommuters, or the teleworker is the sole human inhabitant of the home.

Also avoid locating the office where it can easily be seen from outside the house or apartment or condo, particularly if they're computer users and all that expensive equipment can be seen from outside. Burglars love it!

Face-to-Facing It

Teleworkers should also consider how much contact they are going to have with business visitors. Business callers should find a clear, unobstructed route to the home office.[7] A separate outside door would be ideal. Other household members must find that they and their friends can still come and go freely without imposing on the home business environment.

In these cases, the living room, rather than the teleworkers' office space, may be the best location for meetings. The trick is to have the room easily convertible in appearance between its business and family functions. My own home "conference center" is either the living room or the dining area/table, depending on the number of visitors and the meeting purpose. There is the occasional frantic scurry to get all the newspapers, magazines and crockery stuffed away somewhere (typically on top of the washing machine) before the visitors arrive.

---

[7] This can be an important factor in deciding whether a home-based telecommuter should have meetings at home. The primary issue is liability if a visitor is injured at/in a telecommuter's home. The question of responsibility for maintenance of an environment without unusual physical risk should be settled before telecommuting begins.

There is another issue here for teleworkers operating from home as independent businesses: the local zoning codes. In many cities, Los Angeles for example, there are strict regulations as to what sorts of businesses can operate in homes. Some specific professions are prohibited as home-based businesses (guess what some of them are), and certain levels of street traffic related to the business, as well as most forms of advertising may be outlawed. The general motivation in these cases is to allow home-based business that do not conflict with the character of the neighborhood. Business activities that produce a continuous stream of visitors are generally not good candidates for strictly residential areas. Telecommuting employees of organizations, as contrasted with operators of home-based businesses, tend to be treated more tolerantly in practice.

Inventorying Furniture

For teleworkers who will be spending considerable amounts of time in front of a personal computer or some other "workstation," it is important to have a setup that is comfortable and safe. This often means that standard household furniture is not adequate for the job. What is needed is a good desk, comfortable (for long term sitting) chair, accessible storage space, a place to put a printer and other accessories, and some effective area and/or task lights.

Especially important is the workplace furniture. Aim for minimizing fatigue and maximizing convenience. The furniture doesn't have to be "high tech" for it to be useful. Here are the key requirements, based on years of ergonomic research (For more details on these factors, surf to ErgoWeb at http://www.ergoweb.com.):

Seating Position. Regardless of any computer use, the main requirement is that the teleworker has a chair that lets her sit comfortably erect, with thighs parallel to the floor or slightly up at the knees and spine unslumped. That means the front of the seat should be slightly higher than the rear and the back of the chair should be tilted back somewhat (about fifteen degrees, according to ergonomists). Armrests are OK if they don't get in the way of desk or workstation activities. This works out (for the average-sized person) to a seat height of nineteen to twenty-one inches. An ergonomic secretarial chair is fine for this, but any other that fits the positioning requirements will do if it also has good lower back support. Many regular household chairs fail to meet these standards. Nice, comfortable armchairs are deadly in this respect.

Desk Height. If the teleworker is working with a computer it is likely that a standard office desk will be too high. The key requirement here is that forearms should be parallel to the floor and wrists should be straight (unbent) when the teleworker is keying in information on the computer keyboard. He should also have space in front of the keyboard for the heels of his hands to rest while the keying. For the average person this works out to a desk-top height of about twenty-seven inches.

Display Position. If the teleworker is using a computer regularly, the center of its display screen should be about two feet from the face and about twenty degrees below the horizontal (about eight inches below eye level) for best comfort and ELF[8] safety. If he's a touch-typist and does a lot of working from paper copy then he should have a device for holding the paper at about the same height, to minimize eye and neck/shoulder fatigue. If he's a hunt and peck typist (or somewhere in between, as am I), then he might want to have a copyholder set between the keyboard and the display.

Access to Telephone and/or Electrical Outlets. A teleworker who needs to use a personal computer at home may also need an extension cord or multi-outlet power block. But don't forget, an employer-sponsored home work environment must meet minimum standards to ensure safety of employer-owned equipment and of household members.

For those jobs requiring a computer, grounded electrical outlets are essential. Although newer residential construction will likely have the three-prong outlets (in the U.S., other countries have different standards), older homes may need to be wired for home telecommuting. Special surge protectors also may be desirable to protect the computer from "spikes" in the electrical power line. In areas where there are chronic, or even infrequent, brownouts or other power failures, teleworkers should consider adding an uninterruptible power supply (UPS) to the list of crucial

---

[8] Extremely Low Frequencies; the radiation emitted by many CRT (cathode ray tube) monitors in the range above about 50 Hz. Most very new monitors on the market conform to Swedish standards for radiation safety, so this is probably not a concern. Medical research on what constitutes a "safe" level of ELF is still underway.

equipment. All it takes is one or two power failures that result in lost or damaged files to recoup the cost of the protection—not to mention the screaming and hair tearing that tends to accompany such events.

An additional "work" telephone line will be necessary for the growing number of teleworkers who tele-access another computer frequently or for long periods during hours that a home phone is needed by other household members. Installation of a separate line will also be required for jobs involving a high volume of tele-phone calls to or from your home. Not all teleworkers need extra phone lines, however. In our experience,[9] about 30% of teleworkers have multiple telephone lines—as compared with about 20% multiple-line ownership by non-telecommuters. Telecommuters who need more intensive levels of communication might do better with technologies such as ISDN, ADSL, or cable modems where available (see Chapter 4).

To the degree that one's work requires time-critical contact with co-workers or other people, call forwarding, a telephone an-swering machine, voice or electronic mail, a pager, GroupWare, or some combination of these will be required for efficient job performance.

The problem with many of the message storage systems is that they do not have a fail-safe method of notifying you that a message is waiting. This is particularly the case with electronic mail. The lack of a message-waiting message must be replaced by habit, a pager, or by a telecommunications software package that dials the mail center at fixed times(s) daily.

---

[9] These data are from studies by JALA of City of Los Angeles telecommuters over the period 1990 to 1992.

Noise Abatement

Home-based teleworkers have to be protected from household noise—and the rest of the household has to be protected from their noise.

For computer-using teleworkers, the most likely noise source used to be a dot-matrix printer. That should be considered before teleworkers who need one begin setting up an office in the bedroom or anywhere that its noise will disturb other family members—or the neighbors. Printers are getting quieter every year and laser or ink-jet printers generally minimize discernible noise. Unlike the situation in many on-site environments, teleworkers may be able to insulate themselves by closed doors, background music, or other solutions to achieve the level of sound at which they work most productively.

If telephone contact is part of the job it is the teleworker's responsibility to ensure, for example, that the family dog is not barking—or the vacuum cleaner is not running—next to the telephone. (Of course, this only happens during long distance or otherwise important calls.) It is his responsibility to be thoroughly professional to the degree that the work requires.

Acoustic isolation can get out of hand, however. One telecommuter was so concerned about being able to concentrate on her work that she firmly shut the door to her home office in order to eliminate any distracting noise. She finished about three days' worth of work on her first day of telecommuting. She returned to her principal office the next day, expecting praise from her boss. Instead, she was astonished to discover that he had been trying to get her on the phone all day and—since she didn't answer, the phone being in the other room—became convinced that she was at the beach all day! He didn't bother to listen to her explanation. An instant casualty of insensitive management, she quit telecommuting. It took considerable persuasion to get their communication patterns back to the point where she could resume telecommuting.

Turf Struggles

Some prospective teleworkers already have a workspace established at home, and the rest of their families *know* it's their space. For those people you can skip this part. Otherwise it is important to select a work-place location that has the least intrusion on household space already used by other members of the family, consistent with the other requirements for the teleworker's working comfort. They may have to make some deals with other members of the family to get this to happen. But all parties involved should know whose space gets moved, and whence, before beginning telecommuting. This need not be blown up to a U.N.-level negotiation, a short discussion with the interested parties may be sufficient.

And keep in mind that the territorial incursions can be time limited—that is, working hours only, for teleworkers who have a sufficiently collapsible workstation. In multi-earner households, this is often not a problem—until it becomes a multi-teleworker household!

■ TELEWORK CENTERS

Telework centers resemble conventional office environments. However, there are some key differences. Final selection among the many possible combinations of sites depends heavily on the geography of the implementation city, the location of participant residences, the need for face-to-face meeting sites, and, of course, budget constraints.[10]

➤ Selection Issues

We usually screen potential teleworkers in order to divide them into two groups: home (mostly) and telework center teleworkers. Telework center telecommuter candidates are those who:

➤ Indicate a preference for telework center telecommuting, or whose equipment/facilities requirements or job/behavioral characteristics do not favor home-based teleworking; and

➤ Work in organizations willing to operate with (or test the utility of) telework center employees; and

➤ Live within a *reasonably* short distance of a potential center.

The term "reasonably" above will vary. At one extreme, any center that reduces employee commute times by one-quarter or more might do. At the other end, the goal may be to have all telework

---

[10] The issues connected with marketing independent telework centers are treated separately in Chapter 12.

center telecommuters walk or bicycle to work. In the first case, the center may still be ten miles or more from the average telecommuter's residence. In the other case, it may be around the corner, on a different floor of the high-rise apartment building, or within a few blocks of home. In the late 1990s, I expect to see all of these evolve, slowly moving toward a global network of home offices and telework centers, covering an entire spectrum of sizes.

The next step is to arrive at a list of potential sites, in the cases where telework centers appear to be desirable. Ideally, telework centers would be located in or near clusters of current and/or prospective employee residences. In practice, current company ownership or lease agreements for candidate facilities close to the ideal locations would be used to select the prospective sites, where possible. Long-term leases with large unexpired portions certainly can limit the flexibility of site location unless sub-letting space is a real possibility.

It might also be useful to explore and evaluate one or more of the several forms of decentralized site mentioned in Chapter 1 and expanded in Chapter 10, including the following, ranging from the largest to the smallest in size:

1. A conventional telework complex totally occupied by company workers and otherwise indistinguishable from a central location office building, except that workers would

report to the office on the basis of their residence locations rather than their organization headquarters locations

2. As above, except that the buildings might be shared by other firms in addition to company units

3. Neighborhood office centers, such as "store-front" units, in which only a few workers would work and which would be located in the immediate neighborhoods of the workers' residences.

Final site selection may also involve some design issues. For example, the project might have a situation in which telecommuters are at home much of the time but also require some private, possibly shared office space plus conference facilities for periodic meetings. There are also some internal space design issues related to the extent of computer use at the centers. For example, centers where there is intensive computer use and large amounts of data sharing may require provisions for extra communications network cabling. This requires a different sort of office design than is traditional in buildings housing pre-computer-age information workers.

➤ Telework Centers versus Conventional Office Environments

While relocating an entire organizational unit from a central office to a telework center may be useful in evaluating some aspects of decentralization (e.g., relative lease costs of central versus suburban sites), unless everyone in this organizational unit lives a short distance from the center location, the exercise does little to explore some of the more important dimensions of the problem (e.g., effect of telecommuting on transportation patterns). In fact, the move of an entire organizational unit to another location almost always causes more disruption, loss of key personnel, morale crashes, and other costs than it is worth in facilities rental savings. This is discussed more fully in Chapter 10.

Individuals, Not Organizations

Therefore, most telework centers will accommodate a group of employees whose only other connection is that they live in close proximity to the center. This differs from a common misconception of a telework office, which considers a telework facility as reserved for whole departments or otherwise entire work units.

Shared Support Personnel and Services

Unlike the traditional setting where clerical and other support functions are contained in the organizational unit, the telework center may have personnel performing these services for the diversity of occupants of the center. Or the services may be performed entirely from other sites via telephone and electronic mail connections. Similarly, I anticipate that support spaces and equipment such as conference areas and photocopy machines will be utilized on a shared basis. One set of privately operated telework centers in California has an extensive automatic system for machine-use and support service personnel accounting for its tenants (about 70% of whom were telecommuters in 1992).

In fact, one possibility is to have a telework center that consists solely of meeting and support equipment facilities, with minimal or no permanent support staff at the center. In this arrangement, the telecommuters would work from home much of the time, coming to the telework center only for meetings or for use of the support equipment.

In particular, I suggest that the company provide the basic support services/equipment and the site manager for each telework center. The role of site manager is described more fully in Chapter 9. The site manager's job is that of overseeing the process of activities at the site: availability of supplies and support services, attendance of teleworkers, maintenance of security, and so on. The site manager is *not* responsible for evaluation of the performance of employees from other organizations, except in an advisory capacity to the functional managers of the telecommuters at the site.

Size

At present, most operating telework centers have fewer than 100 occupants, although the center may be shared with other units of the company who are located in the traditional mode. For example, a storefront office in an older neighborhood could be as suitable for a center as a new suburban office building. A telework center might also occupy leased space in a conventional office building amid other tenants. Some Pacific Bell telework centers are located in buildings that formerly were filled with telephone switching equipment; digital switches occupy much less space, thereby allowing the rest of the building to be used for other purposes. The major requirements are suitable space to accommodate people and work activities and ease of space alteration to satisfy architectural requirements.

➤ Organization-Operated (Satellite) Centers

Distribution of Teleworkers between Home Offices and Telework Centers

The distribution of teleworkers depends on the outcome of the screening process. As a first approximation, if you're just starting a teleworking program, you might want half of the company's teleworkers working from home, the other half from one or more telework centers.

Clearly, another major option is available. Many teleworkers who nominally work at home could also be part-time telework center workers. They could spend most of their time either at home or at a telework center, with only occasional excursions to their unit's central office (if it is not at the telework center). Hence we might have all of the teleworkers as telework center workers at least some of the time. The exact final distribution depends on the results of the combined personnel, organization, and site selection process.

Selection Criteria for Telework Centers

The need for locating telework centers close to residences to minimize travel time is readily apparent. If you're trying to get employees out of their cars for commuting, I recommend a somewhat arbitrary limit of one mile as the maximum distance from a telecommuter's home to the telework center in which he or she works. In some cases,[11] such as where a number of employees live at great distances from the main office, it might be desirable to relax the maximum limit and put a "half-way office" into operation.

Transportation-Locational Decisions. The easiest way to get this information is to develop a map of employee residence locations by postal code. That is, for each postal code area in the city, find out how many employees live there. Use your personnel files to get the data. Pick the one or two code areas that have the highest density of employee/telecommuter residences and find a suitable office site in or near the center of those areas. An "eyeball" choice

---

[11] Probably most cases in a new telecommuting program in a mid- to large-sized city.

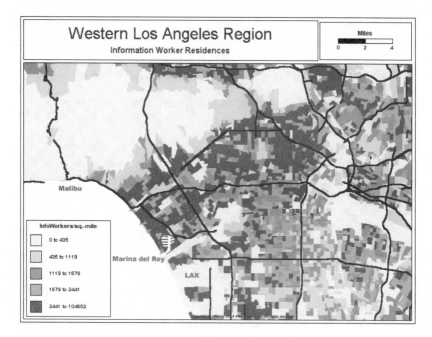

Figure 3.1 An example of employee residence distribution.

is usually adequate to locate a prospective area.[12] Figure 3.1 gives an example for one multi-city telework situation.

If you want to establish or participate in telework centers, then postal codes probably provide too coarse a filter. You may have to resort to mapping the actual residence locations of your employees to find the best spots that are within walking distance of their homes.

In accordance with Murphy's (or Parkinson's) law, if you have multiple facilities now, then it seems that employees who live in the East side commute to the West side while the people who live in the West side commute to the East. If this is the case in your company you might wish to locate new centers or rearrange your existing facilities to minimize that travel. It's also worth considering changing job assignments so that the West siders have jobs associated with the West side, and so on.

Finally, there is the possibility of multi-client centers, in which employees from more than one company may work at

---

[12]This may be easier said than done. In our work with the City of Los Angeles, out of more than 800 prospective telecommuters in a demonstration project, we found that the highest density Zip area contained residences of only 8 of those employees.

a center. Siting of these centers is discussed more fully in Chapter 12.

Parking. Availability of adequate parking (for cars or bicycles, depending on the location) may be an important criterion for the selection of sites and facilities for telework centers.

We do not expect the home office part of teleworking to create major additional demands for parking in residential areas. It is conceivable, however, that 50 to 100 new workers at a regional telework center, if they still drive to work, could overtax the available parking in certain settings (e.g., an older commercial strip), with major impacts on the surrounding neighborhood. Therefore, the availability of adequate parking—or alternative mass transit solutions—should be one determinant of site selection (although what is "adequate" is still open to definition).

From another point of view, elimination of parking space, since close-in telecommuters may elect not to drive to work, may be an important benefit. It could be worth encouraging employees either to walk, bicycle, ride the bus, car- or van- pool, or otherwise not drive to work alone.

Laying Out the Center Space

Space for Work Activities and Support Services. I expect a typical office space requirement for the telework center of approximately 160 square feet per person. This figure includes support space such as corridors and storage areas. So, a telework center for 100 employees would require about 16,000 gross square feet of space. Net square feet, referring to usable office space, would be less, in the order of 145 to 150 square feet per worker.

This estimate is for planning and initial costing purposes only. The final number will depend on such factors as the amount of office sharing done by part-time teleworkers, the ratio of conference room to office space and the amount of shared facilities needed (reception areas, printers, photocopiers, etc.).

Space Arrangements. If the center primarily is to house full-time teleworkers then it will probably be laid out like a traditional office building. The main difference might be in some additional conference space. If, as is more often the case, it is to accommodate a mix of full-time, part-time, and "drop-in" teleworkers, the space requirements are somewhat different.

For example, regular part-time teleworkers might share office space with those who telework on other days of the week. A

Monday-Wednesday-Friday teleworker might share space with a Tuesday-Thursday person without running into other than occasional occupancy conflicts. Often, the part-time center teleworkers will be there mostly for meetings, so that their major need is for conference space, together with access to a small office (possibly with-computer) for telephoning or other electronic messaging. So this kind of center would likely have more conference space and less office space than the traditional office building.

Similarly, you may wish to provide office/conference space for drop-in teleworkers: those from other areas or cities who may be in town on business, or for teleworkers who work primarily somewhere else but who come to the center occasionally.

The initial layout of the center, then, depends on an analysis of the numbers of teleworkers who fit into these categories: full-time, part-time shared space, part-time mostly for meetings, and drop-in. It is difficult to forecast all of this up front so the plan should allow for some alteration of space as experience with teleworking develops. You might want to follow the old maxim for laying out sidewalks—watch where the natural trails develop, then pave them—but apply this to office/conference/support space demands.

Ease of Alteration of Leased Sites. One major cost factor in the leasing of office space is the cost of altering facilities to meet functional and other requirements. For this reason, and because you may have a higher than usual demand for altering the initial layout, the inexpensive adaptation of candidate facilities for telework centers is another important criterion for site selection. It is not anticipated that, with the exception of telecommunications installation, renovation costs for a telework center will be different from the typical renovation costs for traditional leased space.

➤ Multi-Client Telework Centers

Another aspect of telework that is growing in interest is the use of multi-client telework centers, where one organization acts as the landlord and rents or leases space to other organizations and/or individual teleworkers. The advantage to the tenant is that the administrative chores of center operation are undertaken by the center operator. Further, organizations can use multi-client centers as test beds for possible satellite offices—or as halfway houses for potential home-based teleworkers.

The disadvantage is that the tenant generally has less control over such factors as operating hours, security, available technology and the working environment. The security issue is often the most important to prospective tenants. For example, companies are usually not eager to have space in telework centers that house employees of competing firms. On the other hand, government organizations in the U.S., notably the federal Flexiplace program, are expanding their use of such centers. In these cases, employees from several federal departments may work at an individual telework center. See Chapter 12 for more details on these centers.

Chapter 4

Telework and Technology

One main theme of this book is that a substantial amount of telework can be accomplished effectively with only a telephone, paper and pencil as the relevant technologies. Yet, application of more sophisticated technology generally makes life easier, increases the amount of telework one can do, and makes telework available to more people. This chapter is about the impacts of technology on telework.

■ GENERAL RULES OF TECHNOLOGY

We don't discuss the technology here at the level of detail of brand names, model numbers, or prices. The reason is simple. Information technology (computers and telecommunications) improves, in terms of performance per dollar spent—or decreases in cost per unit of capability, at an *annual* rate of between 25% and 30%. That is, the universal cosmic gadget that you paid $400 for this year will probably sell for about $300 or less next year, if it isn't already obsolete. So, the process of turning a manuscript into a book that is manufactured and widely distributed, fast though it is, is too slow to keep up with technology details. Any market details printed here would be out of date by the time you read them.

Having said that, I assure you that the *trends* in information technology development are well established. Therefore, it is fairly easy to forecast what *level* of technology you can expect to have available in the year X—and its approximate price, where X is in the next ten or twenty years or so. Of course, there are technological surprises that can alter this forecast, but history has tended to show more positive surprises than disappointments. This leads us to **Technology Rule One:**

> *If a certain form of information technology is available today, but costs twice as much as you think you can afford to pay, wait a couple of years; it will be down to your price threshold.* If it currently costs ten times as much as you think you can afford, wait about seven years.

This is simply a restatement of the trend mentioned in earlier paragraphs.

In Rule One we're talking about *hardware* technology; things like mainframe-, maxi-, mini-, and micro-computers; telecommunications media, such as fiber optics lines and satellite dishes; and all the gadgets that plug into them. *Software* tends to follow more obscure rules. Suffice it to say that the great new software package that will finally help you to do that tricky part of your job will take from two to five times as long to appear as the manufacturers initially claim. Hence the well-deserved term *vaporware.*

Nevertheless, the software will finally show up, and of a quality sufficient to make it worth your investment. This leads to **Technology Rule Two:**

> *Always buy the best technology available to accomplish a certain job, even if it stretches your budget slightly.* It is at least a partial guarantee that the technology will still be usable in three years. Don't count on more than a three to five-year useful lifetime for computers or telecommunications interface equipment (such as modems), for other than very routine[1] information tasks.

However, all of the foregoing doesn't really have much impact on the fundamental teleworkability of large numbers of jobs. It does have a major impact on some jobs, specifically those that

---

[1] Keep in mind that what is *routine* is also a moving target. Not so many years ago, secretaries did not routinely compile or update spreadsheets or perform sophisticated document processing. Now, with the aid of inexpensive technology, they do.

need the latest high-powered hardware and software to keep ahead of the game. This leads to **Technology Rule Three:**

The absence of a particular technology, beyond the funda-mentals, is rarely a reason (or excuse) not to telework. Almost everyone can telework at least part of the time without any form of "advanced" technology. However, improvements over the fundamentals may enable both significant quali-tative and quantitative improvements in telework.

All of the rules above have to do with deciding the level of tech-nology required in a closed system. By that we mean, all other things being equal, you only have to worry about Rules One through Three. But, in many situations it is not the case that all other things are equal; you exist in a competitive environment. If you are in that situation, you also have to consider **Technology Rule Four:**

Given equal human and economic resources, the person who has the technology best suited for the job wins. If you are able to do the work faster, with higher quality, at lower cost, or with less strain than your competitor, then you have a competitive advantage. The key question: *is the cost of the additional technology less than the value of the increased competitive advantage?* If it is, then the expenditure could be warranted.

At the same time, don't forget that new technology can have a price significantly beyond its purchase cost: *time.* First, it takes time to learn how to use it to do the tasks for which you purchased it. Often, the technology fails to meet your expec-tations in one or more respects. As a result, less time than expected is shaved from those established tasks that the technology was supposed to help. In extreme cases, that user surliness may make you take even longer to do the task with the "improved" technology than without it.

Second, it takes even more time to invent new tasks that use the technology, or to learn how to do them. Third, the cost of producing the "improved" results may exceed the benefits received.

How many times have you spent extra minutes or hours at the computer unnecessarily tweaking that letter or spreadsheet, with no discernible difference to the famous bottom line?

But telework does have an effect on that process, as stated in **Technology Rule Five:**

Telework generally decreases the start-up costs of adoption of a new technology; computer-based technologies in particular.

This is partially the result of greater accessibility. Many offices still have fewer than one personal computer per computer user. In those cases, at least for home-based teleworkers who have personal computers at home, learning the new technology—and inventing new applications for it—is done mostly at home rather than in the principal office.

I have been told repeatedly by teleworkers that the ability to try a new technology at home, without the fear of embarrassment by the snickering power users at the principal office, can be a powerful incentive to someone who is technology-wary. Hence, the learning and innovation time is significantly compressed. This is one of the components of the improved effectiveness demonstrated by teleworkers. Further, the increased emphasis on specifying results (rather than concentrating on a specific procedure that may or may not produce the results) tends to diminish the amount of time wasted in output overkill. Rule Five is particularly important in organizations that ordinarily under-train their employees; that is, most U.S. organizations.

Technology Rule Six is critical:

The technology needed for full-scale successful telework is roughly the same as that required in the principal office—plus some more telecommunications.

No magic here. If you *regularly* need it in the office, you will probably need it in the home office or telework center. The hidden benefit here is that there may be no need for *duplicate* technology. A combination of "older" technologies, such as voice mail and paging, combined with computer sharing in the principal office, possibly with removable hard disks, portable computers for teleworkers and/or teleworker ownership of their own machines, can make the actual startup cost of technology for teleworking range from quite low to nonexistent.

You should also keep in mind **Technology Rule Seven:**

Telecommunications networks are the freeways of telework.

If your organization is not extensively intra-connected by digital telecommunications networks now, it soon will be, if it is to stay in business. The emergence of increasingly sophisticated telecommunications networks—and increasingly uniform international telecommunications regulatory policies—will make telecommuting and teleworking practical for almost all information workers around the globe in the next decade (or so).[2]

Telecommunications networks for telework can range from the familiar ubiquitous public switched telephone network (PSTN) and all its generally available services (call forwarding, conference calling, call waiting, voice mail, paging, caller identification); plus various forms of mobile telecommunications; through the all-digital ISDN (Integrated Services Digital Network) system or switched digital services interconnecting both individuals and arrays of LANs (Local Area Networks); to the next steps: ADSL (Asymmetric Digital Subscriber Line) and ATM (Asynchronous Transfer Mode). The mode of telecommunications can be as simple as voice only, or escalate through voice-and-graphics, and various forms of synchronous and asynchronous teleconferencing. Each of these technologies generally follows Technology Rule One, so that a technology that seems to be out of reach today could be business-as-usual in a decade or less.

Finally, lest you get overly excited by all the possibilities out there, observe **Technology Rule Eight:**

There is no substitute for uniform company technology standards.

At a minimum, the software used by teleworkers should be file-compatible[3] with the software in the principal office. For example,

---

[2] The most significant deterrent to globalization of telework is probably the lack of a single common set of standards for telecommunications, coupled with persistent regulatory barriers. Both of these impediments are the results of the need to get consensus among sets of standard- or regulation-makers with often conflicting interests. That takes time.

[3] That is, a formatted text, spreadsheet, graphics, or database file produced by machine A should be readable by machine B, even if the two machines do not use the same type of microprocessor to run their programs.

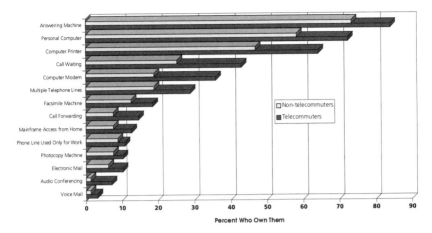

Figure 4.1 Technology ownership rates.

if the principal office uses Macintoshes and one or more teleworkers use PC-compatibles, or vice versa, make sure that one end or the other has software that allows transparent file transfer, either by floppy disk or modem. This problem will recede as (and if) more software becomes platform-independent, but it is a common issue in many organizations today.

Keep these rules in mind—or on your wish list—as you decide what technology is required for a given level of teleworking.

■ REALITY TESTS

Brief descriptions or statements of the type of technology needed for telework are scattered throughout this book. The rules just given cover types of technology needed to perform various teleworking tasks. Now, let's see what is happening at present in non-high-tech, real world organizations.

First, look at some of the results of a survey of a few hundred telecommuters and non-telecommuters, mostly mid-level managers or professionals, concerning the utility of certain types of technology to their work. One test of the importance of a technology is the extent to which it is personally owned/paid for by the telecommuters. Figure 4.1 shows the status late in 1992 for a group of home-based telecommuters and non-telecommuters in a large U.S. metropolitan area, all working for the same large organization. On average, these telecommuters had been working from home for about one year at the rate of slightly more than one day per week.

The results in Figure 4.2 must be viewed with some reservations because not all of the technologies, such as voice mail and electronic mail, were readily available to the participants in the survey. Voice mail in particular tends to enhance teleworking in organizations that have it generally available—yet it is not usually owned by the teleworkers. Further, the survey respondents' jobs covered a very wide spectrum. Some job types are much more dependent than others on a specific technology. Note that price does not seem to be a dominant factor here. Although the most-often-owned technology is answering machines (underlining the importance of voice messaging); personal computers and printers, costing several times as much, rank second. This also demonstrates Rule Six: 74% of these telecommuters owned their own personal computers at the time the survey was made. At the beginning of telecommuting for this organization, half of the applicants already owned their own personal computers.

We also asked the same people how much easier each of these technology types would make their work. The results of that question are shown in Figure 4.2. The scale ran from 1 (it has no effect on my job) to 5 (it makes my job significantly easier).

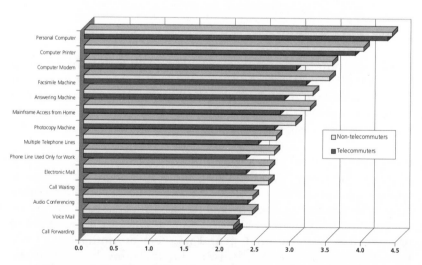

Figure 4.2 The ability of technology to make work easier.

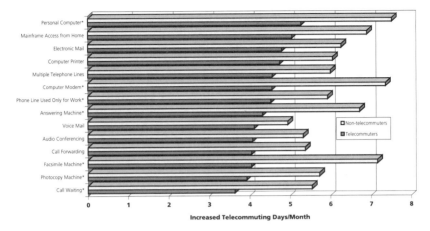

Figure 4.3 The expected impact of technology on increasing telecommuting.

The clear conclusion from these figures is that personal computers, their main peripherals (printers and modems), and facsimile machines should be key components of the future telecommuter's equipage. The differences shown in Figure 4.2 between telecommuters and non-telecommuters are statistically significant only for modems, a further check on Rule Six.

Finally, these same telecommuters and non-telecommuters were asked their opinions as to the impact of each of these technology types on increasing the amount of telecommuting they might do from home. The results are shown in Figure 4.3. The asterisks after the names of the technologies indicate that the differences between telecommuters and non-telecommuters are statistically significant.[4]

The interesting conclusion to be drawn from the graph is that non-telecommuters have expectations of the effect of technology that are not met in reality. Although both groups feel that added technology would increase the amount of telecommuting that is possible for them, experienced telecommuters are more conservative about the likely extent. This is an empirical test of Rule Three above; lack of a particularly nifty technology may not be as impairing as you might think.

---

[4] At or better than the 0.05 level. This means that the probability that the differences are *not* real is less than 5% for those items with asterisks.

■ TECHNOLOGY TRENDS

The previous material concerns the situation in an average-tech organization in the early 1990s. There are some very high-tech organizations using teleworking, as well as some almost no-tech outfits. All of these are successful in the teleworking they do. But, as stated earlier, there seems to be a connection between the level and scope of teleworking in an organization, and the level of technology they use. Here are some general statements about trends in technologies that are particularly suited to telecommuting and to that broader application, teleworking.

➤ Computers

Although about one-third of telecommuters in the late eighties could telecommute at least one day per week without computer assistance, that number has been steadily eroding. Teleworkers are increasingly likely to use computers while teleworking simply because the percentage of information workers who use computers daily in traditional offices is growing.

Technology Rule One is the main motivator for this. Personal computers are delivering unprecedented information processing power to the desktop, regardless of the location on the desktop. By the year 2000, personal computers will be able to perform almost any task that was mainframe-based in 1990 (with the possible

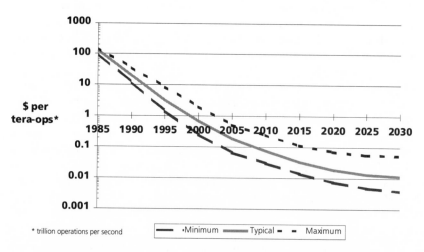

Figure 4.4 Performance improvements of microprocessors.

exception of serving out terabytes of data on line). All of this stems from the growth in power of microprocessors, the "brains" of personal computers. Figure 4.4 tells the story. Similar trends hold for any microelectronics devices, such as memory chips.

In effect, this means that, for most kinds of jobs, the jobholder can soon (if it hasn't happened already) have all the information resources of the principal office at home or in a telework center. Where the telecommunications network can't support enough information transfer, work can be carried between the principal office (if it still exists) and the telework office via some magnetic or optical storage medium. The number of options for this information transfer is continually growing: floppy disk, Zip™ disk, removable hard disk, recordable/erasable CD- or DVD-ROM, WORM disk, and PCMCIA[5] storage card, to name a few.

GOOD MORNING, BOB! NICE TO SEE YOU'RE AT YOUR DESK !

YESSIR!

Another critical outcome of this microelectronics capability growth is desktop video conferencing. That is, the average desktop or laptop personal computer can now display the boss and/or the rest of the gang at the principal office in living color, full motion, and stereo sound, given the proper network connections. In 1997, the cost of this form of point-to-point desktop videoconferencing using ISDN was about $1,400 per seat. By or before the year 2000, look for a price of about $500 per seat. Of course, videoconferencing at lower resolutions and frame rates can now be had, using ordinary phone lines, for under $250 per seat.

Is this an improvement or what? Now the boss can resort to the classical fallback management technique: call all the teleworkers and *see* that they look busy. More to the point, lack of visual contact will no longer be an excuse for prohibiting teleworking.

Further, with multipoint videoconferencing[6] many meetings can be held with all of the participants "present" and no two of

---

[5] CD-ROM means Compact Disk Read Only Memory; WORM is Write Once Read Only Memory; and PCMCIA is an acronym for Personal Computer Memory Card International Association.

[6] Audio/telephone conferencing can also assist in expanding access to many meetings. Add facsimile and/or computer graphics via modem, and most of the components are there for telemeetings that deal largely with routine information

them occupying the same room. Will the outcomes be the same as in traditional, everyone-in-the-same-room meetings? We don't know the full answer to that yet, but some outcomes will be better, if only because many meetings would otherwise not be possible, given the schedule and location conflicts of any group (larger than two) of busy people.

The danger of all this information processing power is that now we can make major mistakes with lightning speed. However, that danger is common to all users of personal computers, not just teleworkers. Many teleworkers have told us that they are far less likely to make computer mistakes while teleworking because of the major decrease in interruptions, as compared to life in the traditional office.

■ TELECOMMUNICATIONS NETWORKS

Telecommunications networks are the freeways of teleworking. At present there are two broad kinds of networks: local area networks (LANs) and wide area networks (WANs). As the names imply, one concentrates on shipping information around a relatively restricted area, while the other has a much broader scope. You have been using WANs for a long time; the most common WAN is called the telephone system. The problem is that these two kinds of networks encompass a bewildering array of different and often incompatible technologies, from good old analog voice transmission at 3 kHz to digital data transmission at gigabit-per-second[7] rates.

As far as telework is concerned, the fundamental question is, what has to be telecommunicated? The answer, for most late-1990s teleworkers, is voice messages, text data and numbers that have been generated "off line." In both of the latter cases, the text and data are represented on the computer by a small number of bits per information element. Therefore, none of these modes of information transfer requires much in the way of transmission capacity. However, that relatively simple demand on the transmission medium is changing.

---

exchange. When the topics get fuzzier, or there is high uncertainty, the need for face-to-face meetings, or a videoconferencing equivalent, increases. However, multipoint videoconferencing is two to three times as expensive as the point-to-point version.

[7] One gigabit per second is a billion 1s and 0s per second.

I THINK MY GIGIBITS ARE GETTING GOOEY!

TECHNICAL SUPPORT LINE

One of the key forces for increasing performance demands on telecommunications networks results from the trends in computers: the move toward high-resolution graphical user interfaces (GUIs—pronounced "gooeys"). A GUI can require thousands of times more data than a system that just transmits codes for characters that are displayed on the screen via a character-memory chip. That is, where a DOS character-mode system simply transmits a byte for each character that is displayed on the screen, a GUI system must transmit a picture of that character. Much more complicated. In addition, GUI systems generally employ color (which further triples the data load) and increasingly complex graphics, so that a super VGA screen requires about 2.4 million bits of data ($1024 \times 768 \times 3$) to display one screenful of information. It needs to do this about 70 times per second. This can be a problem. Even with a modem transmitting at 28,800 bits per second, a GUI interface with a distant LAN can seem painfully slow if the software requires this rate of screen updating.

➤ Wide Area Networks

The first thing to remember is that good old analog transmission is going away; the telephone system is going digital worldwide, although the transition process may extend into the twenty-first century. The most common telework telecommunications appliance today is the modem. Its sole purpose is to convert the digital output of a computer to analog signals capable of being transmitted on the telephone WAN and vice versa. Various tricks can be used in this process so that a phone line limited to voice transmission (nominally covering the frequency range from 300 Hz to 3 kHz) can be stuffed with 50 kilobits per second or more—but not much more. Connecting a high-end personal computer to a modem is sort of like connecting a fire hydrant to a garden hose—lots of ambition but not much production.

The replacement to the Plain Old Telephone System (POTS or PSTN, for you acronym fanatics) is, first, ISDN (Integrated Services Digital Network) then ADSL (Asymmetric Digital Subscriber Line), frame relay and ATM (Asynchronous Transfer Mode), with cable modems coming up fast in some areas. All of these WAN technologies are totally digital and deal with message switching. One consequence of this is that you get to throw away your modems and replace them with other interface devices that plug into the phone lines. The more important consequence is that you can send any kind of information over the same telecommunications line—voice, computer data, video—and have it received reliably at the other end, assuming, of course, that the other end knows what to do with it.

ISDN networks are in place in many countries around the world and by the year 2000 should cover most developed countries. Frame relay is a public data network service that can run at speeds up to 1.5 megabits per second. ADSL, with ATM, promises to be the next major step past ISDN as a service from traditional phone companies. It provides expanded capabilities, but may be a decade or more away from widespread implementation. Table 4.1 provides a rundown of some available options. Finally cable modems, with very wide band download capability, but limited upload capacity, may also show up in some areas. Add satellite data communications to this array to complete the picture.

Aside from the message handling software that constitutes the bulk of ISDN, frame relay, ADSL, and ATM technology there is a parallel trend toward replacing copper wires with optical fibers. The motivation is the same as that behind ISDN and ATM developments: increasing capacity—attaching the fire hydrant to a fire hose (the optical fibers) and putting a wetting agent in the water (ISDN and ATM). As of this writing, an interesting contest is developing over who will deliver this capacity to the end users, the established telephone system or cable companies.

If this isn't confusing enough, Northern Telecom, Ltd. and United Utilities, of Canada and the UK, respectively, have announced a system for providing megabit per second Internet access to homes via conventional electric power lines at rates comparable to those of more conventional Internet Service Providers. However, as of October 1997, there were no plans to provide the services in the U.S.

For mobile teleworkers, such as people on business trips, sales and technical support representatives, field engineers, etc., telecomm technology has also gone digital. With PCS (Personal Communications Service) in the U.S. and GSM (Global System for Mobile) in most of the rest of the world (the two will merge in coming years), mobile digital communications will be ubiquitous. In fact, mobile communications are usually the least capital-intensive way of bringing telecommunications into rural areas and developing countries.

Table 4.1 Alternative Data Transmission Media

Transmission Types	Mode	No. of Channels	Channel kbps	Max. Rate (kbps)	Transmission Limit
POTS (28.8 modem)	Point to cloud	1	28.8	28.8	None
ISDN	Point to cloud				18,000 ft.
US BRI					
B channels		2	64	128	
D channels		1	16	16	
US PRI					
B channels		23	64	1472	
D channels		1	64	64	
European PRI					
B channels		30	64	1920	
D channels		1	128	128	
T-1	Point to point	1	1544	1544	None
T-1C	Point to point	1	3152	3152	None
T-2	Point to point	1	6312	6312	None
T-3	Point to point	1	44376	44376	None
T-4	Point to point	1	274176	274176	None
E-1 (Europe)	Point to point	1	2048	2048	None
ATM	Point to cloud				
Minimum		1	1544	1544	
Maximum		1	622000	622000	
HDSL (single pair)	Point to point				12,000 ft.
Downlink		1	768	768	
Uplink		1	768	768	
ADSL	Point to point				12,000 ft.
Downlink		1	6000	6000	
Uplink		1	64	64	
SDSL	Point to point				
Minimum		1	160	160	
Maximum		1	2048	2048	
DSVD	Point to cloud	1	28.8	28.8	
SONET	Point to cloud			13220000	
Cable modem	Point to point	1	135	135	

Table 4.2 Planned Telecommunications Satellite Systems

Project	Function	Satellites	Operating Altitude	Service Start Date
Teledesic	High-speed data, teleconferencing	288		2003
Iridium	Voice, fax, paging	66	420 nm	Sep-98
SkyBridge	Data	64		
Celestri	Data, broadcast and video	63		merged into Teledesic
Globalstar	Voice	48	~ 400 nm	late 1998
Ellipse		17	medium	late 2000
Odyssey		12	medium	2001
Constellation		44	low	before 2005
ICO Global Communications	Voice	12	medium	2000

Added to the ground-based mobile systems are at least nine global two-way communications satellite systems scheduled for operation over the next few years. The Motorola-backed Iridium satellite system already has launched part of its complement of 66 satellites operating at an altitude of 420 nautical miles with the full complement of satellites scheduled for operation as this book is published. Table 4.2 shows the list of options planned as of this writing.

Finally, the global trend in privatizing telecommunications carriers promises to open competition and eliminate many of the artificial telecomm costs. Whatever the outcome, look for a rapidly growing ability to send any kind of information to anywhere—and from anywhere—at a reasonable price.[8]

The public telephone networks aren't the only forms of WAN. There are many other types, from private networks (PNs) under the control of single organizations (such as the State of California's internal telephone system) to national or global public metanetworks such as America Online, AT&T Mail, CompuServe, MCI Mail, Prodigy, and Internet. While the public telephone networks,

---

[8]The *price* of telecommunications is not often directly related to the *cost* of delivery. Government regulation severely distorts the market in this respect, both at national and international levels. The price of trans-border information transmission, in particular, seems to be influenced—generally upward—by national policy, although the prices are beginning to come down.

and many private networks, include both hardware (the wires/ fibers, communications satellites, microwave relay stations, switching centers, etc.) and the operating organizations, the meta-networks typically operate on top of the public switched networks. The public meta-networks typically offer a variety of services, from electronic mail to travel planning. For telework purposes, the electronic mail possibilities of these networks are probably the most compelling.

➤ Local Area Networks

Local Area Networks are the main means for high-speed, intra-office telecommunications. LANs have grown from a rarity in the mid-1980s to the common means of communications among members of work groups who use personal computers. LANs communicate between personal computers at multi-million bits per second rates. However, the problem with LANs for telework is embodied in their name: they are truly local in the geographic sense, while teleworkers are not.

The first step in solving this problem comes when one of the personal computers in a LAN acts as a telecommunications server. That is, it is connected to the network and, via one or more modems, to the telephone system. Teleworkers can dial in to the LAN communications server and get access to the files of their workgroup. Unfortunately, the teleworkers are limited in the rate of data transfer by the capacities of their modems; the fire hydrant-garden hose problem again. As the WANs go digital, however, this problem will diminish significantly.

➤ The Internet and Intranets

The Internet, a well-kept secret among the military and academic communities for two decades, exploded into public consciousness in 1993 with the introduction of the World Wide Web and MOSAIC, the first GUI Web browser. In just a few years, the Internet has changed the course of the computer industry and materially altered the possibilities for teleworking.

In particular, the Internet has allowed major expansion of the working horizons of small- to medium-sized businesses or any other organizations that could not afford extensive private telecommunications networks. For more on the possibilities, see Chapters 10 and 13. Further, by making telecommunications contact with vendors and clients a matter of daily experience in many offices, the psychological barrier to acceptance of teleworking is greatly diminished. It is a smaller step to go from Internet interaction with a vendor or client to doing the same with fellow employees.

At the minimum, expansion of a company's network to the Internet simply requires the addition of browser software to the arsenal of telecommunications technologies. This will give employees access to the Internet. Toward the maximum end, a company can have its own Internet servers, connected directly to a local ISP (Internet Service Provider) or even one of the Internet backbones. This step can involve extensive technology investments as well as the cost of full-time wide-band telecommunications interconnections.

Intranets generally differ from the Internet only in that they may be isolated from it. That is, a company with multiple facilities could have its own private telecommunications network interconnecting the facilities and providing Internet-like access to all its employees without ever being connected to the Internet. More typically, companies with Intranets are also likely to have Internet access as well. Additionally, companies can have the security advantages of private Intranets through the use of VPN (Virtual Private Network) technology that uses Internet carriers but isolates the company's communications traffic from the Internet.

Some more jargon is appropriate here. Each computer that provides data to the internet is called a *host*. Each separate site on the Web is called a *domain* and is distinguished by an address that is composed of at least the domain name, possibly some subdomains, and either the type of site or country in which the site is located, or both. For example, JALA International's web site address is *www.jala.com*. In this case, the *www* signifies that this is a World Wide Web site for the commercial *(com)* organization *jala*. Figure 4.5 gives an indication of where the Web is going in the next few years.

The fundamental message to the information industry of this growth rate is: *if you don't have a Web address, you don't exist*. The ability to interact on the Internet will be an absolute requirement for commerce in the 21st century.

■ SOFTWARE

One of the means of reducing the demands on the physical transmission of all that data is through recognition that much of it is redundant. This is particularly the case for graphics, and especially

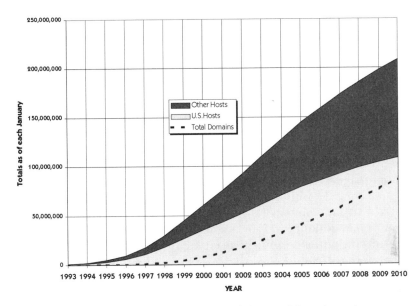

Figure 4.5 Projected growth of the World Wide Web.

video. So, a variety of software packages have been developed, with more advanced ones continually appearing, that compress the data into much more reasonable lengths. So, what seems at first like a hideous problem, sending two million bits of screen information at the rate of seventy times per second, becomes much more tractable; only the changes from screenful to screenful are transmitted.

The result is that the conversion to digital transmission technologies promises to allow enormous expansion in the ability to transmit information between computers at low cost.

One of the most promising, if ill-defined, areas of software development is in what is known as *groupware*. Groupware's goal is to effectively interconnect work groups, regardless of the location of the individual group members. First evolving on LANs, groupware usually migrates to WANs as well, allowing those connections to be global as well as local. The fundamental component of groupware is some form of electronic mail, e-mail.

E-mail allows any member of the group to send messages to any other member, at any time. No big deal? Ah, but the point is that the recipient need not be at his computer when the message is sent; it will patiently wait until she shows up. The Death of Telephone Tag. Furthermore, the sender can require a receipt verification as part of the message, so that there is no question about whether the intended recipient got the message.

For example, I get many e-mail messages via Internet from researchers around the world. Typically, those messages are sent when I am not in the office. This saves not only time, but nerves. If a colleague in Indonesia were to phone me in mid afternoon Jakarta time, I would not be ecstatic; it would be around 1:00 A.M. in California. Conversely, my calling her in mid-afternoon, LA time, might wake her from a sound sleep. The *asynchronous* nature of computer communications can be a significant asset to teleworking.

A variant of e-mail is chatware, software that allows members of small, or even extended groups to intercommunicate synchronously. Once confined to major network service providers such as CompuServe, chatware is now available for corporate intranets. The good news is that chatware allows instantaneous communication among far-flung team members. That may also be the bad news if it is abused to the point of causing as many interruptions as those of the principle office.

Facsimile works almost as well as e-mail, unless you want to keep the messages in digital form for further work or retransmission. This confinement to all-digital formats is particularly important when the group is jointly working on documents, spreadsheets or graphics. Conversion back and forth from analog (fax) to digital form can chew up huge amounts of time—as well as add to the paper storage problem.

Advanced groupware, such as Lotus Notes™—the premiere form of groupware, includes the tools for many such types of interaction. The trend toward multi-media (another ambiguous term) for personal computers increases the likelihood that video conferencing will be almost a standard item on mid-cost personal computers in the late 1990s. Electronic white board software allows group participants to share drawings and sketches, hand-written notes, and other jottings, either live or asynchronously. The main types of Web browsers from Microsoft and Netscape now also include some form of groupware.

Note that the preceding has concentrated on interconnectivity software. One other aspect of software is important for telework costs: duplication. Part-time teleworkers often have the same software at home—and/or on their personal computers at the telework center—as that on their personal computers in the principal office. Many, but not all, software manufacturers allow duplicate copies of their software to be kept on different machines, as long as no more than one copy is being used at a time. Other manufacturers insist on having separate licenses for each machine, regardless of the use patterns. This variance in software producer approaches causes severe hair tearing on the part of conscientious company information system managers. Hence, these usage rules will also evolve to a more standardized form (remember Rule Eight?) as telework becomes an increasing presence in the work force.

In short, as new computer software becomes available for the traditional office, it will likely work as well in homes. Already, technology is not the problem for most teleworkers.

■ SECURITY

One of the main concerns organizations have about distributed work situations like telework is that company-private information may somehow get into the wrong hands or otherwise be compromised. This could happen either intentionally—the perpetrator is an employee who wants to damage the company—or unintentionally. As an example, a report in the trade magazine *PC Week*[9] discusses the claim that the annual disappearance rate of the notebook computers of a company's sales personnel is 8%. This is not believed to be the result of sheer carelessness; the sales people are very protective of the machines. Rather, the disappearances are imputed to competitors' attempts to get access to the company's main computers or to get the sales data that is stored in the notebook computers, or both.

The point is that sensitive company information is easiest to protect from outside intruders if it is kept securely locked in the company's vaulted, main office computers with no access allowed from the outside. This is true, but irrelevant in today's economic climate. It is not possible to totally exclude outside access to the data while operating in a teleworking environment, as most companies must. Teleworkers could be restricted to using only non-sensitive data while they are teleworking but that would ultimately restrict the amount of teleworking—and its benefits—available to employees. Fortunately for teleworkers, the massive acceptance of the Internet has forced many reluctant companies to face up to

---

[9] Jim Seymour's column, September 27, 1993, p. 85.

these problems sooner. Once a general Internet access solution has been found, telework is automatically included in the possible options (whether or not the company realizes it).

There are several technological approaches to this access problem, all of which act either to keep the information out of the hands of unauthorized people or to make it useless to them if they do get it.

In a typical situation, the sensitive information is kept on the company mainframe or a LAN. The teleworker accesses it by modem. Several layers of protection can be built in at this point, such as all or some combination of:

> ➤ Having the telecommunications server either not directly connected to the mainframe or LAN, or examining all incoming data streams for the authorized signatures (that is, the server is a *firewall*).

> ➤ Using "smart cards" that display a password or token that changes every 30 seconds or so, in synchronism with a password identifier in the computer being called (the teleworker pulls out her smart card, dials up the company machine, and enters the password appearing on the card at the moment)

> ➤ Using a call back system—assuming all the password routines are completed correctly (many notebook computers have them built into the communications software, which is why they are desirable theft objects), the central computer dials the teleworker's home or other prearranged phone number

> ➤ Requiring a positive identification of the caller, such as a retinal scan, fingerprint, or hand shape detector

In cases where the sensitive information is stored on the teleworker's computer, there are two (at least) other approaches to denying access to others. First, the sensitive information can be encrypted. Only the authorized teleworker or others who know the key can decipher it. Quality encryption software is readily available (although there is an on-going battle between the U.S. government and the software industry about the allowable quality of encryption software).[10]

---

[10] U.S. law currently treats encryption software as a munition; therefore subject to export restrictions suitable for antitank mines. The software industry points out

Second, removable hard disks or Zip™ disks allow the information to be kept separate from the computer. Contemporary hard disks are small enough so that they are not bulky packages. Zip™ disks can hold up to 100 megabytes of data each. Teleworkers can keep them locked up at home or carry them along as they travel between home, a telework center, and/or the principal office. This has other advantages, such as allowing easier sharing of computers in a telework office. Employee A at the local telework center usually has different software and data requirements than employee B who works at the same computer the following day. If both have removable hard disks, the problem goes away. The growth of the PCMCIA standard is allowing this option to be practical even if the hard disks ordinarily work on different machines.

Like many of the so-called technological barriers to teleworking, security is not an impassable one. Nor need it be a particularly expensive barrier to overcome. Yet, any company that is considering—or practicing—teleworking should put some serious thought into the realities of protection of its sensitive information.

■ SOME REMOTE ACCESS INFRASTRUCTURE OPTIONS

The general issues just discussed provide the background for some specific examples of telework-support arrangements, together with the key relevant decision criteria. The first issue to be addressed is what sort of access the teleworkers need in order to be effective. The design of the information infrastructure hinges on that outcome. The following sections address the decision elements, options, and impacts on the information system operations, beginning with the simplest cases.

➤ Teleworking with a Central Facility

This is the case where all the teleworkers need access to a central facility, typically the company headquarters. This is common for

---

that the rest of the world is free to develop such software, with only U.S. manufacturers prohibited from shipping it abroad. The exportable, short key versions of the software have been shown to be breakable (although with considerable effort). This barrier is very slowly relaxing. However, it appears that the ban against export of encryption software only applies to *electronic* export. The source code for the 128-bit version of PGP (Pretty Good Privacy) was exported to Norway in 1997 and can be downloaded by anyone from the Oslo Web site: The International PGP Home Page.

small organizations or large ones in which the teleworkers are all associated with just one facility or campus. In terms of the numbers of teleworkers working in this mode, this is the most common case.

Decision Criteria

Access Frequency. If each teleworker is only intermittently connected to the network, then dial-up connections are called for. This is the typical situation. In some cases, as call frequency and/or duration expands, it may be more economical to set up dedicated lines to those individuals. At present, this is a fairly rare—and costlier—occurrence although ISDN and cable modems can provide low-cost equivalents to dedicated lines.

Access Scope. In some cases, simple e-mail will suffice. For example, the most common situation is where the teleworker has a complete set of applications software on a PC at his/her work site and simply needs to communicate with clients and/or other work group members via phone, fax, or e-mail, plus send files back and forth. In more complex cases, the teleworkers may need access to most or all of the company's information services and applications.

Security. As always, the dilemma concerns the tradeoff between providing appropriate access to the employees and limiting exposure of the "family jewels" to unauthorized access. The ultimate solution to this aspect of the security issue is probably high quality encryption, as discussed earlier. Still, the encryption and decryption processes do slow things down, possibly to the point where the cure may be worse than the possible disease.

Cost. Not all of these options cost the same. In general, the more complex the solution, the costlier it is, both in money and people resources. My experience has been that the greatest danger in starting a telework program is in technology overkill. The cost of a belt and suspenders approach to telework support may be all out of proportion to the value added by extra bandwidth, security, or other technological whiz-bangs. For IS managers faced with estimating a budget for establishing a telework solution, my advice is to think medium for the demonstration implementation, then test it extensively before and during the evaluation period.

Alternative Technologies

Application Server-Based Connection. The company has a mail and/or applications server to which the teleworker makes a direct connection via a modem bank, possibly through a firewall. For example, a Lotus Notes/Domino server could provide e-mail, database, and other applications services to notebook-equipped teleworkers. This could include sophisticated data entry/editing applications and graphics editing as well. Access is restricted to whatever is available through the server. This has the advantage of enhancing security, because of the limited access, and the corresponding disadvantage of limiting availability of some resources needed by the teleworkers as well as generally slow response times compared to some other options.

Remote Network Node Connection. In this case, the teleworkers connect to their organization's LAN via a remote access device (that also may include, or be connected to, a firewall between it and the network), using Point to Point Protocol (PPP) or Serial Line/Internet Protocol (SLIP). With this technique the teleworker has access to all of the resources available on or via the LAN. This is its primary advantage. The disadvantages of this approach are that security may be more of an issue and the network administration overhead is increased.

Remote Access via the Internet. Here the teleworker connects to the company via a local point of presence (POP), supplied by an Internet Services Provider (ISP) unless the company has its own POP. Because of security considerations, it is advisable to use Point to Point Tunneling Protocol (PPTP) in this connection. As in remote network node connection, the teleworker has full access to the company network, including file sharing, printing, and network-located applications packages. This approach is particularly important in cases where the teleworkers are not telecommuters, because of distance limitations; telecommunications charges are primarily for local phone calls. The disadvantages are those of remote network node connection plus whatever restrictions the ISP may place on the options, such as not supporting PPTP or ISDN access. (are you acronymed out yet?)

Remote Control. The teleworker has direct modem access to one or more central office personal computers, via a common software package such as LapLink™ or pcANYWHERE.™ This gives teleworkers access to whatever is accessible to the host PC(s) which could be the same as the remote network node connection, with the PC acting as the remote access device. One fundamental difference between remote control and the server-oriented options is speed; most remote control packages only transmit screen changes, while server options that repeatedly transmit entire screens are significantly slower.

Hybrids. Systems that work to combine the desirable features of all the previous options while reducing the undesirable ones are beginning to appear. For example, Traveling Software's Point B™ product suite uses several techniques to compress files, minimize hard disk access times, restrict transmissions to changes, and anticipate data flow so that redundancy and connect times are minimized.

IS Impacts

The IS (information Systems) manager has to juggle the various cost and quality factors in these options. For example, if ISDN connections are available, then the system lethargy factor of server-based options may not be important, given the enhanced control over security. If security is the primary consideration, then application server based access may be the best choice and remote control should either be very limited or closely monitored—adding further administrative burdens.

One security option in the remote control case is to ensure that the host PCs do not have network access. Unfortunately, while quite suitable for activities that can be confined to use on a single PC, this approach may unduly limit some teleworkers.

An important factor to consider in designing a teleworker interface is the likely access traffic of the teleworkers. Most teleworkers will be spending less than an hour per day accessing the network—some of them far less—while a few (such as system programmers, people who need constant database access, etc.) may need high levels of access. It is a good idea to have separate high and low load access points, possibly with dedicated modems for the high loads. In the low load cases, one element in the evaluation phase of a telework demonstration project should be a process for testing communication loading. As a first approximation, one modem per ten teleworkers might be sufficient.

➤ Distributed Facilities

In cases where an organization has more than one facility, then further telework options arise. One of these is to allocate some space in one or several facilities as telework center space. Another is to help minimize (or just keep track of) telecommunications costs by assigning inward WATS numbers for serving nearby teleworkers.

Decision Criteria

Inter-Site Access. Quite often, multi-site organizations have a certain amount of electronic interchange traffic just for ordinary, in-office business. Adding teleworkers to this mix may simply increase traffic between some sites, generated by teleworkers who work near site A but work for an organizational unit in site B (see Chapter 10 for details). Similarly, one or more sites may have telework center space, including some additional, more expensive technologies such as high resolution, full-motion, color videoconferencing.

Alternative Technologies

Wideband Site Interconnection. The principal addition to the technologies available at single company sites may be a dedicated wideband link between sites. Pick from among the technologies discussed earlier, with the desired additional bandwidth dependent on the amount of inter-site traffic generated by the teleworkers. Also consider the addition of videoconferencing. Telework may be just the right added use element that tips the scale in video's favor.

IS Impacts

If the title of Information systems Manager includes telecommunications, then the primary impact is in the need to include telework-generated traffic in the inter-site telecomm design. Keep in mind that, once telework proves to be very successful in a company, demand for new teleworkers will accelerate. This may have the added complication that fewer sites will be needed (more of the employees working from home, more of the time) and entirely new site configurations will be in order.

➤ Access via the Internet

For far-flung organizations, or ones where inter-site telecommunications traffic does not warrant dedicated lines, or where there is insufficient staff to handle complex telecommunications issues, Internet access may be the primary work communications mode. This is quite often the case for small companies, particularly those that employ widely dispersed teleworkers. The general arrangement is shown in Figure 4.6.

Decision Criteria

Make or Buy. A fundamental question in this case is: do we have enough staff and resources within the company to handle all of the different telecommunications demands or do we need to outsource part or all of that capability? Given the cost structure of the Internet, it may be hard to ignore its advantages for organizations with even a few distant teleworkers. In fact, for small companies,

Figure 4.6 Teleworking via the Internet.

the Internet is often the ideal medium for connecting workers in the same city because of its ready availability. Another comparable option is to outsource via online service providers such as CompuServe, or some combination of the two options.

Standards. As the number and diversity of teleworkers increases, so does the need for standards in shared/commonly-used applications, especially e-mail. Current Internet protocols limit messages to 7-bit characters. This means that parts of the content of applications and graphics files—which use 8-bit characters—would be garbled unless some form of conversion is used. Unfortunately, there are several varieties of character/data conversion programs available. Hence, Murphy's Law being what it is, chances are pretty good that your message to Sam, attached to an e-mail message by its own character cruncher, will appear at the other end as an indecipherable string of garbage characters. Uniform communication standards for your teleworkers are crucial.

Security. In addition to the security issues already discussed, the Internet intensifies the problem of authentication; that is, how can you be really, really, really sure that the person logging on to your network is actually an authorized teleworker? Some form of authentication less pregnable than passwords may be in order here, such as the smart cards or other authentication techniques discussed earlier.

A- or Iso-chronicity. The Internet uses packet switching as its primary communications mode. This means that each message you send, whether it is e-mail, a file, graphics, or whatever, is diced into small packets, each of which has a destination address, a sender address and an "envelope" containing part of your message. Thus, it is possible that each packet in a message could take a different route to get to the message's final destination, where it is reassembled (if all goes well) into the original version. Often packet 127 will arrive before packet 3 in this process. This is not a problem if your message elements can be *asynchronous.* But some message types, such as live audio and video must be *isochronous*; it is very important that they arrive in the proper order and on time. Although work goes on to allow the Internet to carry such traffic gracefully, your best bet for now is to reserve it for the traditional public switched telephone network (PSTN) or a private network with dedicated lines.

Alternative Technologies

Browsers. The main means of teleworker access to the Internet is via a browser. Microsoft Internet Explorer and Netscape's Netscape Navigator are the main contenders at present. Internet Explorer is confined to PCs running Microsoft Windows/NT or Macintoshes, while Netscape Navigator is available on a number of platforms including Unix and its variants. Both browsers include e-mail client software. The latest versions also include forms of groupware. The prime criterion is that all of your teleworkers should use the same browser and e-mail software.

Servers. If your company is intent on providing full-time Internet access, to clients as well as teleworkers, then you need to have one or more Internet servers. An Internet server is basically a computer that is dedicated to handling Internet traffic. Server software is available in a broad variety of forms, and for platforms ranging from old PCs with Intel 80286 microprocessors[11] to clustered mainframes. Since a server is basically a 24-hour per day, 7-day per week proposition, the telecommunications cost for a dedicated line to an Internet backbone are likely to be the primary operating costs (other than the people maintaining the system).

IS Impacts

The make or buy decision may be the critical one here. An entire industry has sprung up, seemingly overnight, to provide Internet access services. Some ISP's will provide server service, thereby allowing you to share telecomm access with other servers and potentially reducing the communication costs, at the risk of having a server not entirely under your control. The key question is: do you have sufficient spare human, budget, and technology resources, as well as sufficient Internet demand, to handle this yourself or would outsourcing that part of the task be a better option. Still, don't forget that *caveat emptor* is the key phrase here; since the ISP industry is very young, has suppliers whose capacity is chronically less than demand, and is populated by many firms that won't be around next month. As the industry matures, this problem will diminish in intensity, but it will still be around for several years, given the sustained growth rates of the Internet.

---

[11] The Linux operating system with Netscape's Fast Track server software would work on such a system.

➤ Network Isolation—Real or Virtual?

Another approach to balancing the conflicting issues of low-cost free access by teleworkers and strict security for confidential company information is the Virtual Private Network (VPN). The goal is that with a VPN the teleworkers can work via a public network like—but not necessarily—the Internet, while still deflecting attempts by intruders to steal or corrupt company information. The architecture of a VPN is much the same as that shown in Figure 4.6, but there is a difference in the details.

Decision Criteria

Complexity. If you either already have a real private network—and find that its costs and complexity are growing out of bounds—or you haven't the staff or budget to tackle what is essentially the task of running your own phone company, then a VPN may be an ideal solution.

Security. If information security is the paramount consideration, with low-cost access to teleworkers, customers, and suppliers a close second, then VPNs are worth investigating. The market has a growing variety of security options, with various forms of encryption, authentication, and message encapsulation to protect your information.[12]

Cost. A primary attraction of the Internet and VPNs is the possibility of major telecomm costs savings. The level of savings is proportional to the amount of long distance telecommunications you need for your ordinary business and your teleworkers. If your company has leased telecomm lines (i.e., a private network) that are chronically operating below capacity except to peak periods, then you may find substantial savings by using a VPN either for all of your communications or for peak loads on top of a smaller private network.

Alternative Technologies

As of this writing, there are no complete, end-to-end VPNs, although a number of hardware suppliers and telecomm service

---

[12] Relevant acronyms include: IPsec, ESP, DES, MD5, and RADIUS. Pay attention, there will be a quiz on this.

providers are developing pieces of the solution using encryption and PPTP or VTP (Virtual Tunneling Protocol). Service providers include CompuServe, MCI, Netcom, and UUNet Technologies, while all of the primary network hardware providers are working diligently on solutions. The problem, as always in an infant technology, is the lack of standards. The gory details are beyond the scope of this book.

IS Impacts

At present my advice to IS managers is to carefully check the currently available solutions. A well-designed and integrated VPN may well be the key to broad acceptance (or at least the last nail in the coffin of broad denial) of telework.

■ TECHNOLOGY TO FIT THE JOB

Given the general statements above, what do you really need to have in order to support your own teleworkers? Here are some sample setups for teleworkers in different types of jobs. The minimum requirements are based on Rule Six.

➤ Routine Data/Text Processing

Routine information jobs are often considered to be great candidates for teleworking; the jobs are well defined, as is the output, and it is relatively easy to check results. Most of these jobs are computer-intensive by now, or are on the verge of being computer-based. The key technology issues for teleworking have to do with the means of raw input delivery/distribution and output retrieval. The scale of the operation and the required turn-around times affect the approach to use.

At the small workgroup telecommuting scale, sneaker-net technology may suffice: the data/text processing person takes a stack of entry sheets or tapes home at night and comes in with a floppy disk or two after a day of telecommuting. At the next level of sophistication, the paper forms are sent by interoffice mail to the organization's facility that is nearest the teleworker's home for daily pickup by the teleworker. Similarly, dictation could be downloaded to the teleworker's answering machine. The results are sent by modem to a personal computer or LAN in the principal office. In any of these cases, the teleworkers can either be at home or in a telework center. With a little more technology, an ISDN-equipped teleworker can receive photocopies of documents, such as insurance forms, then return the processed action results to headquarters.

A key reason for failure of this simple situation is also simple: *forms fatigue.* As an example, a bank terminated a telesecretary program because of the forms hassle. The telesecretaries did indeed produce more accurate letters quicker. Yet the bank discovered that, because of the many different pre-printed forms it used (designed before the PC revolution), it had to employ another person at the headquarters printer to make sure the right form was in the printer when the data arrived from the telesecretary! Solution: use printers (laser or ink-jet) and/or personal computer software that includes all the necessary form formatting information; the printer prints the form and the data simultaneously. Better yet, it is possible to eliminate internal paper usage altogether by scanning all incoming documents, converting them to electronic form, and dealing exclusively with the electronic versions thereafter. Many insurance companies and other members of the financial industry use this method.

Massive order entry systems also are readily adaptable to teleworking. The most often quoted example is that of the J. C. Penney stores' phone entry operation in Milwaukee. In this case the necessary technology is a telephone distribution system that interconnects the main database functions to individual teleworkers' homes. Personal-computer-based telecommunications network distribution systems that cover this function are commercially available. SWIFNET, a system developed by World Church of God to manage gift-giving resulting from their church's TV religious programs, is an example.[13]

➤ General Mid-Level Information Jobs

Many mid-level jobs are less dependent on technology than the routine jobs just discussed. Often, the only additional technology fix needed (aside from what most mid-level people already have at home, as in Figure 4.1) is some combination of an additional telephone line, pager, fax machine, and voice mail or answering machine. For many manager or professional teleworkers, the primary task performed during teleworking is catching up on reading and simple correspondence.[14]

---

[13] The church is now defunct, for reasons completely unrelated to their teleworking arrangements.

[14] By the way, as I forecast in the mid-70s, mid-level people using personal computers are increasingly performing tasks that once were reserved strictly for secretaries:

The next step in technology escalation is the addition of a stand-alone personal computer. The primary use of the machine is for text processing, with occasional spreadsheet manipulation and preparation of graphics for presentation coming in second and third. Part-time telecommuters are more likely not to use computer telecommunications, preferring sneaker net—or laptop or notebook personal computers—as the primary means of information transfer. The work results are brought in to the principal office on the non-telecommuting days.

As the technology trends become more pronounced, the use of various forms of teleconferencing and/or groupware will spread. Since meetings occupy a substantial amount of the time of mid-level people, the fraction of time spent in non-face-to-face meetings will increase. Certainly, in organizations where networked PC use is common, mid-level people will need appropriate levels of technology support to increase the amount of their teleworking.

➤ Specialists

The primary differences between specialists and other mid-level teleworkers are likely to be in the horsepower of their computers and/or software, and in the extent of their telecommunications usage. For example, actuaries are likely to need large amounts of data on either a mainframe or CD-ROM(s). Attorneys may need access to legal databases such as LEXIS.™ Architects and engineers may need CAD/CAM software and the highest-end personal computers. Programmers may need almost constant access to the mainframe, although possibly not during peak business hours. Information specialists need access to meta-databases such as DIALOG.™

➤ Sales and Field Service People

Laptop and notebook computers have revolutionized sales and field service techniques and processes in many industries. The

---

text entry and editing. This is often decried as a waste of managers' more valuable time, but that quibble is almost always wrong. The initial text entry process rarely slows down a manager or professional who is trying to get ideas out; most of the time is spent thinking up what to say next, even for inept keyboarders such as myself. When it comes to content editing, the idea originator is a far superior editor and time saver than the traditional mark-it-up, send-it-to-the-secretary-for-a-redraft, etc., process. All that is required is a fairly rudimentary knowledge of personal computer text processing software.

prospect of instant access to all the critical information materially enhances the leverage of a sales call. Insurance salespeople can assemble and print policies on the client's premises. An insurance adjuster can complete the transaction in a single visit, using the hard-disk-stored database of replacement or repair costs. A realtor can display prospective homes in a client's own home; with advanced, three-dimensional CAD software, the realtor or an architect can even take the client for a virtual "stroll" through the building.

A teleworking sales representative no longer needs a desk in the principal office. Lists of sales prospects can be downloaded to the representative's home. Final contracts can be printed either by the portable printer or, if a more visually attractive version is wanted, on the laser printer at home. Many large companies have noticed this possibility, in the past year or so, as a powerful means of reducing office space costs. But don't forget the security issues mentioned earlier.

➤ Senior Executives

Senior executives are the most difficult to get out of an office. They tend to spend much more times in meetings, for the simple reason that they are hired primarily to deal with uncertainty and ambiguity—activities that generally require real face-to-face meetings. However, information technology acts to compress meeting time. A few years ago a senior executive of a large corporation told me that he typically used to spend a whole day discussing business problems at one of the regional facilities he visited. Now, with the ability to resolve a good portion of the routine matters by e-mail and telephone conferencing, the face-to-face aspects of the meetings were reduced to an hour or two. The new problem: what to do with the spare time at the regional centers?

Senior executives also tend to spend more time than average traveling, usually more time than they or their families would like. Like everything else noted above, the coming technological changes can allow the executives to substitute telecommunications for transportation for some of the meetings and change their "meeting" location to home from somewhere else.

Senior executives also tend to be significantly less willing to learn to use complex, user-surly software. If they are going to personally use a computer-with-software package, it had better actually be intuitive. Few contemporary systems can make that claim, although the executive gap is closing.

Chapter

How Do You KNOW
They're Working?

This leading question has a very simple answer: **You don't, not every minute!**

Not only that, but I'm pretty convinced that there really isn't a surefire way to *know* whether an information worker is actually working without getting inside his or her head—except in those cases where the work is apparent as physical activity of some sort, such as a secretary's keystrokes (he's not writing a letter home, is he?). Since much of information work is cerebral it is also invisible while it's going on. You can't see it. You can't hear it. You can't feel it.

Even if it's occurring—or failing to—before your very eyes.

So why do we managers have this compulsion about needing to be together with our employees in an office somewhere in order to do useful work? Perhaps it is because many of us have been brought up with the role model of the boss as cop. Those of us who adhere to this belief somehow feel that our personal charisma/

charm/scowl will somehow inspire our workers into new heights of effort. A well placed glare or stroll past their desks from time to time will keep the laggards motivated. Therefore we have to be in the same location with them, *all* of the time, in order to get the best results. Otherwise the whole organization will run down in very short order.

There is a growing body of evidence, including our own measurements over the last quarter century, that suggests that this isn't so, that the most vital attribute of a manager is *leadership,* not authoritarianism, not Big Brother behavior. I suggest that leadership can be practiced very well at a distance as well as up close. Telemanagement requires leadership ability. Leadership can be learned.

■ THE TWO HALVES OF TELEMANAGEMENT

There are several key attributes of leadership. Two are particularly important for teleworking. They are *trustworthiness* and *rapport.* The key to leadership is the ability to inspire others to empower themselves to work toward the same goals that the leader elucidates. Lack of leadership manifests itself by everyone in the group proceeding according to their own private goals and agendas, heedless of the group goals. Here is where trustworthiness and rapport come in.

➤ Establishing Trust

The core virtue of quality telemanagement is trust. If you trust your employees to do their jobs, whether or not you are physically in their neighborhood, and they trust you to provide competent direction and guidance, reward them for work well done—and penalize them for work poorly performed, much of your job is under control. If you don't achieve that level of trust with everyone, then teleworking is not recommended for those for whom the trust factor isn't there.

This is why it is generally easier to have well-established employees as teleworkers, rather than new workers. In fact, surveys of successful telecommuters generally show that they have been with their organizations longer than the average worker. These employees are known quantities. They know how the system works and their managers know how they work. Trust already has been established.

Yet, even in those cases, there may still be some nagging uncertainty. "I trust them to produce as long as they have the stimulation of the office environment, but what happens when they're at home? (or in another, unknown quantity, telework office)" Then we come back to the original issue. How do we arrange things so that we can build up the trust level to the point where we and our employees feel comfortable with it?

The following sections of this chapter treat those dilemmas.

➤ Quality Communications

Trust depends on quality communication. Quality communication helps develop trust. "Quality" in this case refers to the idea that each party to a communication can accurately assess the meaning and intent of the other parties as a consequence of the communication. The law of uncertainty has been defeated, if only temporarily. This doesn't mean that you always *like* what the other person is saying, but it does mean that you *understand* it.

Our usual preconception is that the highest quality interpersonal communication occurs when we're face-to-face with the other person. We rely on a variety of cues—facial expression, body language, tone of voice, the physical surroundings—to help us interpret and expand on the information reaching us through speech alone. In teleworking, at least for the next few years, those visual cues may not be available to us. We have to make do with a reduced palette of psychological colors to help us decide what the other person is *really* saying. This is one of the key factors that makes novice telemanagers nervous. They are concerned that the loss in communications richness will be so high that they will have severe difficulties in getting their ideas across to their employees, and in deciding what those employees are really doing.

Face-to-face situations also allow us to get a little lazy. Because our employees are there in front of us we can assure ourselves that, even though we may not know exactly what they're doing at the moment, we know that they're working, at least. Activity is reassuring. But possibly misleading. The real question is: is all of that activity on our behalf? We depend on our personal charisma, enforced by periodic site visits (that is, management by walking around) to keep the troops in shape and ourselves well informed as to what's really going on.

I don't argue with the claim that face-to-face communication is *richer* than electronic substitutes such as telephones and electronic mail or computer conferencing. But face-to-face isn't necessarily *better* than these other forms in many situations. The key is in the content of the communications. After all, a short, explicit written communication can often be more meaningful than a twenty minute meeting in which the real point never comes out, or is lost in a welter of extraneous comments and remarks.

One point to keep in mind is that you, as a manager, must make sure that the *frequency* of communications is such that the remote employees still feel themselves to be part of the gang at the office. "Out of sight, out of mind" can be a worry for them as well as for you. The delicate balance is between being in touch and being pestered, on the one hand, and being forlorn on the other.

But the answer, of course, the real secret of much successful teleworking communication is this: *Mix face-to-face and electronic communications so that the routine, information transmission types of messages get sent electronically and the very complex or emotion-related ones get sent or received face-to-face.* This is why most home-based telecommuters get into the office an average of two to three days a week. In all cases, the manager's job is to work on maximizing the effectiveness of all of the forms of communication. If the messages are getting through accurately, then we can start to rely on the self-motivational powers of each individual to get the job done. Occasional walking around doesn't hurt either.

Does this mean more work for the manager? In a sense, yes. It means more thought on how you and your employees communicate best and more action directed toward maintaining communications. But, if that work is done well, it means less work in unsnarling the communication foul-ups that can plague the best of offices at times.

■ THE BUYER-SELLER MENTALITY: SETTING PERFORMANCE CRITERIA

Although vital to the success of teleworking, and of quality management in general, high trust and quality communications are fuzzy terms. Warm and fuzzy, maybe, great buzzwords for management seminars, but fuzzy nevertheless. The nexus of teleworking management is the set of performance criteria and assessment techniques that interconnect management and employees.

➤ Focusing on Product instead of Process

Any organization exists primarily to produce some kind of product. Whether that product is widgets, groceries, laws, newspapers, inventions, regulations, or invoices. The product is what the organization's clients get and is the basis for their evaluation of the effectiveness of the organization. It makes no difference whether the organization is a separate entity, like a government agency or a company, or a subunit of a larger group, such as a section or department, the rule still applies. It makes no difference whether you are providing products and services to external clients or to other company work units, the rule still applies. The nature and quality of your product is what counts.

Furthermore, most constituents don't care *how* your product was developed. They *do* care about its quality—in terms of their own needs, its promptness, and cost. But how it was done and what processes were involved are not important to them.

In management we have a similar situation. Ideally, a manager should be able to give his or her employees a set of requirements for what they are to produce, establish the level of quality required, the cost in time and resources, the timing and rate at which the results are to appear, and leave it at that. Get out of their way. The employees skip back to their work places, produce the results as specified, and they all live happily ever after. Ideal organizations really do work like that. The ideal is the goal toward which we are striving.

Why is this so good? Because it is a situation in which there is minimum conflict, a minimum of working at cross-purposes, a maximum of all the pieces fitting well together. Extremely low hassle for the manager—and the employees. Everyone nows his or her job, is competent and eager to produce results, and is able to adapt to the occasional schedule or cost or resource scarcity pressures that come along.

Back in the real world it appears that sometimes things don't work that way. Sometimes we don't specify the desired product adequately, *or* the employees don't have the skills, knowledge, or training to produce the results, *or* they didn't fully understand our specifications, *or* the needed resources just weren't available, *or* it took more effort than everyone thought, *or* . . . *or,* horrors, they are shiftless, lazy, and unmotivated, couldn't care less about getting the product out—and won't do it unless you stand over them like a warden and personally keep them at it.

If that last alternative is *really* the case, you have significant trouble ahead. Fortunately, it's pretty rare, but certainly not impossible. Yet, we often act as if that *is* the case for many of our employees. It's time to examine why. *Are* they shiftless or is it that they aren't sure what they're supposed to do? *Are* they unmotivated or is it because they don't see where they are supposed to be going or why they should go there? *Are* they lazy or just inadequately trained? Maybe what's needed is a better understanding—and agreement—on both sides as to what each part requires of the other. A pact or memorandum of understanding. Something that specifies what each of you will contribute to the common goal of getting that product out; that says it as unequivocally as possible (or as necessary). Then you have the basis for establishing that long term valuable: trust.

Your job is to provide specific, measurable, and attainable standards for the teleworker to meet so that he or she knows what must be done, why it must be done, and when and how well it must be done.

When that is accomplished consistently the relationship is simple: more trust means less contractual detail, less effort in negotiation, a smoother-running organization, less misspent effort on all sides, and probably a better-satisfied set of clients. Furthermore, since most people basically want to do good work, this relationship provides a level of motivation that is more intense and consistent than any nonviolent sort of ruler-subject relationship.

➤ The Agreement between Managers and . . .

Notice that all of this applies to work in general. It is not peculiar to teleworking. But teleworking relies much more heavily on the understanding or trust relationship simply because it is not practical for you to act as the cop or monitor for people who are somewhere else. If you have employees who you feel are just not trustworthy when they're out of sight, they should not be teleworking—unless, of course, they work at a telework center. There someone else can see whether they look busy and you can check on their progress via periodic face-to-face meetings and more frequent phone calls or electronic messages. Your job should be as a coach and mentor, not an overseer.

By the way, all this talk about agreements and memoranda of understanding doesn't mean you have the prospect of a huge stack of legalistic documents in front of you. I mean it in the sense of a mutually binding agreement between you and one or more other parties. You are all free to change it mutually as circumstances change. The key word is *mutual*; all parties must agree on what is required, of whom, and when. The key concept is *attitude*. If you all believe you are in this venture together and you all share responsibility for the group effort, then you have most of it already. And it needn't be in writing. In fact, if you have successfully managed your group for some time, most of this is probably understood already.

➤ Employees

As a manager, your most important asset is your employees. I have spent considerable time on what is required of them. The agreement also must include what is required of you. Sometimes it's very little other than occasional guidance about some difficult aspects of their work. Other times you are required to provide much more: training, hand-holding through some new task, encouragement, access to scarce resources, special equipment. Whatever it is, make sure you *both* understand who is responsible for what. Do this with an agreement session as part of the initiation process for each new teleworker, *before* he or she actually starts teleworking.

It might also help to draw a schedule or flow chart showing when each side gets input from the other. In particular, try to schedule face-to-face meetings sufficiently far in advance so that your teleworkers can set up their home or telework or main office schedules. Make sure those meetings are productive, although this seems to happen naturally with teleworkers. You might also want to ensure that your employees are available during specific hours of the day so that you and others can communicate with them easily.

You may have lots of requirements for input that don't need meetings. Electronic mail, faxes, and phone calls may satisfy most of those requirements. Other employees who come in to the office may act as couriers for written materials and supplies. Whatever the need, try to make it explicit *before* teleworking begins.

This is also a good time, if you don't already use email or some form of groupware, to test the need for a group electronic bulletin board if your teleworkers are using personal computers. In short, make sure the agreement covers the communication resources you'll both need, as well as other resources including paper, forms, stamps, and sealing wax.

➤ Others

Here the issue shifts in flavor more toward understanding than agreement. As a manager, part of your job is to let your colleagues, clients (both internal and external), and upper management know about the new working arrangements. It is important to get their feedback in order to tune your teleworking operations successfully. Colleagues, clients, and upper managers all have their own expectations about what it is that your group is doing for, with, or to them. Part of your task as a manager of teleworkers is to see that their fondest expectations are realized.

It might even be worth a test. Some time ago I came across a case where a senior manager of Company X remarked that he recently had found it much easier to get in touch with Employee Y because Y had installed an answering machine and promptly returned calls. Before, several hours or even days had elapsed in a classic case of telephone tag. The senior manager was astonished to hear that Y was now telecommuting from home, generally was out exercising in the early afternoon, and in mid-afternoon returned calls stored on the machine. Try it with some of your teleworkers—if the demands of your daily operations allow it. Merrill Lynch even goes to the extent of running a telecommuting lab so that future telecommuters can acclimate themselves beforehand.

Attitudes of colleagues are particularly important. Most members of organizations spend far more time communicating with colleagues than with superiors or subordinates. Those colleagues who are not telecommuting will invariably come up with comments like, "Well, did you come back from vacation just for this meeting?"[1] Tensions like this will arise. The telecommuters are suddenly different. At first they are even more visible in the organization because of their difference. Therefore it is of extreme importance to let the non-teleworkers know that the teleworkers are still a vital part of the organization and are contributing at least as much as before to its progress. The trick is to let both sides know that neither of the groups—teleworkers and non-teleworkers—is specially privileged or specially burdened. The adjustment may take some time.

■ MEETING AND REVIEW STRATEGIES

➤ Why Have Meetings?

Why indeed? To share information. To find out what's going on. To gossip. To explore ideas, plans, and alternatives. To reacquaint ourselves with other people. To negotiate. To come to decisions. To politic. To cajole, exhort, persuade, threaten. To keep from getting our other work done. To relax. To be entertained. To feel important. To butter up to the boss. All sorts of reasons.

Teleworking makes meetings more difficult, doesn't it? Certainly it's hard to have a spontaneous get-together if we're scattered all over the countryside. Teleworkers have to plan for meetings in advance so they can arrange to be there. More than one teleworker has told us that this planning does have an interesting side effect: there are fewer meetings and those that do occur tend to be shorter and more productive. Let's examine what happens.

---

[1] As a consultant I am often greeted with similar remarks as, still jet-lagged from an intense business trip to Europe or Asia (ironically, explaining to people how they can reduce travel), I am asked how I enjoyed my vacation.

➤ Formal Objectives

Most officially scheduled meetings have a formal agenda. Certain topics are to be discussed, decisions made, and subsequent actions taken by specific attendees. Ideally, the attendees come prepared to enter into those discussions, make those decisions, and take those actions. In very well run meetings that is exactly what happens. That is what meetings are about. End of subject.

Sometimes.

Often (not in your case, of course, but in some other groups) meetings depart from the ideal somewhat. The agenda is less well defined, the participants are not always well prepared, the discussions tend to wander, and the decisions are not always made, are not well understood, or are a little too vague. It happens. When it does we can always have another meeting very soon to straighten out the ambiguities.

The problem with this is that in telecommuting situations togetherness-time is a valuable commodity, not to be wasted. Face-to-face meetings are more difficult to arrange because the travel time is way up; it's no longer the time it takes to walk from the office to the conference room. Meetings have to be scheduled, people have to show up and the formal content of each meeting must be dispatched expeditiously.

Hence, a few suggestions. Wherever possible, plan the meeting well ahead of time. Decide what must be discussed. What decisions have to be taken? Who should contribute? Are there alternatives if they can't make it? How much time should be spent discussing each item? To what extent are digressions permissible? Get the agenda together (including a statement of objectives), distribute it to the attendees in time for them to get prepared, and stick to it (within reason) at the meeting. This is what makes meetings shorter and more productive.

What can also make them productive for teleworkers is the use of electronic mail (for those organizations that have it) or fax transmissions to exchange information, including progress reports, *before* the meeting. If all the basic information flow has already occurred then the meeting itself can concentrate on the decision process rather than the information exchange that all too often makes up a large part of "normal" meetings.

➤ Informal Objectives

Meetings also have informal, or at least not-formally-stated objectives, hidden agendas, or whatever euphemism is appropriate. The meeting serves as an occasion for A and B to get-together on the side and make agreements about other topics than the formal ones of the meeting. Often the real—but unstated—purpose of the meeting is to establish pecking order or to gather support or test the water for something not on the agenda. One executive told us that she felt she could not telecommute because she had to attend the daily bull sessions (that were otherwise unproductive) just to maintain status in the organization.[2] This, of course, is an admission that career advancement in that organization depends more on political than on objective performance factors. The success of teleworking depends on the dominance of objective rather than political factors for career stability and advancement.

Thus it is important to examine these informal meeting objectives as an indicator of how well the organization can function in a teleworking environment. If the informal objectives serve as sources of inspiration for improving output they are very useful. If they serve as foci for disruptive or inequitable coalition forming— degraders of teamwork—they can be counterproductive.

➤ Scheduling Issues

Since most telecommuters will still need to be in an office part of the time, even though they may not be in the office an equal or greater amount of time, meeting scheduling will not be much more complicated. If you have regularly scheduled staff meetings it probably will be quite effective to continue to have them, unless they are daily affairs.

More problematic are the occasional or *ad hoc* meetings. These tend, by the laws of probability and the perversity of human nature, to be randomly distributed throughout the week. Hence, what starts out, with the best of good intentions, to be an effective home telecommuting schedule can soon degrade to an every-day-in-the-office-as-usual system. No gain. Remember, in the job screening process I concentrated on the ability to clump meetings as a perquisite to home telecommuting. It is therefore important to enforce that as much as possible.

The best way to do this is to regularize most meetings: staff, project review, brainstorming, planning, etc. Try to arrange them, or have the participants arrange them, so that none of the telecommuters needs to come to the office for meetings more than three

---

[2] Her service company subsequently had a severe case of client loss; a possible hint that politics doesn't always pay.

days per week, on average. This does not necessarily mean that all the telecommuters come in the same days, unless they all go to the same meetings. It may be better, for facilities usage purposes, if the group's meetings can be staggered so that the entire group is almost never there at the same time. Make sure that each meeting chairperson distributes an agenda, either in person at a prior meeting, by memo, and/or by electronic mail or fax to the telecommuters, at least a day before the meeting.

This type of scheduling has some beneficial side effects, in our experience. First, meetings tend to be more effective as a consequence of prior, rather than ad hoc, agenda setting. Participants tend to be better prepared when they know they are discouraged from using the meeting as the occasion to "get up to speed" on the subject. Prior electronic messaging of information relevant to the meeting further serves this end. Conference room usage can be distributed more evenly, thereby cutting down on facilities needs.

The cost of this to you as a manager, or to the meeting chairpersons, is some extra time and effort spent in meeting planning. This can be more than repaid by the time released to you as a consequence of the shorter, more effective and less frequent meetings that occur as a result. There are also some computer-based aids for all this, such as outliners (for agenda setting), project scheduling packages, and groupware such as Lotus Notes.™

All of the above is for relatively routine get-togethers. There is always the problem of the special occasions when an unexpected crisis (as contrasted to an expected crisis) occurs. Why is no one ever there when you want them? Here, there is clearly a problem with home, or maybe even telework center, telecommuters. There is a necessary delay before they can get from wherever they are to wherever the meeting is to occur. The real question is: do they really have to *be* there?

➤ Telemeetings and Teleconferencing

Try holding some of these crisis meetings with tele-attendees via conference telephone. Note that audio teleconferences really require special equipment (that is, more sophisticated than a speaker-phone) and multiple phone lines *if* several people are involved. It's not absolutely necessary to have such equipment if such meetings are very infrequent, but it is important when telemeetings become regular events. On the other hand, you don't need to *own* the special equipment (such as a multi-port telephone bridge); the service can be supplied by most local phone companies or long distance carriers—and may be coming soon on the Internet.

A telemeeting may be viewed mostly as a stopgap measure for including people in a conference who otherwise wouldn't be able to make it, as in our crisis meeting scenario. It may also be viewed as a great way of getting people together on other, more routine occasions; people who ordinarily wouldn't attend the meeting because of travel time pressures.

The latter motivation has been driving the growth of video and audio teleconferencing systems for the past decade. Video teleconferencing, in which TV pictures are sent between conference locations, is still relatively expensive, not to be used for the typical routine meeting in the typical office. However, audio conferencing can be a very useful tool for including everyone in a meeting without all of them actually having to go there. This use of telephone technology is not confined to regular teleworkers, of course. It can be used to augment many forms of meeting in traditional office situations.

Another form of electronic meeting is the computer conference, in which it's not even necessary that more than one person be "present" at the meeting at any given time. Computer conferencing is an expanded version of electronic mail: each of the participants sends computer messages to one or all of the other participants over some period of time lasting from a few hours to months. The conference leader sets the agenda, keeps the discussions on track, organizes the summary of proceedings—keeps the messages "threaded," and otherwise acts as the usual chairperson. The difference is that all of this is *asynchronous*; the participants "attend" when they have the time, which generally is not the same time that any one of the other participants can be involved. This is a particularly good tool when the participants are very widely separated geographically.

➤ The Importance of Ongoing Feedback

Another area of good supervision that sometimes is taken for granted in teleworking is the act of giving ongoing feedback about how the work is being done. Many employees—at all levels and in all locations—believe they don't get enough feedback about how they're doing; this is a special problem, though, for teleworkers who don't have as many opportunities to bump into the boss and get that feedback. That's why you have to take some extra effort to provide it.

That *extra effort* doesn't necessarily mean *extra work*. I'm talking about simple, quick, short ways of letting people know how well they're doing. This can include everything from a five-minute chat in the office when the person is in, to a brief message via electronic mail or voice mail, to a quick note you jot down in the margin of a memo or report you return to the employee. Keep it simple—and don't confuse this with the periodic performance appraisal.

Even though your telecommuters may be in the office three to four days a week, on average, don't wait for those times to give feedback. One way to keep them feeling tied in is to give each one a call or send an e-mail or fax message on the home days (for those so equipped). It can be very rewarding for a teleworker to get a call saying, "Nice job!" when he or she has been working hard for several days on a big project. Better still, make that pat on the back public at a staff meeting.

Your department is probably not self-contained; your subordinates may have frequent interaction with customers, clients, or vendors as well as with others in your work unit. It is a good idea to get feedback from those people on occasion to get their views of your teleworker's performance. You can funnel those comments back to the teleworker, taking the place of some of the informal contacts he or she might have with them while both are in the office.

➤ Informal Communications—The Key to Productivity

Most of the above has been concerned with formal communication within work groups. As we all know, there is a lot of communication in the office that does not occur in formal situations.

The Necessity for Informal Communications

This informal communication is absolutely necessary for the mental health of the organization. Meetings take care of the specific work objectives that must be met, set the marching orders for the members of the group, and form the backbone of the communications structure of the group. But those communications, vital as they are, are only part of the picture. Informal relationships between members of a group act as the glue that holds the group together. These relationships do much to establish the feelings of trust I keep harping on. They often serve as the means of surfacing danger signs and problems in the organization, or of spreading motivation, spirit, togetherness, or whatever you wish to call it, that transforms a collection of individuals into an interdependent, intersupportive team.

While formal communication can be packaged into memos, letters, reports, and meetings, informal communications are more elusive. Consequently, they are less easily captured by formal technologies such as computers. This is why I insist that, for most of us telecommuters, face-to-face get-togethers are absolutely necessary. We schedule meetings in the office ostensibly for formal communicating, but the hidden agenda is that a good deal of informal communication happens at the same time.

Keeping Teleworkers Linked into the Office

Nevertheless, teleworkers, whether at home or in a telework center, are potentially bereft of some chances for useful informal communication, compared with what is available in a traditional office setting. How can we compensate for or, even better, avoid that loss?

➤ Remember that the goal is to create the expectation of continued contact, and not to let them drift away from the mainstream.

➤ Don't assume anything about what you think the telecommuters might be hearing; take those extra few minutes to pick up the phone and pass along the word about changes in projects, organization, etc.

➤ Try to include the telecommuters in various social events around the office, especially the informal ones. If the gang is thinking of going out at lunch time or after work, try to do it on a day when the telecommuter is in the office—or do it so that he or she can join you from home.

➤ Make a point of routinely routing memos and other FYI items to the teleworkers; these don't always have to be sent to the home but should be waiting in the person's mailbox on days in the office. E-mail, of course, should be set up to automatically send copies to the teleworkers.

➤ Remember that a big part of your role is as a "buffer" and problem-solver—make yourself available to provide any resources the teleworker needs, such as manuals, supplies, answers to specific questions, etc.

This "linking" role is perhaps the only managerial duty in teleworking that's not a part of your normal job. But it's one of the most important parts because it can make the difference between your teleworkers feeling isolated or still feeling like they're on the same team.

■ NEW EMPLOYEES

One important question is whether to use new employees as teleworkers. For the most part, organizations with home teleworkers start with employees who have been with the organization for some time—at least long enough to learn the ropes of coping with the organization's system. In general this is the safest way to go. However, new employees may make perfectly fine home teleworkers from the start if the candidates:

➤ Have been elsewhere in the organization for some time (that is, they may be new to you, but not to the organization);

➤ Can be quickly trained to an adequate level of competency via teleworking or by a short introductory course; or

➤ Are not in jobs that require much detailed knowledge of organization policies and procedures[3] (or if there aren't many policies and procedures).

If you use new employees as home teleworkers it is very important to get them to regular meetings at first and/or to make sure they get to "meet" their colleagues over the electronic network. New telework center employees, of course, have fewer problems in this respect. There the task is mostly to get them to meet the others at other centers and in the principal office over a relatively brief period.

---

[3] These are usually jobs where either very special or very well-defined skills are required. Two examples are an actuary and a data entry clerk, neither of whom necessarily needs much knowledge of the organization in order to function well.

■ CAREER MANAGEMENT FOR TELEWORKERS

Close behind isolation as a concern for teleworkers is one about their careers: will they be "out of mind" because they're "out of sight?" Experience across many jobs and companies has not shown this to be true, but the concern may be there.

Here are some things you can do to put your teleworkers' minds at ease in this regard:

➤ **Highlighting:** Make sure the teleworker gets the same credit or attention for the work done remotely as if it had been all done in the office. Sometimes this means you have to take pains to put that person in the limelight so he or she may be gone but is not forgotten. Be careful that you don't draw too much attention, especially if it's out of proportion to the task. This can create a backlash among the in-office workers.

➤ **Job or Task Rotation:** Make sure the teleworker doesn't get pigeonholed into doing only certain kinds of tasks because those are most easily managed from a distance. Again, the goal is to mirror the job or task mix that would have happened in the office. Task diversity builds skills and keeps the person from stagnating. This is, of course, true for all employees but a bit more relevant for teleworkers. This is also a way to ensure that the in-office employees don't feel that they are getting all the onerous tasks, while the teleworkers are living it up at home; make sure that both teleworkers and non-teleworkers share in the less popular tasks.

➤ **Cross-Training:** A closely related aspect of career building is that of training several people, both teleworkers and non-teleworkers, to do some key tasks that are not necessarily part of their nominal jobs. This is particularly important in situations where clients, upper management, or other "outsiders" frequently call (or drop by) the principal office to get information on the projects in your unit. There should always be someone there who can "cover" for the distant teleworker without strain. As is the case for job rotation, this expands everyone's horizons.

➤ **Even-Handed Appraisal:** When it comes time for performance appraisals, make sure you realize that teleworkers may use new methods to do old tasks. They sometimes do this to cope with (or take advantage of) their relative independence. Don't penalize them for using new means to get to the same or better ends as before. In fact, their different ways of performing their work may be worth exporting to your other employees. Don't forget: it's the results that count for both the teleworkers and the non-teleworkers.

■ SPOTTING PROBLEMS EARLY

Despite all the training and everyone's best efforts, it's still possible for snags to develop. Teleworkers can run into problems affecting their performance or satisfaction. Your job is to watch for some early signs and act on them quickly. Here are some of the obvious and not-so-obvious "red flags":

➤ Job performance starts to suffer (either in quantity or quality of results).

➤ Absenteeism starts to increase.

➤ You, or the teleworker's co-workers start having communication problems—either decreased or poorer communication.

➤ The teleworker shows less interest in attending department meetings or otherwise shows signs of becoming a "loner." (Don't confuse this with signs of irritation at ill-organized and rambling meetings. Teleworkers tend to become more time-conscious and agenda-oriented as they gain experience.)

If you see these or other signs, don't jump to conclusions that the person is necessarily having serious problems. After you've verified your observations—and are certain that something has changed for the worse—your first step is to get more information.

The best first step is to confront the problem with the teleworker—share your observation as factually as possible, and then ask for his or her comments. Your goal here is to have an open discussion that will lead to a clear understanding of the problem, and a joint commitment to resolving it.

A little bit of empathy goes a long way here. The teleworker might be having problems adjusting to the new routine, or could still be trying to work out the fine points of scheduling her or his time. Sometimes, the relative independence that teleworkers have can be overwhelming, and some more detailed supervision can help.

In summary, you want to get an open discussion going and keep it going until both of you are comfortable with the outcome. Don't assume the teleworker must return to the office full-time, though that's certainly an option. In most cases, that's the *last* resort, not the first.

■ GLOBAL TELEWORKING

Information technology, a key factor in the development of telecommuting, has also made it much easier to consider teleworking on a national or global scale. With the continuing explosion of Internet use, even small organizations might do well to consider global operations. Although the management principles and practices just covered apply at this expanded scale as well, there are some additional issues that may arise in global teleworking.

➤ Why Consider It?

Even if your company has no immediate interests outside of your local community, actions in the rest of the world surely affect it now and will do so increasingly in the future. For many organizations, of all sizes, the necessity to think in national or global terms is here now. One of the principal reasons for this is the growing disparity between the high demand for skilled employees and the local supply of people with the necessary skills; people who may not wish to relocate their homes.

An article buried in the October 7, 1997 edition of *The Wall Street Journal*[4] provides a case in point. The story tells how US West, one of the "Baby Bell" companies, was faced with the refusal by most of the 130 senior executives of a newly acquired subsidiary to relocate from their homes in the Boston area to Denver, US West's headquarters. The reason for the move? ". . . to forge closer working relations between the two units" despite earlier assurances that no such move would be required. It is ironic that the desirability of teleworking, on other than a local basis, was ignored by a Group CEO of a company that markets telecommuting and should know better. By adhering to the traditional industrial revolution mindset, US West seemed willing to risk the loss of a substantial number of its leaders. See Chapter 10 for more discussion on the likely outcome of this centralization strategy.

---

[4] Page A10, titled: US West Says Most Officials in Unit Declined to Relocate.

A second important motivation for global teleworking is the possibility that your company can substantially expand its markets without necessarily investing in extensive physical "bricks and mortar" infrastructure. Using telework centers in other regions or countries you can establish local presences, including hiring local teleworker employees, with a relatively small investment. IBM España, for example, plans to have most of its 3000 employees teleworking by the year 2000 with a combination of home-, client-, and center-based operations.

➤ Infrastructure Factors

All of the large cities in the world that I've visited have major traffic problems and related urban air pollution, a common incentive to explore some form of telework. However, not all of the world's large cities—and definitely not all of the world's more rural regions—have telecommunications infrastructures that will support leading edge teleworking such as interactive video editing. Therefore, one of the first issues to consider when establishing a teleworking component in another country is the adequacy of its telecommunication infrastructure.

This may not be a serious constraint for many forms of teleworking since reasonable telephone and/or Internet access can be quite enough. Ironically, the U.S. tends to be somewhat behind Western Europe in providing widespread ISDN services. Further, Scandinavia—particularly Sweden and Finland—leads the world in the use of cellular services for fixed-base teleworking.

So-called third world countries also are much more likely to use mobile rather than landline telecommunications. As the various new low altitude (that is, non-synchronous) communications satellites come on line, you can expect to see mid-1990s level Internet capability available in most areas of the world. Still, many third world countries have problems in maintaining basic electrical power, even in large urban areas. If frequent power outages or voltage surges are a problem in your target teleworking region, think APU (auxiliary power units) and UPS (uninterruptible power supplies).

Finally, support technology and services, particularly information technology support, may vary widely from country to country. Factors such as import restrictions and scarcity of trained repair people can substantially increase the costs of operating in other countries. For example, computer prices—as well as diversity of suppliers—in the U.S. are generally significantly lower than those in other countries, although the gap is narrowing.

➤ Telework Forms

Homes outside the U.S. tend to be smaller than those in the U.S., by about one-third, making it difficult to establish uncontested space for home offices. Homes are more likely to be apartments than single family detached dwellings. Cities tend to be higher density, with mixed commercial and residential use in the city centers. Consequently, telework center teleworking is likely to be more attractive outside the U.S., with neighborhood and village telecenters a promising option.

➤ Cultural Influences

Not so many years ago I had the conviction that the way things were done in U.S. organizations was pretty typical of companies and government agencies in the rest of the world. Therefore, I supposed that the task of spreading the word about teleworking to the rest of the world simply involved giving speeches and writing articles to appear in these other places.

That, like the requirement that telework must have a positive bottom-line impact, is a necessary but not sufficient condition. Although American style business practices have certainly had an effect in other countries, you cannot assume that the way you do things in the U.S. will work without modification elsewhere.[5] Here are some factors to check as you hone your management style for global teleworking. Most of these comments are based on my personal experiences. You should check culture-specific sources for broader information.

Language

The *de facto* language for international business—and by far the most dominant language on the Internet—is English. This is good news for most English speakers and a source of constant irritation for many of those whose native language is something else (particularly if it's French).[6] If your distant teleworkers' native language is other than your own, I suggest that you try to gain some familiarity with it. No one language seems to be able to capture all

---

[5] This is even true *within* the U.S.

[6] The 10 most widely spoken languages are, in decreasing order of numbers of speakers: Mandarin, English, Russian, Spanish, Hindi, Arabic, Portuguese, Bengali, German, and Japanese. In 1997 I estimate that at least 64% of those using the Internet were English speakers, with Spanish speakers a distant second.

of the subtleties of our symbolic environment, so selected phrases from your jointly understood languages may enhance the quality of your communications. Grammar, syntax and spelling errors do not seem to be significant impediments to information transmission in email exchanges.

Furthermore, if you are using telework as a means of expanding your operations into other countries, it is critical to have bilingual teleworkers on your staff. There is no substitute for someone who speaks the local language when you are establishing a local presence.

In one sense there is an advantage to working with someone whose native language is other than your own: you are more attentive to possible misinterpretation of your and her remarks. When you both speak nominally the same language it is easy to ignore the possibility that, though you both use the same words, you may attach different meanings to them.

➤ Time Shift

Global telework includes 24-hour days. The local time difference between California and Western Europe—or Australia and Eastern Asia—is 8 or 9 hours.[7] This has some great advantages. Foremost is the ability to have teleworkers in one time zone handing tasks at the close of their business day to team members in Europe or Asia, then to teleworkers in India, and so on, for essentially continuous action on high priority tasks. Since there is no way that a single manager can monitor all of these in real time, the prime tenets of telework—establishing trust and quality communications—are especially important.

Customs

Differences in business and social customs, if ignored, can put potholes in your road to success. If you are a business headquartered in the U.S., accustomed to payment in 30 days, note that the European custom may be closer to 90 days (or months, if you're working with government agencies). Working hours vary from country to country. Mediterranean European countries tend to have two-hour lunch breaks and later closing hours than those in the U.S.

---

[7] That is, you *add* 8 or 9 hours to go from West Coast time to that in Western Europe, and *subtract* 8 or 9 hours (then add a day) to get local time in the Western Pacific region.

Germans have strict rules about weekend work (streng verboten). Most of the rest of the world seems to take longer to make business decisions than do U.S.-based organizations. The Japanese, and many Europeans, dislike saying "no"; you may think that they are agreeing to something, only to discover later that no such agreement exists.

And so on. Although individual teleworkers may be more adaptable to your own ways of doing business, it's very important to spend some time investigating these operational differences *before* you set up long-term telework relationships.

► Laws and Regulations

Although the GATT talks and the subsequent World Trade Organization are directed toward ultimate elimination of trade barriers, that blessed (or cursed, depending on your point of view) state is far from reality today. On the other hand, when it comes to information trade—and telework is information trade—the national and global legal and regulatory establishments generally have fallen well behind the real world. The explosion of Internet traffic is changing the de facto rules at an accelerating pace.

Still, there are some fundamental business issues that must be resolved when you are developing international telework arrangements. For example, what taxes need to be paid—and to whom—on salaries of people who work for you but live in another country? What duties are levied on equipment or software that you ship to your foreign teleworkers—or when they ship it back to you? Under what circumstances should your teleworkers be employees or independent contractors—and what are the tax and benefit (particularly health care benefit) implications of each option?

Most of these issues have different answers in each country where the teleworkers reside. For small organizations the best short term approach may be to treat all of your foreign teleworkers as independent contractors with the stipulation that they must be responsible for all local taxes and regulatory compliance. This approach has a definite loyalty risk and still may not get you off the hook for some taxes. Larger organizations, and small ones interested in long term relationships, will find that hiring these teleworkers as full-time regular employees is the best option. In that case the local requirements need to be carefully explored.

Although all of this may sound daunting, in my opinion it is our future. See Chapter 13 for more on this topic.

Chapter
6

Rules and Regulations

It is important to have a core set of rules and regulations for teleworking, whether it is a demonstration project or everyday standard operation. The rules should be sufficiently specific to minimize the risk of ineffective performance but sufficiently flexible to allow tailoring for work unit and individual cases. The following are key issues that should be covered by the formal rules.

■ KEY ISSUES

➤ Allocation of Responsibility

Emphasizing who is responsible for what, such as defining explicitly what is to be done, doing it, and providing help, advice, supplies, maintenance, etc., is of critical importance. Also important is the home teleworker's responsibility for keeping the home office in OSHA-acceptable condition.

➤ Fair Employment Practices

Teleworkers should *not* be special people in terms of the company rewards system. Teleworker qualification criteria should be as objective as possible, based on performance criteria. There are no other restrictions.

For example, your teleworkers should *not* be working on a piecework basis. They should not fear loss of income resulting from an irregular supply of work. We assume that participant teleworkers will form agreements that will afford them a steady supply of work and that they will not be susceptible to income fluctuations like those who labor on a piecework basis. In addition, participants need not fear onerous work speed-ups (that is, an escalation of minimum requirements to turn the home office into the electronic sweat shop conditions feared by labor organizations).

However, although the baseline employment requirements should remain as established by general agreement with all company workers, we expect that teleworkers will realize productivity increases sufficient to offset any additional net cost of implementing a teleworking program. (This "net cost" should be calculated as total additional costs incurred by the company in equipment purchases, designation or provision of new telecommunication lines, et cetera, minus company savings in office space rental and maintenance, parking lot leases, et cetera.)

In a survey we performed in the mid-1980s, my research team at USC found that about 80% of mid-level information workers[1] worked at home *in addition to* their daily stint at the office. Teleworking should not be just another way to get employees to put in extra hours after their office-based workday. Work assignments should be established clearly prior to implementation. We recommend that these agreements not be made subject to rising expectations. That is, the contractual agreement should specify that implementation of this work style shall not be a means of securing computer-mediated overtime, but that teleworking will take place as substitution for more "traditional" working arrangements.

➤ Time Accounting

This appears to be an issue primarily for home teleworkers. How are they to account for hours spent, if at all? Honor system (recommended); the boss drives by every three hours; monitors the telephone or ?? Whatever the details, there should be an agreement *before teleworking begins* as to what the rules are. The issue may also exist for telework center teleworkers in cases where there is no on-site supervisor to take attendance.

However, although it may be important to think about how long it will take to do a specific task—as a means of estimating

---

[1]The survey involved about 1,000 mid-level workers in a number of Fortune 100 firms. More than 3% of the workers responded that they spent at least 8 hours per week telecommuting; that is, without going in to their principal office. At the time, none of these firms had a formal telecommuting program.

effort, your ultimate focus should always be on the results. Was the task performed as expected, and in time for the pre-established deadline? If so, fine; that performance result, not the time spent arriving at it, should be the success criterion. Time spent is primarily useful for estimating how long it will take to get the next similar result. For information work of even moderate complexity, time accounting is at best an uncertain performance measure.

➤ Sick Leave

As above. If you're sick, you're sick. But remember that what once caused use of sick leave, such as attending the kid's school play in the afternoon, can disappear as the home teleworker makes it up early that morning or that evening.

➤ Liability and Insurance

Who's responsible when the home teleworker trips over the cat in the den at three A.M.—on the way to register that great, dream-induced idea—and breaks a leg? Who's responsible for theft of a computer owned by the company from an employee's home? Who's responsible for paying the insurance premiums?

Most successful teleworking organizations have accepted the premise that the home teleworker's office is covered by the same rules as the principal office. Job-related injuries are job-related injuries, regardless of the location of occurrence in this view. However, this theory has not yet been tested as far as we know. In any case, employees should be given clear and adequate information as to the need to document claims as well as the documentation procedures.

➤ Putting It Together

We address these issues explicitly here in the form of a set of guidelines for a telecommuting demonstration project, governing the relationships between the company and the telecommuters. The guidelines are collected in a document called "The TeleGuide." The TeleGuide covers most of the items of contention that have arisen in past telecommuting experiments, as well as addressing potential problems that have not yet arisen. Each employer tends to put a slightly different structure on the guidelines. Therefore, these should be used as a starting point for your own, customized set. The emphasis here is on telecommuting because it is the dominant form of teleworking, although the same principles apply for more general forms of teleworking.

The first step, as an integral part of the program planning process, is to review the TeleGuide and then submit them to the legal staff—with a specific deadline for comments.[2]

After completion of the legal review, your version of the TeleGuide should be sent to senior executives and distributed as part of the training documentation. To ensure that the senior executive doesn't get relegated to the bottom of the In stack, you may want to have the TeleGuide accompanied by a cover letter signed by the CEO. The version for the training sessions may either be incorporated with other materials or serve as a separate document. In the latter case, you may also wish to attach the CEO cover letter, or one from a more immediate manager.

The "we"s in the TeleGuide refer to these managers. These guidelines should be accompanied by an agreement like that described earlier for home telecommuters. There should also be a signature page on which the prospective telecommuter attests that he or she has read and understood the guidelines. A telecommuter's acknowledgment, a supervisor's checklist, an outline of possible department-specific rules, and an outline of a detailed work agreement follow the guidelines.

---

[2] Attorneys love to agonize over every word in the guidelines, so make sure that the legal staff realizes that timeliness is a virtue. This is likely to be a more persuasive argument if the attorneys are also in line to be telecommuters.

TELEGUIDE
AN INTRODUCTION TO TELECOMMUTING

This guide covers the relationships between the Company and the participants in the Company Telecommuting Demonstration Project. It describes telecommuting and the general rules of participation. These rules are effective for the duration of the employee's telecommuting or the duration of the project, whichever is shorter.

The purpose of the TeleGuide is to answer common questions about the Company's demonstration telecommuting project and is for informational purposes only.

Participation in the demonstration project is voluntary and, therefore, management retains the right to determine the job characteristics best suited for telecommuting participation. Moreover, the selection process, as well as the decision to send a participant back to his or her regular work environment, is the sole responsibility of management.

What Is Telecommuting?

Telecommuting is the substitution of telecommunications and/or computers for commuting to work. There are two main forms of telecommuting: home telecommuting and telework center telecommuting. In home telecommuting, a Company employee works at home instead of in the office, possibly with the aid of a personal computer. In telework center telecommuting, the employee works at an office that is close to his or her home rather than at his or her regular location. Telecommunications systems interconnect the home telecommuters, the telework centers and the "principal" offices so that everyone can keep in touch.

Why Is the Company Interested?

For several reasons. *First,* if telecommuting becomes widespread it could have major positive effects on traffic flow and air quality. *Second,* telecommuting may reduce costs and increase effectiveness. *Third,* telecommuting may beneficially alter energy use, the general quality-of-life, and the economy.

Why Should I Be Interested?

If you want to reduce the time you spend commuting, arrange your working hours to more closely fit your off-work plans, feel more in charge of your life and your job, get closer to your family, or reduce some of your work-related expenses, then maybe telecommuting is worth a try. There is no guarantee that all—or even some—of these things will happen for you, but those are among the reasons most often given by telecommuters for their enthusiasm.

The Company Telecommuting Demonstration Project

The Company Telecommuting Demonstration Project is designed to test the desirability of telecommuting for the Company and for Company employees. Other tests of telecommuting in business and government over the past 25 years have shown that employee job satisfaction generally increases, as does effectiveness. Both the employee and the employer are winners in this situation. The Company is testing telecommuting to develop methods for ensuring that both employees and management achieve positive and satisfying results; then the use of telecommuting can be appropriately expanded throughout the Company.

What's Going to Happen?

The project is in five main parts. The first part comprises orientation briefings for potential telecommuters and their supervisors. Part two focuses on deciding who will be the participating telecommuters. Part three includes training for telecommuters and their supervisors. The fourth part starts when the first project telecommuter begins telecommuting. It will last at least twelve months after telecommuting first officially starts. Finally, part five consists of the evaluation of the project. It will result in recommendations to the chief executive officer concerning expansion of telecommuting.

Why Have a Special Project; Why Not Just Do It?

Because telecommuting is a departure from traditional ways of working. It is important to make sure that it is done right. It is not advisable to rely on undocumented or overblown tales of great success or miserable failures, either in Company departments or other organizations. Where telecommuting succeeds it is important to know exactly why—and how much. More importantly, in cases where it doesn't work out we want to know how to avoid those situations and how to make it work. In order to do that, it is necessary to take very good notes about who is involved, what works, and what doesn't, all through the project. This is why it is *extremely* important that you, as a telecommuter, provide information about what works for you—and what doesn't—over the term of the project. In fact, one of the documents you are required to sign (Telecommuter's Agreement, included here) concentrates on that as one of the conditions for participating in the project.

Who Are the Telecommuters?

Participants in the project are being selected from many Company areas. They may include accountants, secretaries, managers, programmers, engineers, secretaries, administrative analysts, resource specialists, clerks—many sorts of "information workers." Basically, if your job primarily involves working with information, you are a potential telecommuter. However, because of some restrictions, such as the need to use very specialized (or very large) equipment, or the necessity to frequently interact with others face-to-face, not all information workers can be telecommuters—yet.

Do I HAVE to Telecommute?

No. All of the participants in the project are volunteers. Furthermore, if, during the course of the project, you feel that you do not want to continue telecommuting then you are free to return to your job as it was before the project started. Likewise, if your immediate supervisor feels that telecommuting is not working out for you, you may also be asked to return to your former work pattern. It is also possible that changes in work circumstances, responsibilities, or assignment, may require that an employee be taken off the telecommuting project if doing so helps to better meet the immediate Company needs. Remember, the intent of the project is to evaluate telecommuting rather than to specially reward or penalize individual workers.

How Many Telecommuters Are Participating?

About 100. Many of them will telecommute from home, the rest from telework centers at selected field locations as they become available.[3] The telework center telecommuters will work at the

---

[3]This is a critical question, to be answered during the planning phase of the project. A rule of thumb is that you should have enough participants to give statistical validity to any data you are taking during the evaluation phase. Don't forget that the standard error of a normal distribution is $1/\sqrt{N}$, where N is the number of participants. That is, a survey involving 100 participants gives you a standard error of 10%; one with 1000 participants produces about a 3% error, etc. On the other hand, since telecommuting is still scary to a number of managers, you don't want to have so many initial telecommuters that management apprehension turns into panic.

center closest to their homes. Some telecommuters may do both: work from home some of the time, and from a telework center at other times. Not all telecommuters will begin at once. The formal implementation part of the project will run twelve months, beginning shortly after approval by the CEO. The first telecommuters will probably be home-based people, with telework-center-based telecommuting starting later.[4]

Who's in Charge of the Demonstration Project?

Normal reporting relationships will not change. Your department has a project coordinator who will act in an advisory capacity to the Telecommuting Advisory Committee, which is responsible for advising the CEO on policy issues and reviewing progress of the demonstration project throughout its term. The overall project is being coordinated by the _____ Department. Your department coordinator should be contacted if you have questions about the operational details of the project.

THINGS YOU SHOULD KNOW
BEFORE YOU VOLUNTEER

There are a few other things that you should know before you volunteer to be a telecommuter or a telemanager. Here are some commonly asked questions and answers about the details of the company telecommuting program.

Health and Safety for Home Telecommuters

What about Accidents?

In order to maintain a businesslike atmosphere and minimize the chance of accidents, you are expected to keep your home office as clean and free from obstructions as if it were your regular Company office.

If you have a work-related accident at home you are expected to report it promptly. You are covered for such accidents as if they were in your principal office.

Will Someone Check Out My Home?

The Company reserves the right to do so, since it is ultimately responsible for ensuring that employees will have a safe work

---

[4]Or vice versa, depending on the extent of your facilities shortages/planning.

environment. Safety inspections may be made of the home office space prior to the beginning of the demonstration and at random times during the life of the demonstration. At least twenty-four hours prior notice will be given before any inspection. Basically, home-based telecommuters will be required to keep their office free of dangerous obstructions, loose wires, and other hazards. They should also have furniture, seating, acoustic isolation, and lighting that is conducive to a good work environment. Routine inspections during the project are not anticipated.

Equipment

Will I Need a Personal Computer to Telecommute?

Your job may not involve computer use and may still be perfectly "telecommutable." Telework center telecommuters may or may not need personal computers, depending on the details of their jobs. We expect that each telework center will have them.

Some home telecommuters may need only a telephone to work effectively. On the other hand, many home telecommuters will need either a personal computer or a data terminal and a modem for their work. If you regularly use a computer in your daily work, you may also need it at home. So all combinations of telephone or no-telephone, computer or no-computer are possible in the project.

Who's Buying?

(Most government organizations we have surveyed do not provide additional equipment. Many large organizations that manufacture personal computers provide them for their telecommuters [usually older models]. Often, we find that telecommuters have better equipment at home than they do in their offices. Further, some departments in large organizations may decide to provide some equipment and/or software, while others don't.) Any such equipment or service provision is solely at the discretion of the Company. This will vary among the participating departments or divisions. This equipment and software remains the property of the Company.

Who's Responsible for Maintenance?

The Company will be responsible for routine maintenance of Company-owned equipment and software used during the demonstration project. However, it is each employee's responsibility to ensure that the equipment and software are used in businesslike conditions, whether at home or in a telework center. This includes ensuring the equipment and software against abuse or other violation of existing policy of the Company concerning protection of its property.

Can I Use the Company-Provided Equipment and/or Software for Personal Purposes?

As long as your personal use of the equipment and/or software contributes to your proficiency with it, does not harm it, and does not conflict with other rules and regulations of the Company, you may use it for personal, non-business purposes.

Can I Use My Own Equipment?

Yes, provided that it is compatible with the equipment used in the principal office. The responsibility for its maintenance and repair is still yours. Whether this occurs should be decided by your supervisor before you begin using the equipment.

Liability

What Happens When Something Breaks or Otherwise Goes Wrong?

You are responsible for immediately informing your supervisor. If you are conducting authorized Company business and your actions are within the course and scope of your employment, the Company's liability is the same whether you are at home, at a telework center or at your regular work location. This means that, unless your actions are fraudulent, corrupt, or there is actual malice, you will be indemnified by the Company for any losses arising out of the use of your private property, both real and personal, for Company business.

If you interrupt Company business to do something that is not related to Company business and an accident occurs, then you are responsible just like any other homeowner.

Travel Expenses

Who Pays for Work-Related Travel?

Existing laws, and rules and contract provisions of the Company, are applicable to all the participants in the demonstration. On a case-by-case basis an employee's home, rather than the principal office may be designated as the headquarters for purposes of calculating mileage or per diem when the employee is required to make business trips.

If I'm a Home Telecommuter, Do I Get Travel Expenses for the Times When I Have to Come in to the Office for Meetings?

No. Remember, a telecommuting day is one where the telecommuter works away from his or her regular workstation, either at a telework center or at home for the entire day. The telecommuting workstation becomes the "regular work station" for that day. Telecommuters and their supervisors would not normally schedule meetings, or travel, on days when the employee is scheduled for telecommuting.

Hours of Work

If I'm a Home Telecommuter, Do I Have to Work at the Telework Office or at Home All the Time?

No. As a matter of fact, most telecommuters will spend several days per week at their principal office. Neither telework nor home telecommuting is an all-or-nothing situation; the idea is to work out a method for splitting your time between telework center or home and the principal office so that the tasks best done at the remote location (such as reading, letter and report writing, calculating, etc.) are done there, while the tasks best performed at the principal office (such as meetings) are done there. Note that *telecommuting is counted in whole days only.* That is, you have to average at least *one full day* per week[5] telecommuting over a six-month period to remain in the project. Two four-hour stints per week don't count.

Note that *average,* as used here means just that. We expect you to telecommute at least twenty-four full days in a six-month period.[6] That does not mean that you have to telecommute one day each and every week. Some weeks you may need to telecommute several days, other weeks not at all. Telecommuting should be tailored to the demands of your job.

---

[5] This requirement is in the rules because of air quality considerations. A significant part of commuting-related air pollution comes from cars being started. So the idea is to eliminate car starts altogether for home telecommuters. If a telecommuter comes in to the principal office for part of a day, the air quality advantage is mostly lost.

[6] The reason for this constraint is to ensure that each telecommuter has enough hours of telecommuting so that impacts measurements taken after a year's experience are with seasoned telecommuters. With only occasional telecommuters, many of the desired impacts on effectiveness, etc., may not have appeared.

Do I Have to Work during the Standard Hours?

Your specific work periods must be arranged with your supervisor prior to your participation in the demonstration and may be revised at intervals throughout the project. Many telecommuters work when they feel most productive; often this is at times other than the standard office hours. Yet it may also be required that you can be contacted during specific work hours. Some telecommuters may be on a set schedule that coincides with their current work schedule.

What about Sick Leave and Vacation?

You will accrue sick leave and vacation time at the same rate as you would in an ordinary office. If you are sick and unable to work in your home office, report those hours, as you would in a normal office setting. We anticipate that home telecommuters will use less sick leave than non-telecommuters; that has been the experience of other organizations involved in telecommuting. If you take abnormally high amounts of sick leave, or if you are not performing up to expectations in your home telecommuting, then we will ask that you discuss the problems with your supervisor if you haven't already done so. Your use of vacation, compensatory time off, sick leave, or any other type of leave is subject to approval by your supervisor, as usual.

What about Overtime Pay?

In all cases your regular hours of work, whether on a fixed or flexible schedule, must not exceed what is normal for you unless it is approved in advance by your supervisor. There will be no change in overtime. As before, prior approval of the supervisor is required for any overtime worked. Other types of premium pay, such as standby, lead, and shift pay, will not be affected by telecommuting.

Do I Have to Be Glued in Front of the Computer All Day?

Not at all. You might not even use a computer at all. Remember, the emphasis is on using these technologies to help you work better, not to dominate your life. If your job requires that you spend time reading, meeting with others, talking on the phone, or just thinking, then that's what you should be doing.

Training

Is There Any Kind of Telecommuter Training?

Yes. Special workshops for telecommuters and their supervisors will be given before telecommuting begins. Each workshop will take about two hours. These workshops will emphasize the practical aspects of telecommuting: deciding when and how much to telecommute, setting up home offices (if applicable), scheduling meetings, keeping in touch with your fellow employees, and generally dealing with the problems and issues that may arise. Every telecommuter and his or her supervisor must enroll in one of these workshops prior to starting to telecommute or to manage telecommuters.

There also will be a continuing series of meetings throughout the demonstration project during which fellow telecommuters can share experiences and ideas for improving telecommuting.

Performance and Workload Standards

Will Performance Standards Change?

Performance standards and/or employee accountability for quantity and quality of output will not change during the demonstration project. What *may* change is your supervisor's method of monitoring and evaluating your performance in this new working relationship.

Who Decides What My Output Should Be?

You and your direct supervisor. The nature of telecommuting, the fact that you are out of sight significant periods of time, requires that a high level of trust be built up between you and your supervisor. This means that you must accept more responsibility for getting the job done. It also means that you and your supervisor must discuss and ensure that you mutually understand what it is that you are expected to produce and when it is due.

What about Work Rules?

The standard work rules already established will still be officially in place during the demonstration project. However, we will be testing another set of performance and evaluation relationships at the same time. These relationships will be more oriented toward the results of your work than the ways in which you get it done. Therefore, if you and your supervisor feel that a nonstandard way of performing your job produces better results, then you may try it during the lifetime of the project. At the end of the project we will evaluate the results to see what works best for both the employees and the Company.

What about the Security of the Information I Work With?

You are expected to follow all appropriate Company rules and regulations regarding security and confidentiality for your computer, its data and information, and any other information you handle. You are also expected to adhere to your department or division's policies and procedures.

Effects of Participation in the Project

How Will Participation in the Demonstration Project Affect My Promotability?

Telecommuting is just another way to do your job. Performance evaluations will be made as usual. The project is not designed or intended to affect your promotability.

Is It Possible to Leave the Project after I've Begun Telecommuting?

You are always free to voluntarily return to your previous work mode if you feel pressured or if you feel that telecommuting is not right for you. However, we want to keep as many telecommuters as possible in the project throughout its lifetime. So please consider carefully your decision to participate.

Your supervisor may also terminate your participation in the project if your telecommuting, for any reason, is not working out.

It is also possible that changes in working circumstances, responsibilities, or assignment may require that an employee be taken off the telecommuting project in order better to meet the needs of the Company.

There will be no ill effects on your work record simply because of voluntary or involuntary termination of your participation in the project. On the other hand, you should realize that participation will not excuse you from operating within existing work rules and standards.

Chapter

7

Measuring Results

In any organization that is based on economic survival for its continued existence—from families to multinational corporations, and even to governments—it is absolutely essential that the economic benefits of its efforts match or exceed the costs. This works for telecommuting as well. No organization will continue to use telecommuting if it decides that the costs do, or will eventually, outweigh the benefits.

Costs and benefits are not always measured in economic terms. Such hard-to-measure factors as quality-of-life and environmental impacts are also important for telecommuting.

The difficulty with telecommuting, as with most other aspects of information work, is that the typical accounting system usually measures the costs much more easily than the benefits. This chapter explores both costs and benefits, using my experience with real organizations as a basis for illustrating the issues. I have examined these experiences from four points of view:

➤ Amount and distribution of telecommuting
➤ Quality-of-life effects
➤ Work effectiveness changes
➤ Environmental impacts

Even though I am including some supposedly non-economic factors in my results measurements, I have tried to relate them to economic measures.

■ DATA SOURCE

The details in much of the rest of this chapter derive from the final results of a multi-year telecommuting demonstration project in a large urban-based organization with more than 45,000 employees, about 40% of whom are information workers. The organization tested telecommuting primarily in response to the demands of air quality regulations. The data reported here were derived from a number of sources: questionnaires given at roughly 9-month intervals to more than 300 telecommuters, their non-telecommuting co-workers, and their supervisors; departmental cost records; and direct interviews of the participants. The participants in the project came from more than 20 different departments and included a wide spectrum of job types, most of them mid-level. The organization also followed the guidelines in this book. Although the numbers given here are from this one organization, the results are similar to those I have obtained from a number of different organizations and can be considered fairly typical.

■ BEGINNING TELECOMMUTING

My experience has been that both the costs and the benefits of telecommuting change with time. The costs tend to be up-front, even before telecommuting begins. The benefits per telecommuter tend to increase with time, growing even after two years of telecommuting. In a typical program, telecommuting begins with a relatively small proportion of the organization's workforce,[1] so that the initial impacts are equally small. Also typically, the initial complement of telecommuters tends to be among the upper half of the employees in terms of proven performance.

Therefore, the absolute results (that is, annual net dollars) after the first year or two may be higher per telecommuter than in later years when less-capable telecommuters have joined the

---

[1] In a large organization, say one with tens of thousands of employees, only a few hundred telecommuters—1% or 2% of the information workers—may be involved in the initial project

group. However, the proportional results tend to match the early results as the programs expand. That is, while the first group may represent only a few percent of the information workers, they may represent a much larger percent of the organization's productivity base. As workers of lower base productivity are added, their per capita marginal dollar contribution to overall organizational productivity is lower.

The nominal initial goal for the project described here was to have participants telecommuting at least one day per week, on average. Some jobs are suitable for practically full-time telecommuting, in my experience, while others might encounter difficulty reaching the one-day-per-week goal, given early 1990s technology availability. Some of the telecommuters found that they could not continue telecommuting at the same rate that they tried the first month. Others found that they could increase their rate of telecommuting. Still others maintained their original rate. The overall average for the first month of telecommuting was 4.0 days, with median and mode also at 4 days and the range going from 1 to 23 days. For the first month of their telecommuting, 99% of the telecommuters worked at home 8 days or less.

In practice, the number of telecommuting days per month tends to increase over time. An analysis of the historic data for this particular project shows an expected average of 4.2 days per month for those who have been telecommuting for a year. Telecommuters with 2 years of experience are likely to be telecommuting about 8 days per month. For comparison, another project, involving telecommuters from a broader geographical area, showed an average of 5.2 days per month at the end of the first year of telecommuting and 6.5 days per month at the end of the second year. A linear regression analysis[2] of the telecommuting frequency data indicates that the telecommuters will tend to telecommute about 2.4 days per week as they gain experience with telecommuting. Figure 7.1 shows the regression line, slightly modified for the first 10 months.

One concern with telecommuting is whether it will increase car use, since an "extra" car may be available when the telecommuter is working at home. Twenty-three percent of the telecommuters said that the car was indeed used by themselves or someone else in their household when they worked at home (the

---

[2] Linear regression is a statistical procedure that fits a straight line to a set of data points. In this case the data points are length of time telecommuting and the number of telecommuting days during that period.

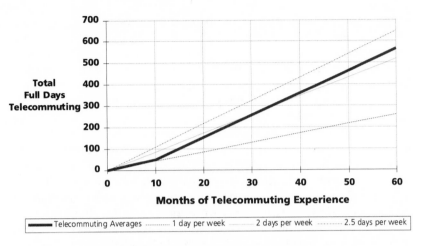

Figure 7.1 Projected telecommuting rates.

remaining 77% maintained that it was not in use). *Of those who stated that their car was available, 23% (6% of all the telecommuters) stated that there was an overall decrease in non-commuting car use in addition to the decrease due to telecommuting!* To counter this, another 23% (6% of all the telecommuters) stated that there was some additional car use, but not enough to counteract the telecommuting reduction. An additional 5% of the car-available group (1% of all telecommuters) said that their added non-commuting car use acted to cancel the reduction from telecommuting. In summary, only 8% of the telecommuters reported any erosion of the car use savings.

Analysis of detailed trip logs that were administered to the telecommuter households, showed that some of this additional car use was the result of telecommuters performing chores that otherwise would have been carried out by other family members. Hence, the slight additional use of their cars by some telecommuters may be overstated, since many of the "new" trips replace trips that would have occurred anyway. The net result of the actual trip measurements was an overall reduction in car use over and above the telecommuting reduction. To be conservative, I concluded that telecommuting produced exactly the car use reduction that equaled the reduction in commute trips. Therefore, it completely satisfied the primary goal of the project: telecommuting-eliminated trips are not replaced by other trips.

The average telecommuter allocated about 37% of his or her weekly work tasks for the telecommuting period. Given the overall

Table 7.1 Activities Performed while Telecommuting

Activity	% Who Engaged in It
Thinking or planning	69.2
Reading	68.6
Text or word processing	58.3
Writing (without a computer)	55.1
Research	55.1
Coordinating by telephone	44.9
Working with data bases	22.4
Computer programming	20.5
Other	20.5
Record keeping	17.3
Graphics or layout	10.9
Coordinating via computer	8.3
Having meetings	2.0

average of 0.9 days per week telecommuting for this group, that works out to 37% *of the work being accomplished in 18% to 23% of the work week; possibly an average 100% productivity increase per telecommuting day.* Table 7.1 shows what the telecommuters were doing when they telecommuted. While 17.5% of the telecommuters viewed telecommuting as a temporary or occasional thing, 82.5% considered it to be a permanent change to their working ways.

■ QUALITY-OF-LIFE EFFECTS

Aside from the quantitative effects of telecommuting, there is the issue of the socio-psychological effects of telecommuting. What is the impact of telecommuting on the telecommuters and their families? We did not develop direct evidence of the effects on the families during these projects; rather we asked the telecommuters about the impacts. We included a section in our evaluation questionnaires specifically oriented toward these impacts. Common factor analysis[3] of the questionnaires allowed us to break a number of the work or social impacts into eleven categories, as follows:

➤ *General Work Life.* This relates to changes in the individual's relationships with his or her supervisor, self-assessment of job skills, feelings of job responsibility, influence, versatility, and scope.

➤ *Personal Life.* This factor includes changes in quality of family relationships, discretionary time, feelings of control of one's life, ability to separate work and home life, success in self-discipline, coordination of family and work time, and knowing when to quit work.

➤ *Visibility.* Do telecommuters feel out of their supervisor's and co-workers' minds when they're out of sight? This factor includes changes in one's influence on organizational strategy, understanding of what others are doing, how well one's suggestions are received, and self-assessment of visibility in the organization.

➤ *Environmental Influences.* This includes changes in home office space, stress from environmental noise, ability to match work and biorhythms, and feelings of self-empowerment.

➤ *Belonging.* Do telecommuters feel themselves to be loners? Here we have changes in involvement in office social activities, amount of job-related feedback, career advancement, job stability, and relationships with fellow workers.

➤ *Creativity.* Changes in: creativity in one's work, the amount of flexibility in job performance, and feelings of self-empowerment are in this factor.

➤ *Stress Avoidance.* Changes in work-related costs, ability to bypass physical handicaps, and avoidance of office politics are grouped here.

➤ *Liberation.* This factor includes changes in ability to concentrate on crucial tasks, the need to cope with traffic, and the ability to get more done.

---

[3] Factor analysis is a statistical technique that helps analyze questionnaire items in terms of groups of closely related questions. That is, if question X in a group was answered with a certain value, the likelihood is high that another question in the same group would be answered the same way. In this case, the participants were given a set of 50 questions that related to quality-of-life impacts; the analysis showed that the responses could be associated into 11 groups.

➤ *Apprehension.* Changes in uneasiness about equipment failure and feelings of guilt about "not really working" constitute this category.

➤ *Interdependence.* This factor relates to changes in the quality of meetings with colleagues and dependence on others to help perform one's job.

➤ *Continuity.* The final factor calibrates changes in freedom from interruptions.

Note that the emphasis is on *changes* in these categories. We asked the participants what had changed since telecommuting began, whether or not they were telecommuters. We asked how much, if any, change there was and how important each issue was to them. We developed composite values (amount of change multiplied by importance to the participant) for these factors, as shown in Table 7.2. The scales for amount of change are from −2 to +2, with −2 signifying much worse, 0 meaning no change, and +2 signifying much better. Importance ranges from 0 (not important at all) to 4 (extremely important to the participant). Thus, the composite factor can range from −8 (i.e., −2 × 4) to +8 (i.e., +2 × 4).

The surveys showed clear differences between the telecommuter and non-telecommuter groups. There are three areas in

Table 7.2 Work or Social Factor Changes

Factor	Telecommuters	Non-Telecommuter	Difference (T − non-T)
Liberation	4.9	1.6	3.2
Continuity	3.1	1.3	1.7
Creativity	3.2	1.3	1.9
Personal life	2.5	1.0	1.5
Environmental influences	2.2	0.6	1.6
General work life	2.2	1.0	1.1
Stress avoidance	1.2	0.3	0.9
Interdependence	1.0	0.5	0.5
Visibility	0.9	0.4	0.5
Belonging	0.6	0.3	0.3
Apprehension	0.7	0.6	0.1

which we might expect to see negative impacts from telecommuting: Visibility, Apprehension and Belonging. Yet, this group of telecommuters, on average, showed net positive changes for all three, although there were some individual negative responses.

Figures 7.2 and 7.3 show two different views of the elements of Table 7.2 as well as the comparable results from the mid-term (first nine months) and baseline (start-of-telecommuting) surveys. Note that, with the exception of the liberation and continuity factors, both groups at mid-term appear to be more positive than they were during the baseline survey; then both groups tended to decline slightly from the mid-term to final surveys. In two of the key factors—continuity and creativity—the telecommuter group switched rankings between the mid-term and final surveys, while the non-telecommuters stayed about the same. This could arise from a possible increase in interruptions to the telecommuters as more people got used to contacting them while they were at home, coupled with a decrease in interruptions in the office as the on-site office population decreased. Interestingly, the telecommuters' responses to the liberation and continuity factors declined after the baseline measure, showing the effects of reality slightly modifying expectations.

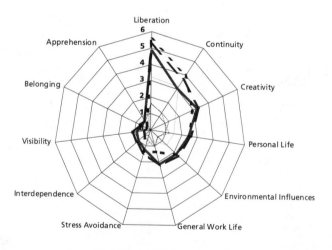

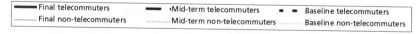

Figure 7.2 "Radar" view of the quality-of-life changes.

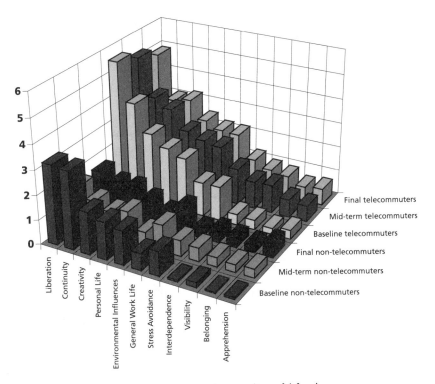

Figure 7.3 Comparative quality-of-life changes.

In any case, the telecommuters showed quality-of-life changes that were more positive in every respect than those of the non-telecommuters.

■ EFFECTIVENESS CHANGES

An important criterion in assessing the desirability of telecommuting is its impact on employee effectiveness. As a minimum acceptance criterion, overall work performance should not degrade from its pre-telecommuting values. As was the case with the quality-of-life factors, I concentrated on assessing changes in, rather than absolute values of, worker effectiveness. Several indirect measures of effectiveness factors were included in our evaluating survey questionnaires. However, the most numerically clear test is a direct question asking each respondent—and her or his direct supervisor—whether, and how much, their effectiveness changed since telecommuting began.

➤ Quantitative Estimates

Of the group of telecommuters, the range in their self-estimate responses ran from no change to increases of 100%. The average response for all the reporting telecommuters was an increase of 30% with a median response of a 25% increase. In the case of the non-telecommuters, the range in responses ran from a decrease of 50% to an increase of 100%.[4] The average response for the non-telecommuters was an increase of 24%, with a median response of 20%. The difference between the telecommuters' and non-telecommuters' average self-estimates of effectiveness change was 6%. The difference was significant at the 0.09 level.[5] About 13% of the telecommuters and 25% of the non-telecommuters indicated no change in their effectiveness since telecommuting began.

Note that the above figures are derived from the *employees'* responses. Typically, supervisors' estimates of employee effectiveness are lower than those of the employees themselves. We also surveyed the participants' supervisors. The supervisors' estimates of the telecommuters' effectiveness changes averaged 22%; their estimate of non-telecommuters' effectiveness changes averaged 9%, a difference of 14%. In this case, the difference was significant at the .008 level.[6] Twenty-five percent of the telecommuters' supervisors and 48% of the non-telecommuters' supervisors indicated no change in effectiveness. Hence, the telecommuters showed clear effectiveness improvements relative to the non-telecommuters, particularly in the estimation of their supervisors.

When the effectiveness changes are ranked by the salary of the employee, the pattern becomes even more interesting. Although the data fluctuate widely, a reasonable estimate is that the improvement in effectiveness, as estimated by the telecommuters' supervisors, is roughly 0.005 times the annual salary of the telecommuter. That is, a telecommuting employee with a salary of $50,000 would likely have an increase in effectiveness of about 25%; a $80,000-salaried

---

[4] Non-telecommuters can increase their effectiveness through such means as more experience or training, fewer interruptions from (telecommuting or other) co-workers, greater maturity in work attitudes, etc.

[5] That is, the odds are 10 to 1 in favor of the difference being meaningful.

[6] Here, the odds are 127 to 1 in favor of a meaningful difference.

Table 7.3 Estimates of Effectiveness Increases by Level of Training

Training	Supervisors' Estimates		Self-Estimates	
Received by	Telecommuters	Non-Telecommuters	Telecommuters	Non-Telecommuters
Neither	21.4%	6.0%	33.3%	21.3%
Telecommuter only	14.7%	11.0%	31.8%	21.2%
Supervisor only	38.3%	8.8%	30.7%	33.0%
Both	23.3%	12.5%	28.9%	26.9%

employee would have a 40% improvement, and so on.[7] No similar relationship was observed for non-telecommuters.

There were some clear differences of opinion between supervisor and employee concerning effectiveness change. The telecommuters' self-estimates tended to agree more closely with that of their supervisors. Nineteen percent of the telecommuters and supervisors agreed exactly on the effectiveness changes; only 8% of the supervisors and non-telecommuters agreed. Twenty-six percent of the telecommuters received higher ratings from their supervisors than they gave themselves. Twenty-one percent of the non-telecommuters received higher than their self-ratings from their supervisors. The most interesting aspect of these results is that the supervisors' estimates differ much more between telecommuters and non-telecommuters than do the individuals' self-estimates.

➤ Training Influences

One of the elements of the analysis is to see whether the initial training sessions for the project had any influence on the effectiveness outcomes. Table 7.3 shows the effectiveness estimates as a function of who was trained. A direct reading of the table can be slightly misleading, since there are only a few cases among the telecommuters where either no one or only the supervisor was trained. The overall evidence is that it is particularly important that supervisors receive training.

---

[7] Since there were fewer employees at these higher salary levels, the average of the entire group was lower than the values just used.

■ ENVIRONMENTAL IMPACTS

The most important environmental impacts of telecommuting come from the fact that most home-based telecommuters do not drive during their telecommuting days. These telecommuters are reducing their daily air pollution production and energy use. At the individual level this may not seem like much but, magnified by thousands or millions of telecommuters, it can become a major means of improving environmental quality.

➤ Air Pollution

For our example case of an organization with about 16,000 telecommuters working from home an average of 1.4 days per week, the annual pollution reduction would be on the order of:

- ➤ 6,150,000 pounds of carbon monoxide;
- ➤ 380,000 pounds of nitrogen oxides;
- ➤ 1,150,000 pounds of unburned hydrocarbons; and
- ➤ 26,000 pounds of particulate matter (mostly from brakes).

As a further example, Figure 7.4 shows the annual levels of reduced car mileage for the Los Angeles CMSA[8] under what appears to be the current telecommuting growth trend in the area.

Since at least half of this mileage reduction involves automobile cold starts—the most polluting phase of car use—telecommuting promises to be a significant reducer of air pollution in coming years at least until zero-polluting cars dominate the market. Figure 7.5 shows the area-wide pollution reduction impacts for that trend. Since the pollution reduction data were calculated using a constant ratio of pollutants per vehicle-mile, the results are somewhat understated for the 1990s and, perhaps, overstated for the years past 2000. The early understatement is because the data used were for highway travel in the mid-1980s and did not include an increase in pollution for the startup and idling periods. An overstatement could result from a steady improvement, over the mid-1980s levels, in the quantity of pollutants emitted by cars.

For comparison, air pollution data from California's South Coast Air Quality Management District show the annual pollution

---

[8] Combined Metropolitan Statistical Area, an area in southern California that includes almost half of California's population.

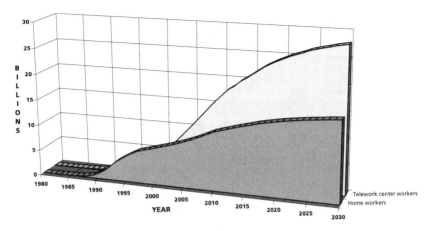

Figure 7.4 Annual mileage reductions from telecommuting: High growth scenario.

contribution from cars in 1991 to be 1,580,000 tons of carbon monoxide, 221,000 tons of hydrocarbons, 243,000 tons of nitrogen oxides, and 20,000 tons of particulates. If the telecommuting growth trend of Figure 7.5 continues, we could expect reductions by the year 2000 of 19%, 23%, 8%, and 4%, respectively, from those levels.

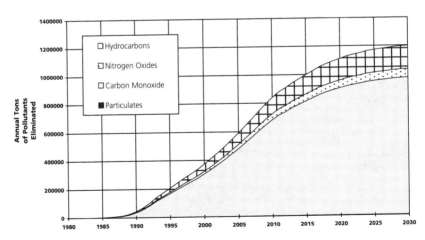

Figure 7.5 Air pollution reductions from telecommuting: High growth scenario.

Clearly, these air pollution reduction values provide a persuasive argument for further development of telecommuting. In addition to the air pollution factors, there are the energy conservation consequences of telecommuting. My forecast model calculates the net effect of telecommuting on energy conservation. The net effect is derived from the reduction in automobile fuel use by telecommuters, combined with the possibly increased use of computers and the clearly increased use of telecommunications.

➤ Energy Consumption

The forecast of the energy conservation impacts of telecommuting is based on my analysis of the commuting patterns of thousands of urban area employees. The particular estimate shown here is derived from a 1990 survey of the employees of our example organization. The average estimated one-way commute distance for these employees was 19.8 miles, slightly less than that of the telecommuters in the project.

I also assumed that future telecommuters would have the same pattern of compressed work week schedules (that is, fewer workdays per week but more hours per workday) as were followed by the employees in 1991. This produces an average effective workweek of 4.8 days. The telecommuting rate was assumed to be an average of 1.4 days per week—all from home—based on the observed trends among the telecommuters.

The calculations produced an average annual energy saving of 4,200 kilowatt-hours per telecommuter,[9] for a total annual saving, assuming about 16,000 active telecommuters, of 60 million kilowatt-hours, about 1,600,000 gallons of gasoline.

The forecast model calculates the net effect of telecommuting on energy conservation. The net effect is derived from the reduction in automobile fuel use by telecommuters, partially offset by the possibly increased use of computers and the clearly increased use of telecommunications.

Three factors are not included in the model. First, notwithstanding the contrary experience of our sample project, I expect that telecommuters will tend to use slightly more home heating and cooling energy while they are telecommuting. At present, there are no data to show an offset of this energy use by a comparable

---

[9] This is a conservative estimate, based on a lower rate of telecommuting than I think will actually occur in a few years. The cost-benefit model later in this chapter uses a higher figure: 6,000 kilowatt-hours per annum.

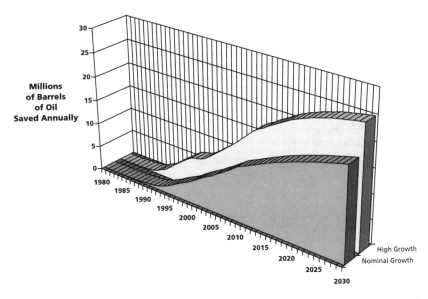

Figure 7.6 Estimated area-wide energy conservation impacts of telecommuting.

reduction in the heating and cooling of the "downtown" offices of the telecommuters—largely because there are not yet enough telecommuters for the effects to be noticeable. The model assumes a wash between these two energy uses in the long run.

Second, the model does not include my finding that about 20% of telecommuter households have a reduction in car use over and above the telecommuting-specific reduction.[10] Given these caveats, I feel that the projections shown in Figure 7.6 provide a conservative estimate of home-based telecommuting's energy impacts.

Third, the model assumes only home-based telecommuting. Telecommuting from telework centers is more problematic in its environmental impacts. The key is whether or not telework center telecommuters drive to work. If they walk or bike to work, ride share (without driving to the ride share pick up point), or take some form of mass transit, then the impacts are as shown for the home-based telecommuters. If they drive to the telework center, then the environmental improvements may be substantially reduced.

---

[10] See our report: *Telecommuting Travel Impact Analysis: Los Angeles Telecommuting Pilot Project* (Los Angeles: JALA International, Inc., 1990) for details.

In reality, there will be a mixed bag of environmental results for a few years. Most contemporary telecommuters are home based. Most telework centers at first were regional centers that reduced, but did not eliminate, driving to work by telecommuters. Therefore, the environmental improvement produced by these centers is only partial. Beginning in late 1993, California began testing the feasibility of neighborhood telework centers. These centers, as defined in Chapter 1, are located so as to service neighborhood residents who walk or bike to work. For them the environmental impacts are essentially the same as for home-based telecommuting.

■ COST AND BENEFIT CONSIDERATIONS

A key issue in evaluating telecommuting, or any other change in organizational behavior, is whether the net economic—the infamous bottom line—result is positive, neutral or negative. Although some factors, such as quality of work life, necessarily must be somewhat subjective, other factors can be quantified relatively readily. I have also included actual measured costs and benefits to date. The costs include the time-plus-overhead costs of the employees who participated in project administration. The numbers in the cost-benefit model reported here are for 300 active telecommuters in our sample organization.

➤ Costs

These are the main factors for analysis.

Direct Costs

There are twelve main cost categories:

- ➤ Additional training
- ➤ Telecommunications hardware, software and operating costs
- ➤ Computer hardware and software
- ➤ Moving expenses
- ➤ Facilities leasing
- ➤ Construction costs
- ➤ Furniture

➤ Insurance

➤ Miscellaneous rental

➤ Project administration

➤ Additional travel

➤ Liability

In most cases the costs are quantifiable relatively easily and are available routinely. In some cases the costs must be estimated. This approach of including quantifiable as well as estimated costs provides a conservative view of a project, so that the actual costs might be lower than those shown here.

Additional Training. This category deals with the costs for training that are specifically telecommuting-related (for example, interpersonal communications and management instruction). Training costs may be computed as the total of time spent by the trainer and trainees, times their respective hourly rates (including indirect costs), plus costs of equipment and materials used for training. Training costs for the more than 400 employees (and their supervisors, etc.) who were trained in the example project were estimated at about $65,000, or $150 per trained telecommuter. This figure includes the costs of the organization's personnel who were involved in administering or coordinating the training sessions, amounting to 34% of the total. Per capita training costs may decrease with time, both as the training becomes more efficient and as telecommuting becomes an integral part of the organization's normal culture.

Telecommunications. Telecommunications costs (such as equipment purchase or lease, software services, etc.) can be primarily telecommuting-related or, as in the case of training costs, may be incurred as a normal part of office automation with telecommuting accounting only for some of the additional service charges. This allocation must also be made on a case-by-case basis. This particular employer did not provide any telecommunications equipment for the telecommuters. The final survey shows that the telecommuters had an average monthly telephone bill of $3.59 more than the non-telecommuters, but a median telephone cost of $7.50 *less* than the non-telecommuters. I could not determine the costs of additional calls from the office to telecommuters' homes, as the organization's telephone billing system does not break out such calls. I have found that this situation is fairly common.

For the sake of conservatism in the benefit-cost model, I assumed that the average telecommuter telephone bill increased $4 per month ($48 per year) and that there was a corresponding $48 annual increase in office-to-home telephone charges for telecommuters.

Computers. Computer charges could constitute the largest portion of a telecommuting budget, depending on how they are allocated. These are the options:

➤ *Total Duplication.* These are cases where a computer is purchased solely because of telecommuting. Either there would be no computer use by an employee except for telecommuting, or there would be no duplication of computers without telecommuting. For these cases, all the computer costs should be charged to telecommuting.

➤ *Partial Duplication.* If the computer capabilities would be made available to an employee in any case, then only those costs peculiar to the telecommuting situation (such as telecommunications interconnect equipment purchase or lease, make-ready costs, software, maintenance, etc.) should be charged to telecommuting.

➤ *No Duplication.* This covers cases where either the telecommuter does not use a computer while telecommuting, or where the necessary equipment and software is already owned by the telecommuter (telecommuters' costs are analyzed separately), or where necessary software duplication is allowed without charge by the software providers and no computer communications software or hardware is used.

At present, I know of no cases of total duplication by the employer among the organizations with which I have dealt, and only a few cases of partial duplication, generally involving duplicate software packages for telecommuters' own personal computers at home. In general, almost no computer charges were incurred by the organization represented here. However, in many cases this is because employees who were trained and needed computers were not allowed to telecommute because they did not have computers at home and employer-supplied computers were not available. Over 70% of the active telecommuters in this organization owned their own computers and used them for telecommuting by the end of the project. Those employees invested just over $100,000 in telecommuting-specific computer hardware, software, furniture, office equipment, telephone services and maintenance during the last year of the project.[11] More than half, 56%, made no telecommuting-specific investments in equipment. Note that, of those who did invest in equipment, about 85% of their total investment was specifically related to telecommuting. For conservatism, I estimated that the investment required for the average new computer-using telecommuter will be about $2,000, to be made either by the telecommuter or by the employer. For the purposes of the benefit-cost model, I assumed that the employer will make this purchase for 40% of the telecommuters added each year after the end of the demonstration project.

Moving Costs. This category includes all the costs of moving existing equipment from offices to either homes or satellite center offices. It also includes telephone installation costs and costs of any related interoffice moves by non-telecommuters. There were no costs for moving telecommuters on the part of our example employer. I was not able to assess costs of moving non-telecommuters. Therefore, this amount is zero in my current model.

Facilities Leasing. This cost applies to any telework center set up as part of the telecommuting program. The differential cost should be charged here. That is, the cost of the leased space (or amortized purchase or construction costs) minus the cost of any space eliminated from the inventory of the facility previously occupied by the telecommuter(s). Our example organization had no telework centers; all telecommuters were home based. Therefore, this amount is zero in the benefit-cost model.

Administration. There are several components of the administrative costs of telecommuting, some of which are difficult to assess. These include the special management costs of the pilot project itself (including evaluation); telecommuting-related changes in the administrative system of the employer (such as changes in time accounting); possible duplication of effort or supplies caused by telecommuting; and costs of system integration and coordination. Administrative costs include part of the salaries of the Project Manager, the department coordinators and consulting costs other

---

[11] The per-telecommuter cost for those who made telecommuting-specific investments averaged $2000, split into $1840 for hardware and $210 for software that was telecommuting-specific.

than training. I estimated the total administrative costs for the completed demonstration project at $307,000, including the planning phase of the project—about $700 per trained telecommuter.

Additional Travel. This category applies to two factors:

1. Managers and professionals who find themselves traveling between their "home" offices and other centers during the day for meetings that would otherwise require only a short walk to a conference room
2. Losses to car- and van-pools because of telecommuters who no longer use them

None of these costs appeared in the example project. Although some telecommuters were members of car- or van-pools, their participation as telecommuters did not appear to have disturbed the pools significantly, according to our interviews and trip survey data.

Liability Costs. One largely unresolved factor is the possibility of increased exposure to worker's compensation claims resulting from work-related accidents in the homes of telecommuters. Although I do not know of any worker's compensation claims arising to date from telecommuting in any organization, this factor is included for informational purposes. No participants in the example project have claimed telecommuting-related worker's compensation claims.

Indirect Costs

The following are indirect cost factors that are analyzed, since they relate to general support of office work.

Increased Building Energy Consumption. Shifting work to homes, or to smaller buildings characteristic of telework centers, may increase or decrease energy consumption related to space heating and cooling. Persuasive arguments have been made to support either net increases or net decreases in building energy use.

To estimate this I checked the differences between average reported home gas and electric bills. Telecommuters paid an average of $4.01 *more* for electricity and $4.51 *less* for gas than the members of the control group, for a net energy cost decrease of $0.50

per month per telecommuter. For conservatism I assumed that there was no change in the energy consumption of employer office facilities when the telecommuters were away from those offices. My conclusion is that there was no significant difference between telecommuters and non-telecommuters in building energy consumption.[12]

Increased Local Traffic Congestion. By diverting automobile traffic from freeways to local streets, telework center telecommuting may cause an increase in local traffic congestion, with associated energy and pollution costs. On the other hand, one objective of local and neighborhood telework centers was to reduce the fraction of telecommuters who still drive (rather than walk or bicycle) to work. I have no clear data of any effect one way or the other. Therefore, it is set as zero in the model.

➤ Benefits

Direct Benefits

Although many of the cost elements are easily established, many of the benefits of telecommuting are less easily defined in quantitative terms. Most important of these benefits is employee effectiveness. The following are the benefit factors that generally appear in non-quantitative terms.

➤ *Increased Employee Effectiveness* including output quality and quantity. I compute the effectiveness impact by multiplying the estimated effectiveness change by the individual's salary. Suppose we adopt the conservative view that the differential effectiveness change of the telecommuters (that is, the telecommuter estimates minus the non-telecommuter estimates) is that of the employees. Then the monthly effectiveness-change-benefit per telecommuter after 18 months or so of telecommuting is

---

[12] As a counter example, the author's tele-office has two high-end personal computers and monitors running 24 hours per day, every day including weekends, plus a laser printer and other computer accessories, lighting, etc.. The office is electrically air conditioned. The total annual energy use of the office is about 1900 kilowatt-hours. The annual cost of this (all in electricity use) is $176, or about $14.70 per month (about the cost of ten gallons of gasoline). Ten gallons of gasoline will suffice for about six 36-mile round trips between the author's office and downtown Los Angeles.

about $369 (as contrasted with $344 at the project mid-point and $155 after a few weeks of telecommuting). If we average the supervisor's and employee's estimates we get a monthly effectiveness-change-benefit of $642 (as compared to $508 at the mid-term evaluation and $295 in the baseline survey). If all of the employer's 400-odd telecommuters maintained or increased these effectiveness differences in the future, then the annual benefit would be between $1,920,000 and $3,330,800, depending on one's point of view, or between $4,800 and $8,300 per telecommuter.

➤ The average telecommuters' self-estimate of effectiveness change increased by 19% between the mid-term and final surveys, and by 22% between the baseline and mid-term surveys, while the non-telecommuters' self estimates increased by 41% between the mid-term and final surveys, and decreased by 7% between the baseline and mid-term surveys. The supervisors' estimates of their telecommuters' effectiveness changes increased by about 28% between the mid-term and final surveys, while their estimates of non-telecommuters effectiveness decreased by about 2%. The mid-term estimates from the supervisors showed about the same amount (46% and 50%, respectively) for both groups over the baseline estimates. The conclusion is that the tele-commuters' effectiveness was still increasing at the end of the project, while the non-telecommuters effectiveness was staying about the same, at least in the estimates of their supervisors.

➤ *Decreased Sick Leave* can be derived from employee records. My conclusion from the data derived to date is that telecommuters will take two days less sick leave per year.

➤ *Decreased Medical Costs* are difficult to assess. No one has performed a long-term study of the health impacts of tele-commuting. For the time being, I assume this impact is zero. However, I expect long term medical costs to decrease for telecommuters because of the clear reductions in stress stated by participants in our focus group sessions. These benefits are not likely to show up in statistically significant terms for several years.

➤ *Increased Organization Effectiveness* including output quality and quantity. A quantitative answer to this question requires a survey that has not yet been made, to the best of my knowledge. Anecdotal evidence from focus group meetings leads us to believe that there is a slight overall increase in effectiveness of the telecommuters' organizations. That is, effectiveness is also increasing among the non-telecommuting office mates of the telecommuters. This is primarily because the non-telecommuters also became better organized because of telecommuting. For the purposes of the benefit-cost model, I estimate that the improvement, in dollar terms, amounts to 0.5% of the telecommuters' salaries (that is, about 3% of the supervisor-estimated effectiveness increase of the non-telecommuters).

➤ *Decreased Turnover* and attendant reductions in personnel search, hiring, and training costs. Of the telecommuter respondents, 23% replied that they had seriously considered quitting. Among that number, 74% (or 18% of all the telecommuters) said the ability to telecommute was a moderate to decisive influence on their decision to stay. My conservative estimate is that it would cost about 25% of the departing telecommuters' annual salaries if they had to be completely replaced.[13] I multiply this by an additional factor (ranging from 0 to 1) related to the influence of telecommuting on their decision to stay. The computed result was a benefit of about $206,000 for the group of about 160 telecommuters who completed this portion of the final questionnaire.

➤ *Reduced Parking Requirements.* If advantage were taken of the fact that telecommuters are not using parking space part of the time, and the space were reassigned to, or used by, non-telecommuters, then the monthly savings would be roughly one-fourth of the $90 monthly parking cost per telecommuter, or about $22.

➤ *Office Space Saving* as telecommuters share office space. We did not yet test office space saving methods for this particular employer. However, my experience with other organizations indicates that companies or government agencies employing large numbers of home-based telecommuters can readily realize up to 33% reductions in office space.[14]

---

[13] For highly skilled individuals the figure can be significantly higher. For example, G. Alan Hunter of the California Franchise Tax Board estimated that the cost of replacing a skilled auditor of multinational corporations is more than $100,000.

[14] For example, AT&T estimates that annual savings from telework-related office space reductions amount to $2,000 per person, as reported in the *Harvard Business Review* (May–June, 1998, p. 126).

In the case of some departments of our example employer, telecommuting allowed existing groups to work more effectively with what was previously severe overcrowding. To be conservative, I set this factor at zero for the cost-benefit model.

➤ *Increased Ability to Attract Staff* as prospective employees consider telecommuting an attractive work option. Although this is related to the turnover reduction benefit, I was not able to get unambiguous data on the impacts because the organization had a hiring freeze at the time. Although this factor has been used successfully by other organizations, particularly government agencies, as a hiring tool. I did not count it as a benefit in this particular instance of the model.

Indirect Benefits

As with the cost elements, there are indirect benefits, some of which are most easily measured in dollar terms. These are largely related to reduced use of automobile transportation, as the following will indicate.

➤ *Decreased Energy Consumption* as commuter automobiles are not used. I estimate that the average telecommuters' energy use reduction, assuming current telecommuting trends persist, will run in excess of 6,000 kilowatt-hours per year.[15] At a gasoline price of $1.30 per gallon, this amounts to an annual saving of about $214 per telecommuter. Although there is no direct saving to the employer, there may be an implicit saving in decreased wage demands by telecommuters.

➤ *Decreased Air Pollution.* The air pollution reduction is directly proportional to the overall decrease in automobile use. However, dollar costs of air pollution are difficult to

---

[15] That is, a continuing trend toward telecommuting an average of two days per week, replacing an average round trip of 45.7 miles, with 10% rideshare offset and an average car fuel efficiency of 24 miles per gallon. The average work week is 4.7 days for this group of telecommuters, since many are also on modified work schedules, with an average of 49 weeks worked per year. This produces a total annual saving of 187 gallons of gasoline (or about 6800 kilowatt-hours) per telecommuter. We deduct 800 kilowatt-hours to account for any additional home energy use.

establish, are not generally assessed directly to the employer, and are not included here.

➤ *Decreased Traffic Congestion.* As in the air pollution case, it is difficult to make a firm estimate of the dollar costs of traffic congestion. An indirect measure is that of one primary impetus for the telecommuting project: compliance with air quality regulations. At the time the project was begun, fines could be imposed of up to $25,000 per day of non-compliance with Rule 1501 of the South Coast Air Quality Management District. The Rule required that all employers with more than 100 employees in a given location had to achieve certain average vehicle ridership levels. This particular employer was facing millions of dollars in fines. Although the Rule was subsequently relaxed, efforts continue to restore it. This pollution penalty trend, although apparently originating in Southern California, is migrating to the rest of the world as urban air pollution problems worsen.

➤ *Increased Access for the Mobility Handicapped* including disabled, working parents, retirees, etc. The group of telecommuters includes individuals with mobility handicaps. Their reactions in this respect are included in the overall improvements in quality-of-life indicated by the telecommuters. However, indirect benefits in this category include the reductions in welfare costs as a result of returning people to the active workforce via telecommuting.

■ RESULTS

➤ Employer

The factors above have been included in a cost-benefit model. The major one-time project costs are those of the project itself: planning, selection, training, evaluation, and administration. These costs cease at the end of the project. Recurring costs are primarily those of telecommunications (phone charges) and training. All of the benefits are recurring. Figure 7.7 shows the historical and expected costs and benefits from the development of the project plan through completion of the evaluation phase and five years thereafter. The figure includes an assumption that telecommuting will increase after completion of the demonstration project. The assumed growth shown here was to 600 telecommuters in the first

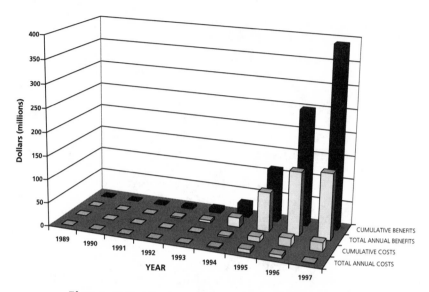

Figure 7.7 Summary of project costs and benefits.

year, 2,400 in the second year, and 9,600 in the third year after the end of the demonstration project. We identified almost 16,000 "telecommutable" jobs for this employer.

It is also informative to review the ratios between benefits and costs. Clearly, at the beginning of the project—during project planning, participant selection and training—there are no benefits, just costs. In the case illustrated here, more than a year elapsed between initiation of the planning phase and the start of participant selection. Once the participants begin telecommuting, however, the benefits begin to accumulate. At some point, if all goes well, monthly benefits begin to exceed costs. At some further point, the payback or break-even point, cumulative benefits equal and begin to exceed cumulative costs. That break-even point for this project was at about month 11 after the selection process began. Figure 7.8 shows the historical and anticipated results for the project. Note that the computer and software costs mentioned above are included as costs to the employer in this analysis, even though those costs were borne by the telecommuters.

Table 7.4 shows these results in numerical form. The drop in benefit-to-cost ratios in years 6 and 7 is a result of training and computer purchases for the large numbers of new telecommuters assumed in the model. If future experience matches the data derived thus far, the post-project benefit-to-cost ratios could regularly

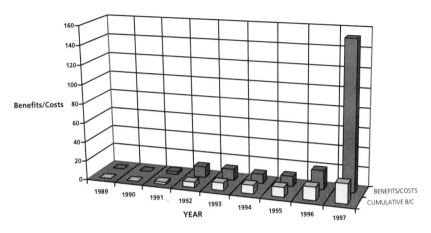

Figure 7.8 Summary of benefit-to-cost ratios.

exceed 100 to 1, once all of the telecommuters are trained and computer purchases are completed! **The average annual net benefit per telecommuter in this example project—and in similar ones for which I have data—is about $8,000.**

This model assumes that only 40% of new telecommuters would receive employer-furnished computer equipment. This is felt to be conservative, since almost three-quarters of the telecommuters are now providing their own equipment. In a broader operational situation, those computer costs might be higher—or

Table 7.4 Summary of the Benefit-Cost Model (Costs in $ Millions)

	Year						
	1	2	3	4	5	6	7
No. of telecommuters	0	0	211	300	600	2400	9600
Total annual costs	0.05	0.06	0.30	0.25	0.44	2.39	9.57
Total annual benefits	0.00	0.00	0.90	2.82	5.19	21.65	90.37
Cumulative costs	0.05	0.11	0.41	0.66	1.10	3.50	13.06
Cumulative benefits	0.00	0.00	0.90	3.72	8.91	30.56	120.93
Benefits/Costs	0.00	0.00	2.96	11.36	11.68	9.05	9.45
Cumulative B/C	0.00	0.00	2.18	5.63	8.06	8.74	9.26
Development costs	0.048	0.041	0.086	0.157	0.034	0.810	3.240
Operating costs	0.000	0.020	0.217	0.092	0.410	1.581	6.325
Benefits minus costs	- 0.05	- 0.06	0.59	2.58	4.74	19.26	80.81

lower. Similarly, expansion of telecommuting to a broader selection of employees might result in lower effectiveness increases. In any case, the data at this point make it clear that telecommuting is working very well for this employer and is far above a simple break-even situation.

➤ Employee

Most of the above discussion focuses on the employer. What about employee costs and benefits? Home-based telecommuters are the only ones with added monetary costs of telecommuting. These include: space in their homes that is reserved solely for telecommuting, and any added costs of office equipment and furniture, computers, software, telecommunications equipment, and telecommunications service charges that are not compensated by their employers.

In our sample case, home-based telecommuters, on average, used 170 square feet of their 1,850 square-foot homes; 130 square feet were reserved exclusively for telecommuting (the remainder also being used for other purposes). That is, the size of the dedicated office space at home, for which the employee pays the rent, taxes, and insurance, is about the same as, or larger than, the office space in the employer's facility. The most popular locations for the home office are a spare bedroom and the study or den, in that order. Note that in many countries, home sizes are roughly half that of the U.S. homes in our example. This does have an effect on the extent of home-based telecommuting in those countries.

WHAT ABOUT US?

There is generally no monetary compensation for this use of home office space, which I estimate has an annual cost (equivalent rental cost) of about $200. Employers typically do not reimburse their employees for the rental or related costs (except telephone); and, if they did, the Internal Revenue Service would probably count it as extra income since current IRS rules make it practically impossible to deduct home office space costs in tax returns.

Many employees already had office equipment and personal computers at home before they even heard about telecommuting. Almost exactly half of the applicants to large telecommuting projects in the late 1980s and early 1990s already owned personal computers. Of the remainder, about half stated that they would buy a computer if allowed to telecommute at least one day per week.

However, don't jump to the conclusion that the equipment investment is not a problem. Most of the telecommuters in these projects were mid-level employees, about two-thirds of them living in multi-earner households with household incomes significantly above the U.S. average. Some applicants were turned down because they needed a personal computer to telecommute and could not afford to buy it. This is why I used a value of 40% employer-purchased computers for new applicants to telecommuting projects. Employer purchases of portable computers—or even zero-interest purchase loans to employees—can greatly expand the use of telecommuting to lower-income employees.

As explored earlier, I can not find clear evidence of a net cost to telecommuters of utilities such as gas, electricity, and telephone. The differences seem to be buried in the inter-household variations in such costs. However, personal computers do use electrical energy, say, 1.6 kilowatt-hour per day. Thus a computer-using, one-day-per-week telecommuter might incur added annual electricity costs (at $0.10 per kilowatt-hour) of about $8.

The monetary benefits to telecommuters are generally in the form of reduced operating expenses: car use, clothing, food, and child care costs. The average telecommuter in the example case traveled 22.8 miles each way to work. Given an average automobile operating cost (including depreciation, fuel, insurance, and maintenance) of $0.42 per mile, the average one-day-per-week telecommuter saves about $920 per year.

I do not have accurate information on telecommuter savings in food and clothing. Typically, home-based telecommuters do not dress formally for their home office, nor do they eat out for lunch. My personal estimate is that the annual clothing bill is down by $200 for a one-day-per-week telecommuter, while lunch savings can amount to at least $2 per telecommuting day, or another $200 annually for one-day-per-week telecommuters.

Telecommuting is not a substitute for child or parent care; telecommuters cannot work effectively and supervise other household members simultaneously. However, telecommuters may be able to hire lower cost in-home supervisors for either small children or invalid relatives. I do not have estimates for these savings.

Because of the wide variation in home-telecommuting scenarios, I do not have a number for the net monetary impact of telecommuting on an individual telecommuter, except that it is probably a net benefit. The most significant benefit for home-telecommuters is psychological: stress reduction; feelings of greater control of one's life; increased family interaction, as discussed earlier.

Telework center telecommuters can have most of the benefits just described, with fewer costs, particularly in equipment and housing. This is most apparent for neighborhood telework centers, which are almost at home. Regional centers, to the extent that they are relatively distant from employees' homes and have more formal office atmospheres, may have somewhat lower net telecommuter benefits. There is simply too little experience to date with either of these forms for us to reach quantitative conclusions.

➤ The Community

In the case examined here, the primary motivation for the telecommuting project was a community cost problem: air pollution. The community, via its regulatory powers, decided to transfer that cost to the polluters, or the employers thereof, by means of fines imposed on those who did not meet or exceed minimum standards.

If the telecommuting were to be extended to all of the potential participants in the example project, there would be an annual reduction in air pollution of about 6 million pounds of carbon monoxide, 1.2 million pounds of unburned hydrocarbons, and about 400,000 pounds of nitrogen oxides. The impact on reducing traffic congestion is harder to determine. Yet, eliminating about 3,000 cars from the downtown commute every day (just from this employer) would likely have a significant impact on traffic flow.

That, in turn, would reduce air pollution further. The reduced traffic flow, since it would also proportionately reduce roadway wear and tear, would diminish highway infrastructure costs. Further, if large numbers of organizations were to adopt telecommuting, the existing transportation infrastructure could serve adequately for many more years, even under conditions of increasing local population growth.

Telecommuters also appear to be more likely to participate in local activities, participating in local political and service groups more frequently. The telecommuters are less fatigued from the daily commute and have more discretionary time. There may also be a reduction in the crime rate; as residential neighborhoods increase the numbers of people who are present during daylight hours, property crime and drug sales are likely to drop.

None of these community-impact speculations can be proven as of this writing. The population of telecommuters in the U.S., although more than 14 million strong, is still too dispersed for the effects to show unequivocally.

Stick around, you'll see.

■ A SIMPLIFIED ANALYSIS FOR TEST PURPOSES

Often it is useful to present a simplified cost-benefit analysis to senior management (or your own supervisor) as part of the preliminary stages of setting up a telework program. A few years ago we developed such an analysis as part of a handout to executives in companies considering telecommuting. We have also posted a similar version on JALA International's Web site *(www.jala.com)*. The analysis naturally omits many of the finer points discussed above but has proven to be very popular. So here it is, encapsulated in 3 spreadsheets (Tables 7.5, 7.6, and 7.7).

Table 7.5 Simplified Home-Based Telecommuting CBA

Sample Cost-Benefit Analysis for Home-Based Telecommuting (At end of first year of telecommuting)			
Assumptions: Av'g annual salary is: $26,000 TCing days/week: 1.5			

Costs to Employer per Telecommuter			
Direct Costs	**One-Time**	**Recurring (Annual)**	**Notes**
Selection and training	$175		Both telecommuters & supervisors trained
Telecommunications			
New installations	$505		ISDN phone line (2 B + D) and interface card
Services		$912	Will vary, depending on need for telecommunications, local tariff structure
Computers	$3,200		Cost of docking station, extra monitor, laptop instead of desktop computer
Moving costs			
Computer equipment	$0		Usually zero if employee handles this
Renovation/installation	$240		Some employee-specific materials, lock boxes, etc.
Facilities leasing		$0	Assumes employee reports to principal office on non-telecommute days
Furniture purchase/lease	$350	$0	
Insurance		$0	Company is self-insured
Equipment purchase/rental costs	$350	$0	Inkjet printer
Performance evaluation	$700		Will vary, depending on level of detail required
TOTAL DIRECT COSTS	$5,520	$912	

Benefits to Employer per Telecommuter Direct Benefits			
Increased employee effectiveness		$3,900	Average 15% relative to non-telecommuters @ 1.5 days/week
Decreased sick leave		$226	2 days per year reduction; 230 work days per year
Increased organizational effectiveness		$520	Average about 2%
Decreased turnover rate		$1,300	Equivalent to 5% of salary in search and training costs avoided
Reduced parking req'mts		$360	30% reduction in $100/month space requirements for non-carpooler
Office space savings		$1,620	150 square feet in the central office, proportionally reclaimed
TOTAL DIRECT BENEFITS	$0	$7,926	

Table 7.5 (Continued)

Direct Costs	One-Time	Recurring (Annual)	Notes
Benefits to Employer per Telecommuter Indirect Benefits			
Decreased air pollution			Put your own number here for compliance with AQ regulations
Increased competitiveness			Put your own number here for the effect of your new productivity
TOTAL INDIRECT BENEFITS			
ANNUAL NET BENEFITS	($5,520)	$7,014	
FIRST YEAR NET BENEFITS		$1,494	

Table 7.6 Simplified Telework Center CBA

Sample Cost-Benefit Analysis for a Telework Center (At end of first year of telecommuting)			
Assumptions: Av'g annual salary is: $26,000 Telecommuting days/week: 1.5			
Costs to Employer per Telecommuter			
Direct Costs	One-Time	Recurring (Annual)	Notes
Additional Training	$150		Both telecommuters & supervisors trained
Telecommunications			
New installations	$505		ISDN phone line (2 B + D) and interface card
Services		$912	Will vary, depending on need for telecommunications, local tariff structure
Computers	$960		Telecommuter uses company laptop and docking station
Moving Costs			
Computer equipment	$20		Move from central facility to telework center
Renovation/installation	$50		Some employee-specific materials, lock boxes, etc.
Facilities leasing		$0	Will vary from telecenter to telecenter
Furniture purchase/lease	$0	$0	Included in lease costs
Insurance		$0	Included in lease costs
Equipment purchase/rental costs		$0	Included in lease costs
Performance evaluation	$700		Will vary, depending on level of detail required
TOTAL DIRECT COSTS	$2,385	$912	
Benefits to Employer per Telecommuter Direct Benefits			
Increased employee effectiveness		$3,120	Average 12% relative to non-telecommuters @ 1.5 days/week
Decreased sick leave		$226	2 days per year reduction; 230 work days per year
Increased organizational effectiveness		$520	Average about 2%
Decreased turnover rate		$1,300	Equivalent to 5% of salary in search and training costs avoided
Reduced parking req'mts		$360	30% reduction in $100/month space requirements for non-pooler
Office space savings		$0	150 square feet in central office, proportionally reclaimed
TOTAL DIRECT BENEFITS	$0	$5,526	

Table 7.6 (Continued)

Direct Costs	One-Time	Recurring (Annual)	Notes
Indirect Benefits			
Decreased air pollution			Put your own number here for compliance with AQ regulations
Increased competitiveness			Put your own number here for the effect of your new productivity
TOTAL INDIRECT BENEFITS			
ANNUAL NET BENEFITS	($2,385)	$4,614	
FIRST YEAR NET BENEFITS		$2,229	

Table 7.7   Home-Based Employee's CBA

Sample Cost-Benefit Analysis for Home-Based Telecommuting			
Assumptions: Av'g annual salary is: $26,000 Telecommuting days/week: 1.5			
Costs to Employee			
Direct Costs	**One-Time**	**Recurring (Annual)**	**Notes**
Telecommunications			
New installations	$200		Extra phone line and modem, if necessary
Services		$348	Will vary, depending on need for telecommunications
Computers	$1,850		If employee buys the computer, monitor and printer
Facilities leasing		$234	Factored as a % of monthly rent allocated to the home office
Office furniture purchase	$450	$0	Office chair, desk, lamp
Home heating/cooling increases		$0	Will vary with location, weather; this is Southern California value
Insurance		$30	Addendum to homeowner's policy
Office equipment	$50	$0	Miscellaneous office equipment for telecommuting
TOTAL DIRECT COSTS	$2,550	$612	
Benefits to Employee			
Fuel consumption reduction		$132	See OTHER ASSUMPTIONS sheet
Car maintenance cost reduction		$109	See OTHER ASSUMPTIONS sheet
Reduced lunch costs		$324	One-third the cost at home
Child/elder care cost reduction		$1,512	Also assume a 30% reduction on telecommuting days
Lowered clothing bills		$150	Assumes you don't refit annually at fashion's dictates
Income tax reduction		$0	Forget it!
TOTAL DIRECT BENEFITS	$0	$2,228	
Indirect Benefits			
Stress reduction			Put your own number here for analgesic savings
Increased discretionary time			Put your own number here for the impact of your new freedom
TOTAL INDIRECT BENEFITS			
ANNUAL NET BENEFITS	($2,550)	$1,616	
FIRST YEAR NET BENEFITS		($934)	

Chapter

8

Issues for Home-Based Teleworkers

TRAFFIC IS LIGHT IN THE HALLWAY TODAY....

Very often telemanagers are also teleworkers. In case you now (or will) belong to that illustrious group, here are a few factors that may apply to your own case—and will certainly apply to many of your teleworkers. This chapter is written as advice that you might want to give to your teleworkers, or even take yourself.

There are two parts to getting started at home teleworking. The first part is establishing your home office and setting up a good working environment. The second part is getting yourself together and rearranging your head so that it, too, works well in this new situation.

■ DESIGNING YOUR WORKSPACE

Now, with all these thoughts in mind, become an instant architect. Get some graph paper with a square grid and lay out your proposed workspace (or, if you have an architectural program on your PC, use it). Pick a scale; for example, $^1/_2$ inch on the graph paper equals 1 foot in the house ($^1/_4$ inch on the paper equals 6 inches in the real world). Make cutouts for all the pieces of furniture—and large equipment—you think you will need: desk, chair(s), table(s), telephone, modem, printer stand, exercise machine, file cabinet(s), bookshelves, lamps, whatever you feel is necessary. Lay out the walls, doors, and windows on the graph paper, including the swing space needed for doors (if any). Don't forget that you need room to walk in and to have access to drawers.

If you're using a computer and you get direct sunlight in the room, lightly draw in the angles of the incoming light rays. You'll want to avoid direct reflections from the computer display into your eyes. You'll also want to avoid reflections from well-lit walls behind you onto your display screen.

Finally, you need to avoid having the screen between you and a bright area light source behind it. If you can't avoid these by workstation placement, be sure that you can screen off the offending light source when necessary. There are screens that you can buy to fit over the display screen and reduce glare, but these add costs and often are dust catchers. Many recent monitor screens have built-in glare-reduction features that further help reduce the problem.

You also may be able to adjust light levels with available lamps or drapes. Or supplementary lighting may be part of the equipment that you or the company should supply to achieve the proper work environment. Task lighting may be sufficient, and is generally preferable to area lighting.

Think of the activities you do most. Arrange the furniture so that whatever is required for those activities is within arm's reach—or a short roll of your chair.[1] Other, less-frequently used items can be placed farther away.

---

[1] Don't try this if your chair doesn't have rollers on the legs!

Try to arrange any electronic hardware so that:

➤ It is near electrical outlets and can be connected via a surge protector/master switch. If you live in an area that has frequent power fluctuations or outages, think about getting an Uninterruptible Power Supply (UPS) to prevent your screams of agony when the computer loses all of the stuff that you have been inputting but haven't bothered to save for the last two hours

➤ Interconnecting cables are out of the way, tied together, or covered to minimize the danger of tripping over them and to reduce the amount of dust they catch

➤ Heavy items are on secure stands, preferably near a wall, and as child-proofed as possible (even if the kids are only occasional visitors). If you live in earthquake country you may want to secure them to a wall or desk with a flexible cable. You may be able to use Velcro strips on the bottom of lighter objects.

If you're a smoker, remember that ashes and computers are bitter enemies, as are spilled coffee and floppy disks.

Keep the telephone ringer, or anything else with a magnet— like those nice little paper clip holders, away from floppy disks.

Keep frequently used manuals or other references on a shelf next to or above your computer display. Remember to put them back right after you've used them.

Add your own inspirations here:

■ SECURING YOUR EQUIPMENT, MATERIALS, AND SUPPLIES

First, a fundamental point. Make sure you list the supplies you'll need at home *before* you embark on your teleworking adventure. The list should include the obvious things, such as paper and pencils, but keep an eye out for those not-so-obvious things: stapler, staple remover, phone number file, ruler, address or appointment book, calendar, manuals, and so on.

Particularly if you have children who love to play with mom's or dad's fascinating equipment, or who really need some of those supplies for school, it may be necessary to have a secure storage place for critical items. Paper and printer supplies can be in a cabinet that is locked or otherwise established as solely yours. (If you have a printer stand, the paper often can be kept in a box below it.) In any case it is your responsibility to ensure that your home office is a safe place to work in and that it is always in good shape for the work to be performed.

➤ Computer Security

The computer can be kept in a desk or cabinet that is lockable. Floppy disks can be put in lockable (non-magnetic) storage bins. Many computers have lockable keyboards to foil the attempts of the kids to play with the machine while you're off somewhere else. Computer viruses are a growing worry; never boot your computer from a floppy disk unless you are sure it is an original or has an exact copy of the manufacturer's operating system software and boot tracks.[2]

Computer bulletin board systems (BBSes) and the Internet are particularly worrisome, even nightmare producing, to company computing executives. Publicly available BBSes are a favorite target for hackers whose idea of entertainment is destroying someone else's data. The Internet also has that reputation, although hordes of programmers are working feverishly to correct it. Either don't connect to BBSes with your computer or, if you must try it, make very sure that any downloadable files of the BBS are well

---

[2] If you don't understand that sentence, check with your local computer guru.

policed by its operator and/or that you habitually use a good brand of virus-protection software.[3] If Internet access is the means you use to connect to the principal office, however, make sure that your use of it still avoids these hazards.

■ GETTING DOWN TO WORK

Home is definitely not the office that you are used to. Working at home gives you great new freedoms. That's the trouble. You have to find that balance between the new freedoms and the responsibilities of getting the work out. That involves cultivating some self-discipline that you may not have needed in the office. Here are some pointers for keeping yourself working when you should be—and not working when you shouldn't be.

➤ Training Yourself

While I'm on the isolation question, someone who has supervised a teleworking employee once observed, "the office environment has evolved for a reason." Going to work separates one from all but the most urgent non-work responsibilities. Establishing an office environment in the home is not only a physical problem but, more importantly, a conceptual task. The worker, household members and neighbors must be convinced that the teleworker is at work. A three-year-old's demands for attention are difficult to ignore. Some double duty is a benefit of being at home: accepting a United Parcel Service delivery at the door is a more efficient use of time than driving to the depot. In effect, the home worker is substituting a new set of interruptions for some of those he has become accustomed to on site.

Some such interruptions require imaginative solutions. If a responsible relative is not available, it may be necessary to hire supplemental child care and insist that while Mommy or Daddy is "at work" she or he is not to be disturbed. This is particularly true for pre-school children. The neighbor will have to be "trained" not to drop in. With no hard and fast rules, the overriding guideline is that it is the worker's responsibility to improvise whatever adjustments are necessary for him or her to do the job on time and up to standard.

However, it is possible to set up a system of protocols for handling the most common sources of interruption listed above and

---

[3] If you don't understand that sentence, check with your local computer guru.

provide training in dealing with them. Each protocol is of the type: "In this situation . . . here are the steps to be taken to deal with the problem." (This is described in Chapter 9.)

➤ Achieving the Office Frame of Mind

The first thing to settle is getting your mind to believe that you're in the office even though the evidence of your eyes and ears is that you're at home. That is one reason why it is important to establish a definite workspace in the home that is clearly different from the rest of the space. The environment around your desk gives you the clues that it's an office. That extra easy chair may be tempting, but do you really work better while sitting in it?

The next important factor contributing to that frame of mind is the schedule. Set one up for every day that you're at home—and try to stick to it. That's the bad news. The good news is that it doesn't have to be the schedule you would use if you were actually in your principal office. It may overlap your ordinary schedule, particularly when you have to make phone or computer calls to others, to the public, clients or colleagues. But those times when such contact is unnecessary can be rearranged to suit your style. Many people stick to the regular office schedule anyway. Others work for a few hours early in the day, followed by some leisure time, then another stint in late afternoon and/or evening. Try a few of these options, after first discussing and agreeing upon them with your supervisor. Ultimately it is easiest if you get into a specific pattern of work hours that is consistent from day to day.

➤ Clothes May Make a Difference

The first impulse of many teleworkers is to get away from office garb entirely; stick to jeans and sweatshirt, bathing suit, birthday suit, very informal wear.[4] If it makes you feel more energetic, do it. Some teleworkers find that wearing more formal clothes helps keep them work-aware, even to the extent of wearing a suit in the

---

[4] A series of TV ads in 1997 featured a teleworker wearing bunny slippers.

home office. If you feel uncomfortable in casual clothes (or in a suit) change to the reverse.

➤ Getting Organized

One of the hardest tasks at first may be sorting out what belongs where. I call it "The Two-Briefcase Syndrome." You may be familiar with it already. If you're at home the report you need to reference is in the old office. If you're in the old office the report you need is at home. So what do you do? You trudge back and forth between home- and old-office with two briefcases full of papers that you just might need.[5]

While this may be great for bodybuilding it is not an answer to your quest for serenity. Start keeping records on what is needed where. In some cases you can move non-sensitive files or references permanently home. In other cases you might want to have duplicates at home. In either case get into the habit of planning ahead of time what you'll need to have with you either at home or in the old office. The test of your success is when you graduate to a single—or no—briefcase.

Here's another trick. Think about what you do at home in terms of communicating and non-communicating time. Try to bunch the communicating time into coherent groups. That is, try to make all your phone calls (or return calls), fax transmissions, etc., in a specific time interval. This way, you can increase the amount of uninterrupted time you have. That, in turn tends to both increase your effectiveness and decrease your stress levels.

Many teleworkers notice a positive side-effect of this. They become generally better organized. They plan more carefully, visualizing exactly what's needed for the next step, the next job. This carries over into tasks that have nothing to do with teleworking.

➤ "Leaving" the Office

Sometimes it's harder to leave the office at home than it is to leave the distant one. "Just one more calculation (or paragraph) and I'll quit for sure, dear." One of the prime dangers for happy teleworkers is workaholism. As in the case of getting in the frame of mind to do work at home, you may want to set up a schedule of sacrosanct non-work hours.

Some teleworkers have gone to the extent of having an outside door installed in the room they use as an office. In the morning

---

[5] One telecommuter had a trunk full of files in the car—just in case.

they go out of the front door of the house (or apartment if they have an understanding landlord) and go in the new office door, reversing the trip at day's end.

Then, of course, there's the topic of brief visits. Sometimes you have really brilliant work-related ideas during non-working hours. Should you try to remember them until the next work period or rush right into your home office and get them into action? Our experience is to do the latter; it is much more satisfying and quite possibly takes less time than if you try to remember it all later—or lie awake worrying whether you'll forget it.

We also advise you to keep going on those occasions when you're really on a roll; get those great ideas down even if you are working past your schedule—just don't make a habit of it.

Our experience also shows that working at home is more intense than working in the traditional office. You tend to get much more done in a given amount of time, provided that it is the kind of work suited for a home office. Make use of that intensity in scheduling your hours, both in and out of the office. Work when you feel that you can best exert that intensity, do something else when you feel a need for change. But keep in mind that the measure of success in this new work environment is output.[6]

➤ Exercise

Working from home also gives you a chance to get that exercise that you never had time for when you had to commute every day. Make pushing yourself away from the refrigerator one of your first daily routines. One teleworker gets up in the morning and goes straight to the home office for an hour or so. Then this teleworker runs or goes swimming, comes back for a shower and breakfast. Then it's back to the home office. The exercise time also turns out to be useful for arranging or re-examining the thoughts from the earlier work session. Both the thoughts and the teleworker end up in better shape.

---

[6]This doesn't mean that you should feel free to reduce the *length* of the workday. After all, teleworking does cost the company extra and your increased productivity is one of the ways of compensating for those costs.

If you're a constant computer user it's also a very good idea to take regular breaks to walk around, water the plants or the pets, or otherwise loosen up from the time you've spent in a fixed position at the keyboard.[7] There are even exercise books for the office-bound.

■ TRAINING THE HOUSEHOLD

You are not the only one who has to get in shape for working at home. Removing the distractions of home can be a—or *the*—major task in setting up a good working environment. The hardest part is usually training the rest of the family that when you are working you are working and are not to be disturbed any more than you would be if you were in the principal office. You are not available for running down to the store for groceries. You are not available for random questions and interruption from the spouse and kids. You are working.

➤ Business Visitors

One of the issues for setting up a home office is how much contact, if any, you are going to have with business visitors. Although business visitors probably won't expect to see a duplicate of a traditional office in your home, they should find a clear, unobstructed, hazard-free route to your home office. An entryway separate from the rest of your home would be ideal. That way, the rest of the household can continue their usual routines without concern about disturbing you—or vice versa.

If you need to have a dual-purpose location for such meetings, the best place is probably the living room, rather than your office space. One reason is that it's likely to be more readily convertible to meeting uses than other rooms in the home. I often use either the living room or the dining area/table as a conference center, depending on the number of visitors and the meeting purpose. The primary constraint is that I have to plan far enough ahead of the meeting time to clear out any clutter that may be left over from other family activities. My wife does point out that it is a good motivation to keep the area reasonably neat (although possibly at the expense of piles of papers stacked elsewhere).

---

[7] About 15 minutes every hour for constant computer users; about 15 minutes every two hours for intermittent computer users.

➤ Noise

As I mentioned earlier, one of the common distractions is background noise while you are on the phone. Vacuum cleaners, washing machines, crying children, barking dogs and parrots with colorful vocabularies make poor impressions of businesslike behavior to the party on the other end of the line. The best solution is to have your home office in a room where you can shut the door and isolate those noises. Failing that, if there is someone else at home to take care of the noise sources, make sure that that person takes care of the problem promptly.

On the other hand, if you miss some of the office sounds, fear not. Tapes are available of typewriters clacking, copiers copying, water coolers glukking, and other office environments.

➤ Toddler Tension

The subject of noise triggers the issue of teleworkers with young children. Contrary to one's initial hopes, it is not a great idea to try to telework and personally take care of an active three-year-old simultaneously. Although it can be done, and is more satisfying than leaving the job to a sitter, it is much better to try to arrange the schedule so that you are working while the child is asleep or is being supervised by some other responsible person. In the latter case, this may also take some training of the prospective sitter.

This does not mean that you can't telework if you're a single parent, or have pre-school kids or invalid parents. It does mean that there should be someone else present in the household who can handle the non-emergency, routine care of those dependents while you're working. You're still available for the occasional crisis.

➤ Diplomacy

You are not a flaming tyrant, I hope. The best policy seems to be to get the family together before you start working at home, explain the situation carefully, then reinforce the rules, gently, as such situations arise when you are actually working at home. Many teleworkers have found that everything settles down after a few weeks. The kids or spouses no longer disturb them, but still feel better for having the teleworkers around even though they are nominally not available.

Keep the assertiveness image in mind, though. One of the advantages of working at home is that you are available for those really special occasions—or emergencies—that come up from time to time. Firmness combined with flexibility is the key.

One teleworker did have an unusual problem, though. His dog loved having him home; got so accustomed to it that, when he did go to the principal office once or twice a week, the dog was inconsolable and howled all day. This did nothing to improve relationships with the neighbors. What would you do in that situation?[8]

■ DEALING WITH THE NEIGHBORS AND DROP-IN TRAFFIC

Speaking of neighbors, they can present a few challenges. The first is convincing them that you really are working, not loafing or unemployed. It might help to have a little home-office-warming party to demonstrate your new operation.

That party might also be a good time to mention that you are not available as a baby sitter, parcel drop-off point, message taker, or coffee klatscher while you are working. This, too, might take a little polite reinforcing during the first few weeks of your new lifestyle. That doesn't mean that you can't have lunch with the neighbors, or go out for short shopping tours, provided that these fit into your new schedule. One of the greatest appeals of teleworking is that you can arrange many of these previously impossible conflicts in your newly flexible schedule. Lately, neighborhood coffeehouses seem to be filled with teleworkers on mid-week midmornings—and they still get their work done.

In Japan the social mores about having a respectable job are particularly intense. I heard, but cannot verify, the following story: This social status situation quickly became painful to some Japanese teleworkers whose neighbors were completely unconvinced by explanations that they really hadn't lost their jobs (and major status). Their employer not only came to their rescue but materially increased their status by sending around a company cleaning squad, complete with uniforms bearing the company logo, to the teleworkers' homes once a month!

---

[8] Our solution: get another dog to keep the first one company. It worked.

■ LIVING ABOVE WHAT YOU CAN'T CHANGE

Try as you might, some of the distractions and interruptions of working at home are unavoidable. You also must try to adapt yourself to those as well. Remember, there are many unavoidable distractions and interruptions in the traditional office as well. You may not be able to isolate yourself visually or acoustically from the other doings at home. If you can't arrange the schedule so that you miss particularly busy periods, try some mental conditioning (or local background music) so that you learn to ignore the distractions. It does work. On the other hand, don't get so isolated that you miss important calls, such as those from the boss!

Also, don't get frustrated if not everything works well at first. We routinely find that new teleworkers need a few weeks to make adjustments and get the work patterns smoothly developed. Your attitude is really important during that time. Use your ingenuity to get around obstacles that may come up. We have yet to find a difficulty that can't be surmounted by some careful planning or attitude adjustments on your—or your supervisor's—part.

■ MANAGING YOURSELF

Successful management *of* teleworkers is covered in other chapters. This section covers successful management *by* teleworkers: the aspects of telework management that are important for each teleworker to understand.

➤ New Working Relationships with Co-Workers

One of the worries of new teleworkers is that they will lose contact with their fellow workers, that they somehow will become different in the eyes of their colleagues. This fear is sometimes abetted by the treatment they get when they do come into the office, sort of a new form of hazing. "Oh, I see you've finally decided to come in to work for a while!" "Well, stranger, how was the vacation?" "Didn't you used to work here?" These and similar remarks are not too successful in easing your tensions.

A related problem is the: "Gee, I hate to call you at home, but . . . ." The hidden meaning: you are somehow different (and worse, or luckier, or otherwise less understood) than everyone else. So here, as well as at home, there is some training and adjustment needed.

The first rule is: *Be positive, not defensive, about teleworking.* Admit that you've been having a great time at home and, by the way, turned out that big report a week ahead of schedule and with much better insight than you could with all the interruptions at the office. Mention that you can now exercise regularly with no problems, now that you don't have to waste an hour or two on the road every day. Tell about the time you went sailing last Wednesday afternoon, having finished your work at home by 10:30 that morning. Or the play that your ten-year-old starred in that you went to see at her school. Or the town council seat that you're running for now that you have the time and energy to go to meetings. You get the idea. Just don't be obnoxious about it. On second thought, maybe you should keep some of those things to yourself. Just smile; make them wonder what you've been up to.

The second rule is: *Business as usual.* Make sure that your colleagues know that they can call you at home any time they would normally try to contact you at the office. One technique, probably a good one in any case if you have lots of phone traffic, is to have a separate phone line that is solely for business purposes. Give that number out to people. Print it on your business card.

Have call forwarding (together with an answering machine at home) or voice mail installed in the principal office so that calls get to you as expeditiously as possible. The trick here, as mentioned earlier, is to balance communications with uninterrupted think-work. To keep the interruptions down, the best trick may be to use a pager. If the people at the principal office really need you, you get beeped. Otherwise, you pick up the recorded communications in accordance with your schedule, not the callers'.[9]

Many people, particularly those not in your immediate office group, won't even know you're working from home. Make a particular effort to keep in frequent touch with your close colleagues via telephone, fax, or electronic mail (if you have the equipment or software). Don't wait for them to call you, call them. Try calling first thing in the morning a few times—before they've made it through the traffic. Or just before quitting time—after they've left to catch the car pool; they'll get the message.

The real secret to breaking down those misunderstandings is frequent communication. What we're doing in teleworking is substituting some telecommunication for face-to-face conversation. We do not eliminate communication. Nor do we eliminate face-to-face

---

[9]This advice is given on the assumption that your primary job requirement is other than immediately responding to external calls.

conversation. We may actually increase the amount of total communication by this new combination. But it may take some real effort on your part to keep the communication going.

Which brings us to rule three for telecommuters: *Go to the principal office regularly to reinforce your telecommunications.*

"Regularly" can mean anything from a few days a year to four days per week, depending on all those other job factors we covered earlier. For the average contemporary telecommuter, it means about three days per week. One of the important parts of this rule is that you may have to schedule meetings more tightly, and make sure that the meetings you do have are short and to the point. This tactic allows you to move your meetings into as few days as possible. (This in itself is a productivity enhancer.)

Many teleworkers find that they can set agendas for the meetings and transmit the necessary background material to the attendees by electronic mail and telephone or facsimile from home (or via a secretary who just might be at home). They also find that this preparation significantly shrinks meeting time. In some cases, you can attend the meetings electronically, via telephone or video teleconferencing.[10]

Try to have at least one day per week when you are always at home. This helps get you, your family, and your colleagues acclimated to teleworking. Of course, this is not always possible; occasional crises do seem to intervene, but it is a good idea to try. In a matter of a few weeks to a few months your teleworking will be routine to all concerned.

➤ Job (Re)design

Sometimes it seems that, no matter how you try, you can't arrange your schedule—or the schedules of others—so that you can telework effectively. Maybe this situation calls for some rethinking of the content of your job and the jobs of your co-workers. For example, one teleworker was responsible for certifying that new test equipment shipped to her organization was operating properly. The rules of her job also required that the certification be made

---

[10] *ITAC*, the International Telework Association and Council, is a non-profit educational organization dedicated to disseminating information about telecommuting. ITAC holds periodic telephone teleconferences (as well as annual national and regional face-to-face get-togethers) to report on the status of telecommuting activities and discuss telecommuting-related issues. Participation in the teleconferences is limited to people on Earth, so far.

within twenty-four hours of the equipment's arrival. Unfortunately, the equipment never arrived according to a preset schedule; often it appeared when she was teleworking from home. She began missing those twenty-four-hour deadlines, her co-workers were getting upset because they couldn't handle the inspections. Her supervisor, uneasy about teleworking from the start, was preparing to stop it all.

What should be done? One possibility is for the teleworker's job to be redesigned to share inspection responsibility among two or three of her co-workers. This is usually known as *cross training*. Each is responsible for equipment inspection on the specific days when he or she is in the principal office. This has extra benefits: co-workers who could not telework before (because of similar job restrictions) are free to telework; job responsibilities and knowledge are expanded for all concerned.

In a situation like this the important first step is to look at your entire work group as a collection of tasks to be performed. See how reallocation of those tasks among the existing workers can free up more people's time for teleworking. Don't forget, if you want someone else to take over some of your responsibilities then you have to take over some of the other person's in return.

The buddy system is a variation of this. Many teleworkers keep a file cabinet in the principal office with copies of the current "hot" project materials in it, together with an easily identified index of what's where. When the inevitable crisis comes and the boss wants to know *now* about project X, your designated buddy in the office can retrieve the key material, after a phone call to you. The crisis gets solved without the necessity of your coming to the office.[11] As in the previous case, make sure that you return the favor for your buddy.

➤ Communicating with Your Supervisor

What nags at managers' nerves the most is the thought that you really might be out playing instead of working! This is exacerbated when the manager calls you in mid-day and you really are out playing golf—even though you got up at 4:00 A.M. to get the day's work out of the way first.

Quality communication with your supervisor can be even more important, at least to your career plans, than communication with

---

[11] This doesn't always work; some crises really **will** require your in-person attendance. Be willing to make those appearances cheerfully.

others. One of the central management issues of teleworking is the shift from focusing on how many hours you put in to something that is more performance-oriented.

Attitudes are crucial here. The real secret of successful teleworking rests on *mutual trust* being established between you and your supervisor. If your supervisor already trusts you to deliver the goods regardless of whether you are at home or in the office, and if you trust your supervisor to reward you justly for work well done, then that is all you need. If you have established this bond of mutual trust and respect you can work anywhere that is feasible within the other constraints of the job.

If some of this is missing on one or both sides, or even if you are a little uncertain about this new venture, it may be worth getting a little more formal about teleworking. What seems to work best for teleworkers is almost a contractual relationship between you and your supervisor. You jointly have to agree on the following:

➤ What is the product—what *specifically* it is that you are supposed to do

➤ What resources you will need to do it

➤ When it is supposed to be finished

➤ How you recognize the finished product (and, for long duration projects, the intermediate stage products)

➤ Quality or success criteria for the results

. . . just as if you were an independent consultant hired by the Company.

If possible, get the main points of your mutual understanding in writing, although it need not be nearly as complex or intimidating as a formal contract. Then be sure that you fulfill your end of the bargain. As you start teleworking it is particularly important to build up your supervisor's confidence (and possibly your own) that you can do the work well, and on time, even though you're not always in the office.

Part of the task of setting up that first understanding is agreeing on performance standards. If you have a very well-defined job, and it is perfectly clear to both you and your supervisor what it is that you are supposed to do, this is easy. The less well-defined your job is, or the more subject it is to sudden changes in direction, the harder it is to nail down the performance criteria—and the more important it is to arrive at a joint understanding of what it is that you are supposed to do, and how well you are to do it. Try to work out a description anyway, as well as the two of you can. Then reexamine it at appropriate intervals to ultimately fine-tune it or, better yet, find out that you don't really need it at all.

The length of the interval for reexamination also depends on your job. Think of the tasks you do in your job. How long does it take to do the longest duration task? Hours? Days? Weeks? Months? If it's one of the last three, pick an interval about one-fourth of that for your initial performance reviews. As your mutual confidence grows, the interval between reviews may also. Don't forget, the boss may be a teleworker too.

An example of a written understanding is in Appendix B.

■ FEEDBACK AND HELP

One of the first worries about home teleworking is that you're alone out there! What happens when things go wrong?

➤ Technical Problems for Computer Users

This may be particularly important if your teleworking involves intensive use of a computer and you are new to the foibles of the machines. Microcomputers do break, although it is fairly infrequent. More often they do inexplicable things, like becoming suddenly catatonic, that are nerve-wracking even in the office where there may be ready help at hand. At home such ill-mannered machines can be even more threatening. What to do?

First, don't be afraid to ask "dumb" questions, either over the phone or in person when you are in the principal office. If you don't completely understand how something works, or can be fixed, ask. If your machine suddenly seems to die, before you do anything else ask someone how to fix it. (Remember Murphy's Law, Corollary 53: the machine will usually die just before the report is due and you have worked the last seven and a half hours without once saving your data on a disk.) Dumb questions are not at all dumb if they save you later grief. We know of many pairs of teleworkers who have solved equipment and software problems over the telephone. This can work very well indeed. In fact, one of the things we would like you to do is jot down the technical problems you have had, or are having, so that the Company can come up with a more extensive "how to" for future teleworkers.

Meanwhile, the Company may have established a guru service for your hardware, software, and other technical questions. Check this out. If so, write down the particulars here, so you can find it later.

Your local guru's name is _____. Your guru can be reached at ____-_____. If you have problems, contact the guru first. However, you should also write down the solution or recovery process for each problem you run into. Keep those notes in an easily accessible place (your memory?) so you won't have to bother the guru with incessant repeat performances.

The Company should also have a series of workshops and other available types of training to help get you off to a roaring start as a computer teleworker. Information on these training sessions usually can be obtained from the Company human resources department.

➤ Physical Support

Despite all the forecasts to the contrary, the "paperless office" seems to be a long way off. Mail, supplies and materials still have to travel to and from your desk, wherever that desk is. If it is at home, the interoffice mail system won't reach. There are some ways to meet this problem. First, change the address on periodicals so that they come to your home instead of the office. Second, if you telework extensively arrange with a co-worker to drop off and pick up your interoffice mail daily or at appropriate intervals. Third, when you do go into the principal office pick up your mail and that of other nearby teleworkers; it still beats a car pool. Finally, try to convert most of your interoffice messaging to electronic mail, voice mail, facsimile, or telephone conversations.

Some equipment problems and repairs just can't be done easily at home. They require that the offending box be taken somewhere for surgery. As the background information says, sometimes you may have to go into the principal office until the culprit is repaired or replaced.

➤ Dealing with Personal and Household Compulsions and Relationships

There are problems and issues that a book this general in nature cannot handle. For down-to-earth advice on how to deal with

problems of overeating (the teleworking refrigerator syndrome), kids or mates who can't seem to fit themselves into your new role (or vice versa), technical problems that the guru can't handle effectively, and similar problems, there seems to be no substitute for advice from others who have been through it. To that end, the Company should have periodic group sessions to explore problems and solutions offered by fellow teleworkers.

For issues that have to do with management or organizational problems, the best approach is to see your supervisor.

➤ Dealing with the IRS

This is not a source of legal advice on the tax laws. You should consult your accountant for the latest information. However, current tax law makes it *very* difficult for you to have any tax advantage from an office at home, although the 1997 tax law changes have improved matters for some types of home-based workers.

■ BAILING OUT

Sometimes, in spite of all our good intentions, you or your supervisor feel that teleworking just isn't working out for you. If attempts to resolve the problems are not successful then the best solution seems to be to quit teleworking from home. All that is necessary is that you tell your supervisor that you want to quit the project and you can arrange to return with no questions asked.

This project is for volunteers and that commitment works both ways: you do not have to telework if you don't want to (provided that there *is* an office to go to); similarly, your supervisor can ask you to stop teleworking at any time. So, if you enjoy teleworking, keep in mind the fact that teleworking has to work for everyone concerned if it is to work at all.

Chapter

9

Training

The importance of proper training of teleworkers, telemanagers and of those non-teleworkers with whom they deal regularly cannot be over stressed. Employees and managers alike may be intimidated by the concept, non-teleworking colleagues have misapprehensions about the nature of teleworking, families need to understand the changing roles of home teleworkers, and the work patterns of the teleworkers themselves tend to change. It is extremely important to provide pre-implementation and during-implementation training (and assessment) for all of those who are directly affected by teleworking.

■ TRAINING ISSUES

Central to the training plan is the identification of the differences between traditional work situations and those of teleworking. For example, techniques of supervision (as discussed in Chapter 5) are likely to be different, as are performance indicators. Employees with limited or no prior computer experience will need familiarization training as well as a readily available "hot line" source of advice during work if they will be using computers as teleworkers. Home teleworkers may need training or advice on how to work with their families to eliminate distractions during working periods.[1]

---

[1] Actually, my experience has been that, in our contemporary world of two-earner households, there is fairly little interaction with the rest of the family for many teleworkers. This is because the non-teleworking earner is usually at work somewhere else. This will change as the number of two-teleworker households increases.

The nature and details of the types of training required will depend on the types of work and work situations of the prospective teleworkers.

Teleworking by large numbers of employees may be a novel concept but it is not a work style without precedents. Many employees of large organizations already work remotely from organization or district headquarters: forest rangers, detectives, construction managers, sales people, and field engineers all work "off site" with varying degrees of contact with their supervisors. For those workers and their managers the training to work independently and to monitor from a distance are already ingrained in the system. To achieve the same level of confidence regarding teleworking requires attention to:

➤ How each participating work unit functions now and

➤ What training and procedures (in addition to those for the new technology) will optimize productive functioning in the future.

■ BUT FIRST, GENERAL ORIENTATION

At the early stages of telecommuting in an organization, even before any telecommuters are selected or "how-to" sessions begin, it may be necessary to brief both managers and prospective telecommuters on the concepts, issues, costs, risks and benefits of telecommuting. Foremost among the objectives of these briefings is that of presenting telecommuting in an evenhanded, practical way. The briefings should include explanations of what telecommuting is—and isn't, for whom telecommuting may—or may not—be appropriate, what changes can be expected, what the costs and risks are (especially important for managers) and what the implementation schedule is.

These briefings serve as the catalyst for enlisting the initial group(s) of active telecommuters. Typically, they are followed by a formal process of selecting the participants in the initial pilot project. Once the selection is completed the focus changes to preparing the selected telecommuters and their supervisors for active telecommuting.

In cases where an impact evaluation is planned as part of the initial project (or an expansion process) it is also desirable to include in the briefings members of a control group (that is, individuals who have been selected to closely match the telecommuters' work characteristics but who will not telecommute during the evaluation period).

■ TRAINING WHAT?

How do you know how much training is required? We recommend that you develop this information by means of a survey of potential teleworkers, as described in Chapter 10. One of the products of the survey should be an estimate of the extent and nature of the changes facing individual teleworkers, their managers and their peer groups. This estimate will serve to scope the types and nature of training that might be required.

➤ The Book(s)

As one part of the training approach, I feel that it is important to have an easily readable book or manual for teleworkers that can serve as a valuable aid and reference during the acclimatization process. This book was designed with that thought in mind (portions of it have been used by thousands of teleworkers), although it may be "overkill" for some teleworkers.

It is also desirable to have the participating teleworkers and telemanagers develop a company-specific addendum to the book as their experience with teleworking progresses. Although the book you are reading at this moment can act as core material, specific additional anecdotes and rules appropriate to your organization may make it more personal and positive as a learning tool.

➤ Training Face-to-Face

In addition to such written aids, it is important to have face-to-face training sessions with the prospective teleworkers both prior to the initiation of their new work styles and at intervals throughout the start-up phase of the project. In the latter case, for example, focus group sessions, or the formation of "users' groups" can serve as excellent means of self-training and maintaining group communications.

The active participation of some prospective teleworkers can materially aid in development of the training plan. You can help employees identify their own training needs and requirements, through meetings and telephone interviews during the initial period of implementation, and during or shortly after the participant selection process. Thus, the training plan, as well as other key parts of the implementation plan, will be guided by those who are or will be the ultimate recipients of the training. Then, when the actual personnel training begins, the training aids will be optimally matched to the requirements of the participants.

The following sections describe the issues and approaches in more detail.

■ TRAINING TOPICS AND METHODS

The most extensive training requirement is for those teleworkers who will be working at home. In many cases, particularly among professionals and those individuals who are accustomed to working independently, very little extra training may be required. For some individuals, such as those who are used to working under detailed supervision, fairly extensive training may be in order.

➤ Learning to Work in the Home

Objectives of Training for Off-Site Work

Learning to work at home requires developing or adopting self-supplied cues to "go to work," continue, and stop working. At the office, group behavior, whether or not it is formally imposed, sets times to start and stop work within "allowable" variances, exercises peer pressure to keep working, and provides a hierarchical supervisory structure that sets productivity standards and maintains the group routine.

When an individual travels for business, work periods are structured by scheduled appointments, flight departure times, and the group behavior at each place she or he conducts business.

During overtime work periods, the task overload which necessitates the extra work time tends to be stimulus enough to continue working even if one is alone and without direct supervision.

In teleworking situations, however, either an externally imposed structure or self-imposed artifices may be required to maintain discipline equivalent to what one has in the office.

Employees beginning to telework from home may need training in the following areas:

Scheduling Work Periods

Most home teleworkers work on schedules that are either evolved to fit their individual preferences and household constraints or are determined by the nature of the job. Programmers, for example, tend to work late at night during hours when response times are fastest on mainframe computers. Most people work by the clock, but not necessarily by the same time periods as for on-site work.[2]

A common change is *schedule chunking*: from the traditional nine-hour continuous day[3] (with lunch in the middle), to two or more chunks of two to four hours, only some of which are during conventional office hours. As another variation, some teleworkers change to a more flexible twenty-four-hour day, seven-day week of interspersed work and leisure. If interaction with on-site peers is required as part of the tasks performed at home, those work hours need to be synchronized. Where use of electronic- or voice-mail satisfies the work communications needs, the time periods worked at home need not overlap on-site work hours.

Accepting Shifts in Household Responsibilities

A worker coming home to work, even for intermittent periods, must be prepared for his or her new role within a shared habitat. Assuming traditional role models, "he" must be prepared to meet expectations that now he is home he can . . . and "she" must be prepared to give up household territory (aural as well as physical). Persons who successfully home telework find that, although the tradeoffs of being at home are positive, there may be adjustments to be made.

Controlling Interruptions

This is probably the most difficult adjustment home-based teleworkers may have to make. Establishing an office environment in

---

[2] Several teleworkers list the main virtue of teleworking as its *metabolism equalizer* nature. It allows them to work during their most energetic periods—that are not consistent with normal office hours.

[3] Many teleworkers also work on compressed schedules such as 9–80 (8 nine-hour-plus-lunch days and 1 eight-hour-plus-lunch day in two weeks) or 4–10 (4 ten-hour-plus-lunch days per week). The same principles apply here. However, managers are even more reluctant to accept teleworking for compressed-week employees, arguing that they are already spending diminished time in the office. Our data indicate that the benefits of teleworking are relatively insensitive to these different schedule options; they work for all of them.

a house that "has a life of its own" requires setting new precedents for which interruptions are permissible and which are not. Most teleworkers cannot isolate themselves totally within the household. They and their families can mutually agree, however, that the family exchanges routinely will take place during times set for breaks so that home workers are not continually distracted from their jobs.

Even having trained all members of the household, including himself or herself, the teleworker must take some interruptions in his stride. Stopping to answer the delivery person's knock on the door may be no more distracting than a co-worker's interruption unless one is fighting a grievance over spousal responsibilities. Frequently, these "interruptions" are themselves useful for relaxation and posture realignment breaks, particularly as a means of dragging teleworkers away from their computers.

Resisting Temptations

When does freedom become license? With all those on-site restrictions lifted, it's an opportunity for bad habits to take over. Snacking, drug abuse, watching a TV soap opera, and other temptations lurk just around the corner. *Impulse-stifling* is another key arrow in the experienced teleworker's quiver.

The most effective approach for this aspect of working at home is to heighten the teleworker's awareness that such problems often arise and to suggest immediate counter-activities, such as:

- ➤ Relaxation techniques;
- ➤ Development of positive rewards for not succumbing;
- ➤ Avoiding the source of temptation (for example, not working in the kitchen); and
- ➤ Developing strict break schedules.

If lecture style techniques have insufficient impact, then group discussions with fellow victims of temptation may work.

For several years we have taken informal polls of the net weight gain or loss of home-based teleworkers as a measure of the TTD (Tele-Temptation Differential). The answers are still inconclusive; weight losses are reported about as often as gains. At home, the refrigerator may be too close. At the office there are the birthday, going-away, and any-other-excuse parties, not to mention the doughnuts in the morning.

➤ Telemanagement Topics

Management of Home Teleworkers

A major incentive for employees to work in their homes is the opportunity to set up a more flexible schedule of work and personal activities. From the management viewpoint one consequence of that work mode is that the worker can no longer feasibly be monitored by time. The time the employee arrives and remains more or less in view has been a measure of performance for many managers. A supervisor who permits employees to work remotely *must adopt the management style of monitoring by results instead of by process.* He or she must set a completion time and level of quality for a given task and send the employee off to do that job. Not every supervisor now has the management style that supports remote work. Not every manager will want to employ that style.

Topics that pertain specifically to monitoring remote employees include the following:

Setting Performance Standards

"It is extremely rare to find any valid or validated standard of performance on any level. Some units may have some fragmentary standards and some directors may think they have them [but don't]."[4] It is better not to attempt a universal performance measure per se because it is likely that most situations will contain numerous exceptions to the "rule."

Although generalized performance standards may be lacking, any manager usually has in mind a level of expectation for each employee under his or her supervision. Many projects have an historic background on which to base person-hour estimates. Thus work can be assigned with some confidence as to the timeliness and level of quality with which it will be delivered. With the same degree of predictability, the manager can assign a task to be performed at home.

There is a major difference that requires training to overcome: the teleworker and supervisor must comprehend the verbal understanding to which they are jointly agreeing. For example, they could reach agreement on milestones. *The worker must accept responsibility for accomplishing the project, but the manager must ensure that the desired results and milestones are clearly and fully stated.*

---

[4] A comment by one of the telemanagers we have trained.

Communicating with Remote Workers

Managers find that they must be more aware of how they communicate to personnel who telework. Instructions must be more complete when they cannot be continually amended. Thus, vaguely stated requests are less easily upgraded to specific requirements when the manager is no longer "looking over the shoulder" of the task in progress.

Managers become more skilled in giving directions because they are forced to define to themselves what it is they want accomplished. This differs from saying, in effect, to an employee "I'll know what I want when I see it."

Training in communication skills must focus on (1) task definition and (2) performance expectations.

Setting Guidelines for Remote Work

The process of setting guidelines for working at home must involve coming to a mutual understanding between supervisor and employee. Each case will be somewhat unique, since the major benefit for the employee is a work mode that fits each one's individual situation. The agreement can be formalized, however. One of the objectives of the demonstration project is to set up model formal agreements.

Troubleshooting

Training for managers of remote employees must include techniques for dealing with below-standard performance. Role playing might be an effective way to practice differentiating between "excuses" and valid reasons for non-performance. As a last resort, the manager can bring the employee back on site to work. But particularly during the demonstration project, focus should be kept on finding the solutions that make teleworking beneficial to both manager and employee.

Self-Identification of Management Styles

The first step in defining a training program appropriate for a given manager is to identify her or his current management style.

The offices responsible for management training in departments have developed management training programs. Validated instruments are available for supervisors to identify their own management styles. Those should serve very well as the first step in screening candidate supervisors for the teleworking demonstration.

➤ Training Methods

In a teleworking program of any size it is not possible to train everyone on a one-on-one basis. Group sessions are inevitable. Our practice has been to hold initial training sessions with teleworkers separately from the manager sessions. A typical session should have from fifteen to twenty-five participants. Fifteen is used as a lower target figure because you would like to have enough interaction among the participants to stimulate discussion—smaller groups will often just sit there. The upper limit is suggested in order to keep the interaction from getting out of hand. These numbers apply to the final initial training sessions, completed after the orientation briefings have been given.

The purpose of these sessions, which are generally in a traditional lecture format, is to provide practical applications—how-to ideas—for home teleworkers to show them how to organize their work and to set up a home office. In the latter case, you might include a slide show of sample offices plus descriptions of the techniques for deciding what equipment is needed and where it should be placed, space selection, and related issues. However, we have found that most teleworkers at the professional or mid-level management level already have offices established at home. Therefore, as in most of these training topics, it is a good idea to test the pre-existing level of expertise of your audience before boring them with information they already have.

Here is a typical training agenda for a 3-hour session for home-based telecommuters:

Teleworkers' Workshop (15 to 25 participants)

0:00 **Introductions**

0:05 **Overview**
—Concerns List (that is, what uncertainties do you have about teleworking?)

0:20 **The Rules**
—Company Guidelines and Procedures

0:40 **Analyzing Your Job**
—Telecommuter Work Planning Exercise: This should cover the nature of each person's job in terms of its "teleworkability"

1:05   **Break**

1:20   **Communicating, communicating, communicating**
—Introduction on why maintaining communication is so important
—Have each teleworker analyze his/her current communications
patterns: who; how (what mode is used); why; how often
—Analyzing On-Site Communication: exploring the difference between—and rates of occurrence of—formal (scheduled) and informal (ad hoc) meetings
—Scheduling and Work Planning: Adapting the traditional schedule
to teleworking; clumping location-dependent and independent
tasks; developing a proposal to the boss for your teleworking time

2:00   **Break**

2:10   **Developing Your Telecommuting Skills**
—Managing Your Boss and Career
—Administrative Details
—Developing Your Home Office
—Facilities and Equipment

Coping with the Home Environment
—Dealing with Family/Friends/Neighbors
—Working in a Home Office
—Sharing the Household
—Household Roles

2:45   **Crisis Management**
—Potential Pitfalls: What to do if things don't work out as planned

3:00   **Adjourn**

   A similar agenda can be used for telemanagers, although the
emphasis shifts to the management issues, rather than the factors
related to working at home.

Manager's Workshop (15 to 25 participants)

0:00   **Introductions**

0:05   **Overview**
—What's A Telemanager? Duties and responsibilities of telemanagers
—Concerns List: As for the teleworkers, make sure that the uncertainties are noted and subsequently covered

0:25 Selecting Telecommuters and Structuring Jobs
—Job Analysis: What makes a job teleworkable; analyzing jobs in terms of task location independence
—Telecommuter Selection Factors: Key attributes of successful teleworkers, including motivational and home environmental factors; review of the company's formal selection process (if any)

0:50 Break

1:05 Analyzing Office Information Flows
—Communication Needs: A review of the communications that must continue if work is to be performed successfully
—Develop analyses of the communication patterns in each telemanagers' organizational unit to establish the required links to be maintained; discuss changes in the mode of communication from face-to-face to technology intermediated options (phone, email, fax, teleconferencing)
—Importance of Ongoing Feedback: This stresses the need to keep the teleworkers informed as to their progress—and vice versa
—Keeping Teleworkers Linked into the Office: Ensuring that the teleworkers are not out of mind even if they may be out of sight for extended periods
—Analyzing On-Site Communication: Exploring the difference between—and rates of occurrence of—formal (scheduled) and informal (ad hoc) meetings

1:50 Break

2:05 Establishing Performance Measures and Evaluating Results
—The Rules: Company Guidelines and Procedures
—Working Out the Specifications: Establishing performance requirements for teleworkers. This is a key component and is the core of all of the telework management practices. The telemanagers should be able to set up a reasonably formal means of specifying the products of their teleworkers' activities as if they were hiring a subcontractor to do the work
—Making the Teleworking Contract: Set up a simple list of items to be covered in the agreements between each telemanager and his/her teleworkers
—Telework Work Planning Exercise: This includes setting up a typical work week schedule, including some mix of telework and in-office working
—Watching It Work, Career Management for Teleworkers: Making sure that the teleworkers have equal opportunities for advancement

—Spotting Problems Early: Making sure that any operational problems are nipped in the bud

2:45 **Summing Up**—What have we forgotten?

3:00 **Adjourn**

The Joint Workshop

After these general how-do-we-do-it sessions, a third session is required. In this session, the teleworkers and their direct supervisors meet to establish mutual expectations and agreement on the guidelines for remote work. We anticipate that within your organization's overall policies there is a reasonable amount of flexibility in the working agreement between a supervisor and a given employee. The details of how and when work is to be performed will be first, task-related, and second, dependent upon individual home circumstances. This session need not be a formal one as long as the supervisor-teleworker groups engage in the session *before* teleworking begins. Here is a typical agenda (note that it is shorter then the other two):

0:00 **Review** of the formal company agreement for teleworkers

0:10 **Who Needs What?**
—Comparing the communication pattern requirements of the teleworkers with those of the telemanagers and coworkers.

0:30 **Setting Goals and Expectations**
—This component focuses on ensuring that all three parties involved—the telemanagers, the teleworkers, and their co-workers—are considered in the forthcoming teleworking activities; as with all of these sessions, the objective is to avoid unpleasant surprises in the future

1:10 **Break**

1:20 **Dealing with Change**
—This continues the discussion and expands it to include contingency planning (what happens if X doesn't turn out to be as expected?)

1:50 **Completing the Agreement**
—This is the final formal step prior to beginning teleworking

2:00 **Adjourn**

The goal of the three sessions is to produce agreements—of whatever formality and length of term are appropriate—between the teleworkers and their supervisors. It is important to emphasize that the agreements are just a tool to increase confidence in the process on the parts of both telemanagers and teleworkers.

➤ Focus Groups

I have found that follow-up workshops or focus group sessions are invaluable both as a neutral forum in which to share successes and resolve problems and as a vehicle for reinforcing the messages of the initial training. These should be held at decreasing intervals after teleworking has begun. The first ones should be within a few weeks of the initial training sessions. There is more on this in Chapter 10.

Employees also may need access to a "guru" for technical help and to an ombudsman, a peer network, and co-worker groups for work-related counsel.

■ MANAGEMENT OF TELEWORK CENTERS

Managers affiliated with telework centers may require training according to their status. He or she may hold one (or a combination) of three functional positions:

1. Supervisor of employees working at telework center office(s) at other than the supervisor's location;
2. Supervisor of, and location with, his or her entire staff at a telework center; or
3. Manager of the telework facility.

Group 1 should have the same training options as supervisors of home telecommuters. Added to their training should be guidance on how to relate their telework center employees to those located at the principal site in terms of the work process and identification as a single group. (It is possible that some telework center workers will be operationally totally independent so that they are treated as a "branch" office.)

Group 2 may not need any training different from that given to on-site supervisors. If however, they must relate functionally to other staff within their parent—and distant—departments, they may profit from a workshop on how to coordinate their assigned tasks with the primary operation. Supervisors, like employees who volunteer to work remotely, will have questions as to how this will effect their pay and promotion.

Group 3, which will be few (or zero) in number, should be given a workshop designed to meet their unique responsibilities. They must be offered direction on how to set priorities for use of the telework facility that covers space, use of shared equipment, maintenance etc. *They need to be connected to a chain of authority that backs up their position as arbitrator of sometimes conflicting requests from other users of the facility.*

Chapter

10

Getting It Together

The purpose of this chapter is to assemble the previous components into an outline or checklist for a telework demonstration project. My assumption here is that you will be the program manager and need to present a formal plan—or, more likely, a series of plans—to upper management before and as the program progresses.

The assumed program includes the demonstration project and, after its successful conclusion, a rollout phase to extend telework to the rest of the company. I assume further that you are proactive in this respect; that it is not a job thrust upon you for which you have little regard (which is probably true or you wouldn't have read this far). This chapter is based on our work with organizations employing thousands of potential teleworkers; your program might not need as much formality.

In order to begin a formal telecommuting program it is necessary to convince a number of key people that telecommuting is worth trying. In order to do that, you probably need to have a well-organized and well-thought out plan. Once you have accomplished those tasks, the next step is to select and train the telemanagers and telecommuters. Neither the ability to be an effective telecommuter, nor the fundamental understanding that telecommuting may be a better way of doing business, springs fully formed into a person's brain at birth. Yet the principles and disciplines of telecommuting are relatively easily learned through a combination of planning, communication, and training techniques, discussed next.

■ THE PRELIMINARIES

Any organization with more than a few employees has some sort of decision structure and a set of individuals who make the key decisions. Because telecommuting is a new concept to many, and because reluctance to change does appear to be a common trait among managers, it is very important that the new telecommuting program get the support of these key decision makers right up front.

➤ Convincing the Executive Suite

Not everyone in the decision structure has to agree that telecommuting is the greatest thing since the invention of the wheel. But the chief executive officer (and/or chief operating officer) and all of the chain of command down the line to each and every prospective telecommuter should be at least neutral to the concept. The CEO should be positively behind it—or at least willing to try it for a suitable period. Therefore, your first step in mounting a telecommuting program is to convince the members of the executive suite that it's worth trying.

The fundamental job of every CEO is to ensure the organization's economic viability. Therefore, a presentation aimed at that aspect is the most likely to get the CEO's positive attention. The CEO needs to be presented with a set of cogent, quantitative reasons why the organization should expend any resources to develop telecommuting, as well as a convincing plan for making it happen. Chapter 1 contains the most common basic arguments. Your job as a telecommuting instigator is to particularize those arguments to your organization; to emphasize the issues that are of most concern to your CEO.

Almost always, the key economic issues are some combination of these top four:

➤ Maintaining or increasing productivity

➤ Decreasing office space needs

➤ Attracting or retaining critical skills among the staff

➤ Complying with air quality or other environmental regulations

That is, increasing output at the same or lower costs.

As an erstwhile presidential candidate was so fond of saying: Here's the deal. Convert those four issues (or as many of them as you think the CEO worries about) into numbers.

➤ What's the average salary (plus fringe benefits?) of your potential telecommuters? What's the annual dollar impact of a 12% improvement in their productivity?[1]

➤ What's the annual cost of your office space? What if you could eliminate the need for one-third of it for your telecommuters?[2] [Or, for telework centers, what's the differential between the costs of headquarters office space and the space at the local telework centers?]

➤ What does it cost to replace one of your potential telecommuters? Figure a year's salary for each replacement[3] in other than very easily replaceable jobs. Turnover rates for telecommuters tend to be near-zero. What's the usual rate for your organization?

➤ What's the tab for failing to meet your local air quality regulations? In Southern California, it might be as high as $25,000 for every day of non-compliance!

You also have to think about the costs of getting these benefits. Figure on spending about 5% of the telecommuters' salaries for the job of starting the program, acquiring some extra equipment and/or software, training the telecommuters and telemanagers, and evaluating the results for at least a year. The *net* benefits (that

---

[1] Our data indicate effectiveness changes ranging from 0% to 300%, with averages from 10% to 20% or more *as estimated by direct supervisors.* There is also some correlation between salary and productivity improvement. That is, higher paid employees tend to get a larger productivity boost from telecommuting than do entry level workers. However, I would not bet the store on this relationship.

[2] Be careful about this one if your CEO has just spent the last five years convincing the board that the company should move into new quarters, at the cost of many megabucks.

[3] That includes the loss of the services of the person while the replacement is being found; the costs of finding the replacement; the diminished productivity of those who are filling in for, or depending on the services of, the departee; and the diminished productivity of the replacement until s/he gets up to speed in the organization.

is, benefits minus costs) to the organization, for properly managed telecommuting programs with mid-level participants, should be on the order of $8,000 or more annually (in 1998 dollars). That is what we have found in several programs in both the private and public sectors. That figure does not include any benefits to either the telecommuters, their families, or the community at large.

■ DEVELOPING THE DEMONSTRATION PLAN(S)

Rather than say: "Just do it," the boss is likely to ask for a more fully developed plan than can be delivered in a twenty-minute briefing. In a sense, this book contains the elements of a project plan. What remains for you to do is to particularize it for your organization. Make sure it answers the main what, why, where, who, how, and when questions. Put in the names of the potential participating groups. Develop an implementation schedule, together with a description of what has to be done. Assess the operating costs of the project. Estimate the potential benefits for each participating group (what's in it for them?).

By far the best way to avoid problems in developing teleworking, as in any innovation process, is clearly to state what you expect to go well, and to anticipate everything (and everybody) that could go wrong, well before you start implementation. The project plan is simply a structured record of your (and the company's)[4] expectations and concerns. It must contain at least the following components.

➤ Critical Success Criteria

Why are you considering teleworking in the first place? What will have to happen in order for at least a certain percentage of your company's employees to be teleworking two years from now? More to the point, who will need to approve the program in order for it to become company policy?

The answer to that last question is: The Board of Directors, all of the Senior Executives, and most of the mid-level managers who will be involved in supporting telework or managing teleworkers. You need to know what will motivate them to endorse teleworking.

---

[4] Although I use the term "company" here, the points apply equally well to government and other organizations.

Well, not *all* of them at first. Your initial task is to get a senior manager's attention; a manager who will help convince the rest of this group once he/she has solid evidence to back the decision.

Which brings us to the critical success criteria. What specific facts have to be demonstrated before this senior executive and, subsequently the CEO, Executive Committee, etc., will be satisfied that telework is good for the company? This list (like "It's the economy, stupid!") should be glued to your office wall, wherever that is.

Be as specific as possible. For each criterion, make an exact statement of what it is, how it is to be measured, and how important it is. For example: "We need to eliminate 150,000 square feet of office space in our main campus, or the equivalent in other campuses, by 19XX (or 20XX); this is an absolute requirement. A goal is to eliminate 250,000 square feet." An invariable requirement is "Whatever else is accomplished, there should be no loss in productivity." The initial goals stated by the Mayor and City Council of Los Angeles for their telecommuting program were:

➤ *Air Pollution.* The Air Quality Management Plan calls for a 20% reduction in commuting via telecommuting by 2010.

➤ *Cost Effectiveness.* Experience with telecommuting in the private sector and by the State of California has shown significant and lasting increases in the productivity of telecommuters—averaging from 5% to 20%, decreased rates of turnover, space and energy savings and other net cost reductions.

➤ *Traffic Congestion.* It is reaching unmanageable levels in the downtown area—and in many other Los Angeles locales. It is slowing work and frustrating commuters. Just in Los Angeles millions of hours of potential productivity— and billions of dollars in economic output—are being lost annually from congestion. [A specific requirement was added later.]

➤ *Energy Dependency.* Commuting continues to account for almost half of the automobile transportation energy use in California, making us increasingly susceptible to fuel shortages and supply interruptions.

➤ *Office Space.* The City is running low on affordable office space in central Los Angeles. Costs of parking space are rising as well.

➤ *Information Technology.* Computers are showing up on more and more desks of City workers. Computers connected to telephone lines provide a significant opportunity to make many forms of information work partially "location independent" and ideal for telecommuting.

➤ *Attracting/Retaining Personnel.* Telecommuting as a work option has been found to be an effective tool for helping to attract and retain qualified personnel in a competitive market.

➤ *Access to Jobs.* The mobility disadvantaged, whether it's a result of physical impairments, inadequate transportation, or other factors, can have easier access to jobs via telecommuting.

Notice that most of these goals are general. It is better (if riskier) to get some more quantitative goals, with success criteria for each. The goals and criteria statements may have to be revised a few times during the planning phase as you get more input from the stakeholders in the program.

➤ The Advisory Board

It is very useful to have an advisory board comprising key people from the organizational units that may be participants in the program. This includes service providers (such as Human Resources and Information Systems) and union leaders as well as units that will include teleworkers. The Advisory Board has two functions:

➤ To give you sound advice on what will and won't work, and

➤ To help pave the way for acceptance of—and enthusiasm for—the program.

Consequently, try to choose Board members who are both knowledgeable about the processes and are opinion leaders in their units. Still, don't try to include all possible stakeholders in the Board; you want useful advice, not a debating society. The Board membership should include at least the following functions:

➤ Corporate Legal
➤ Facilities
➤ Finance/Accounting
➤ Human Resources/Personnel
➤ Information Systems (including telecommunications)
➤ Union(s)

Remember, though, that this is an *advisory* board. They do not make either the strategic or operational decisions for the program, although you should listen carefully to their advice. In cases where you get conflicting advice, see if you can arrange the project so as to test which option turns out to be the best course; but, if possible, do so in a way that won't anger the advice givers.

➤ Champions

 Almost as important as the Advisory Board in giving advice, and probably more important in making telework happen in your company, are the department champions. These are individuals selected by the participating departments (or whatever you call your major organizational units) to act as the primary overseers of the implementation and evaluation. They are responsible for scheduling briefings, shepherding the selection process, answering questions about the program, and making sure that the evaluation data are forthcoming. They are your key lieutenants in the program.

The ideal champion is:

➤ Self-motivated and reasonably enthusiastic about the program.
➤ At a fairly high level in the company; possibly not as high as the Advisory Board members but with enough clout and experience to be able to get things done within the system.
➤ Willing to put in the time to make the program go even though it might be in addition to all his/her other duties.
➤ Sufficiently diplomatic so that the implementation can proceed with minimal friction.

You do *not* want a champion who lacks these qualities; someone who is assigned the task and reluctantly carries it out can be
more of a liability than an asset.

➤ Key Documents

The purpose of the planning process is to produce a set of baseline
documents describing the project in sufficient detail to get approval by whatever senior executive is empowered to do so. The
principal document is *The Demonstration Program Plan*. The Plan
should contain at least the following.

1. A list of the program goals and
   critical success criteria.

2. A description of the program elements and proposed phasing, including personnel, technology and
   site selection, training, implementation, and evaluation processes.

3. The program budget, including
   any subcontracted services.

4. A preliminary cost-benefit analysis (see Chapter 7) emphasizing
   the long-term bottom line results
   and estimated time before return
   on investment.

You should also develop the following supporting documents
during the planning phase:

➤ Preliminary work rules. This should include any temporary variances from standard rules, as discussed in Chapter 6, and as reviewed by your legal staff (one member of
which should be in the Advisory Board).

➤ A description of the selection processes, in more detail
than what appears in the main plan.

➤ An evaluation plan that describes how the degree of satisfaction of the critical success criteria will be measured.

The size and complexity of The Plan and its associated documents will depend on program magnitude, as well as the level of
formality in your company about such matters. But, whatever the

size of the plan, it is important that you, your Advisory Board, your champions, and your legal staff have spent enough time thinking about all of the what-ifs and their consequences—and that the results of this thinking are reflected in the plan.

If the CEO doesn't buy the project at this point, you have a problem. If you can, find out what objections still exist. See if you can mount compelling arguments to overcome them. The most common objections tend to be of the "I have too many more pressing worries on my plate" variety. Good. See how telecommuting can address each of them and revise the plan accordingly. Let's face it; if increasing profitability and smoother sailing won't help your organization, it's time to begin looking for other career opportunities.

➤ Timing

There are two aspects about timing of the program plan that are important. First is the time span required to produce the plan. If you are in a small company, or will restrict teleworking to a small part of the company, a suitable plan may be produced in a few days or weeks. In large companies, with thousands of employees and possible widespread adoption of telework, the planning period can take as long as six months, possibly more. The deciding factor is the number of people to be involved and/or approvals needed before the plan is ready for adoption.

The second factor is the phasing of the plan with the company's budget process. This is particularly important if capital expenditures are needed for the demonstration; you must get the expenditures required by the plan included in the current or next annual budget. In any demonstration project it is easiest if the costs of the demonstration come out of the corporate budget. If each participating department is required to support its share of the costs, then you have the added task of convincing each department head that this is a good thing.

■ PARTICIPANT SELECTION

The purpose of a demonstration program, as the title suggests, is to prove to the key people that telework works. The key to success in that regard is the selection and training process for both teleworkers and telemanagers. Almost all of the claimed teleworking/telecommuting disasters I have read or heard about stem from poor selection and training rather than technological failures.

With one important exception: changes in senior management. If a new CEO appears,[5] either during the demonstration phase or before teleworking is extended to the rest of the company, you may have to start all over again.

➤ The Rest of the Hierarchy: Orientation Briefings

Informed consent is the watchword for a smoothly run telework program. From the top executives down, each group of prospective participants and stakeholders should be told about the project plans and the impacts of a successful conclusion on their own futures. Although a company's formal interest in telework often comes from a grass roots movement by employees, its long-term success has to be a result of senior managers' endorsement of the concept. Therefore, it has always been our practice to start at the top, once the plan has been approved.

Once the boss is convinced, it is time to develop the rest of the chain. We always adopt a strict rule of volunteerism for telework demonstration programs: *if manager X does not want to participate, then neither X nor any of X's subordinates are to participate.* The reason for this is very simple: people can become incredibly ingenious at defeating a system that they don't like. Therefore, either convince them that they are going to like it or leave them alone. Most organizations have a treelike reporting structure. The volunteer rule simply lops some of the branches and twigs from your opportunity tree.

Usually, in a demonstration program with more than a few teleworkers, several briefings are needed before formal selection begins. Each briefing is a review of the reasons for the program, its goals and objectives, schedule and milestones, and anticipated results.

Naturally, the emphasis in the briefings will change as you go from the executive offices, to mid-level management and ultimately to the prospective teleworkers. Senior executives are most likely to be interested in the bottom-line impacts and any capital budgeting required. Mid-level managers will focus on the practical issues of management techniques. The prospective teleworkers will want to know about the details of work rules and procedures. You don't need to have all the answers at this point

---

[5] Usually cleaning house in the executive suite as well, so that more than one of your key supporters can disappear.

but it is important to convey the fact that you, your advisory group, and your champions have made the effort to cover every aspect of the program.

The briefings also constitute the first part of the selection process. If the Chief Executive Officer doesn't like it, then the rest of the process is easy; the program is over. Barring that unfortunate event, it should be the option of anyone in the company to not participate in the program. Note that if any manager, having heard the briefing(s), does not want to participate, then the manager and his/her subordinates do not participate. Still, make sure those managers realize that, when the demonstration project[6] is deemed to be a success and telecommuting is extended to the whole organization, they will have missed out on months of vital experience. The purpose of the program is to demonstrate success, not to test how long it takes some people to come around.

Finally, brief the prospective telecommuters in the organizational units that have decided to stick with the plan. These people are your first volunteers and, most of them, trainees. It is often a good gauge of the informal communication network in your company to test how accurate the prospective teleworkers' view of the program is *before* you brief them.

Unless your organization is incredibly tightly organized, you will find that the steps up to this point will have to be repeated several times as managers in your organization have second thoughts. (Gee, maybe I'd better check this out after all!) This is what tends to make the briefing and training phase of the project last several times longer than your most conservative initial estimate.[7]

---

[6] Don't call it a pilot project (as I have done). Apparently, *pilot* connotes: "after it's over we can forget about it"; while *demonstration* or *initial* seems to mean: "they're serious about this and the purpose of the project is just to work out the bugs."

[7] My personal record, so far, is a "one-month" training series that has extended over more than 15 months as more managers changed their minds.

➤ Formal Selection Procedures

Chapter 2 reviewed several ways of selecting teleworkers. Whether you use one of those or some other system for verifying the participants in your program, you should have a formal system. This has several advantages:

- ➤ It helps assure uniformity of procedures
- ➤ It minimizes claims of favoritism
- ➤ It provides a database of "before" capabilities and attitudes that can be compared subsequently with the realities of telework experience.

The focus of the procedure should be on testing how well the prospective teleworker will do as a teleworker, as well as how well the teleworker is likely to get along with his/her supervisor and co-workers. The teleworker-telemanager link is especially important in this testing. Finally, all responses by prospective teleworkers and their direct supervisors should be kept strictly confidential. Several of our clients have asked us to do the formal selection in order to deflect any worries about private personal information getting out to co-workers.

■ SITE SELECTION

Site selection can be important in telecommuting programs where telecommuters need a place to work other than their homes. The selection process for telework centers needs special attention if only because it has been done so poorly so often in the past.

➤ How Many Sites and Where Are They

The fundamental question to be answered during the planning phase is: where are the teleworkers going to work? If they are all telecommuters, that is, relatively local employees who would otherwise be coming in to a central or regional office each day, how many should be home based and how many, if any, will be working at a telework center? If you are considering teleworking on a more geographically distributed basis, that same question applies, except "local" applies to clusters of teleworkers, not just your main facility.

The rule of thumb for assigning teleworkers to telework centers is: try to locate centers that are within about a 20-minute walk (or ride via mass transit) from their homes. That works out to about 2 km or a little more than a mile. Beyond that and people tend to drive to work, at which point many feel that it is just as easy to come all the way in to the main facility. Hence, you probably will need a map showing employee residence locations and the sites for potential telework centers to make that decision.

In our original telecommuting study in 1973 we did just that and decided that the company (with about 2500 employees) would reach a halfway point (in terms of commute-mile savings) with 4 or 5 telework centers. If one of your company's goals is to reduce air pollution while also minimizing the additional administrative load, then relatively small numbers of telework centers might suffice.

➤ How Long

One very practical question in telework center selection is: is this an existing facility or is a new one needed? If an existing facility (such as a regional office) does the company own or lease it? If it is leased, what is the remaining term of the lease? (This is also a key question when you're trying to assess the impact of taking teleworkers out of an already-leased facility.) If you have to build new quarters, how long will it take—and how does that relate to the duration of the demonstration project.

As you can appreciate, the complexity of these issues is often what leads the planners of demonstration telework programs to say: "We'll wait until the follow-on program to test telework centers, unless there is a suitable commercial center that will rent space on a monthly basis."

➤ Site Redesign

If one of the reasons for demonstrating telework was to reduce facility costs, then it is also important to explore options for redesigning the remaining space. Telecommuters will still be coming in to their former sole offices some of the time, but they will most probably be there for meetings, rather than for the use of isolated workspaces.

The demonstration phase is a good time to test that hypothesis, with an eye toward rearranging space allocation for the time when there are more teleworkers. Remember that space usage in the principal office will also change when there are numerous teleworkers: more conference/meeting space, fewer isolated offices.

■ CREATING THE TECHNOLOGY INFRASTRUCTURE

Although I have kept maintaining that lack of the latest nifty technology is rarely a reason for not teleworking, improper or inadequate technology can surely slow down telework and possibly derail an otherwise successful telework program.

➤ What's Needed

Both as a part of the planning process and continually during the selection phase of the program, you need to make sure that all of the technology support need by the teleworkers will be available and working properly when actual teleworking begins. Possibly using Chapter 4 to review the options, you and the IS manager (in case you're not the IS manager) need to decide exactly what each teleworker will need in order to function effectively. Your list may vary in details as the participant selection process continues, but the primary issues should be decided early on—at least early enough so that you can survive missed ship dates, unexpected debugging (as contrasted to expected debugging?), and other Murphy's Law delays.

Most important for the early list are the possible bottleneck items such as installation of ISDN lines and/or major new technology changes. But also make sure that you have backup equipment or process alternatives as well.

➤ Assembling the Pieces

Keep concentrating on the overall system design. The objective of a telework support infrastructure is to make itself transparent both to the teleworkers and those with whom they work. This is also one of the reasons to begin with a demonstration program rather than a full-fledged rollout of teleworking.

The telework technology support components should be in place, at least in their first incarnation, at least a month before the first teleworker is trained—more if the installation is very complex. Make sure that whoever is responsible for this part of the program is on top of the schedule and has the resources to get all of the parts together.

➤ Testing, Testing, Testing

Then test it all many times. Given the vagaries of telecommunications systems, particularly if you're just starting on a VPN or other Internet-mediated venture, thorough testing is vital to ensure that desired transparency. Software incompatibilities are common here. Often they are mind-numbingly simple; such as the teleworker who couldn't get his e-mail because the dialup interface automatically dropped his call if it appeared to be inactive for more than three minutes—and didn't count downloading as activity.

There are many more similar stories but all point to the axiom that there is no substitute for testing, preferably by a select set of people who had no part in design of the system. They won't know how it's *supposed* to work, just how they *want* it to work, a rough test indeed.

Clearly, testing takes time and is expensive. But so do system crashes and, if enough of them occur, the program is scrubbed. Since the purpose of the program is supposed to be about testing teleworking, your operational phase is not the time to be testing the technology.

Finally, your experience with the novice testers will give you insight as to what, if any, technology training should accompany your management training for the program. Microsoft used massive amounts of user testing of its beta versions of Microsoft Windows 95. It's no accident that Windows 95 has the largest market share of GUI operating systems for PCs.

■ TRAINING

Most of the reports in the media about failures of telecommuting can be traced directly to training failures: the telecommuters and telemanagers made all of the classical errors that would have been avoided had they been trained properly. Training is particularly important in telework because it has to alter "traditional" business attitudes and behavior patterns in a very short time.

➤ Review the Training Plan

I DON'T WANT TO TELECOMMUTE AND I DON'T WANT ANYBODY ELSE TO EITHER!

The training plan, along the lines discussed in Chapter 9, should get a final review before the actual training begins. Does the plan include all of the company policy and procedural issues that are to be tested during the demonstration? Make sure that all of the major—and most of the minor—department-specific operational issues are covered. Also make sure that any needed technology training has been included in the overall training package.

The plan should cover at least the prospective teleworkers and telemanagers. If the budget allows, you should also consider sessions for the in-office co-workers as well. This can be very helpful in deflecting any possible sabotage of the project by co-workers.

➤ Make or Buy Decision

In some cases, such as a shortage of in-house staff, you may wish to have the training performed by outside experts. Make sure that they are experts by requesting—and checking—references. Do not confuse enthusiasm with expertise—or confuse expertise on some other topic with knowledge of telework management. The ideal trainer will be thoroughly informed about every aspect of telework management (or telework-related technology; they're rarely the same person), be able to give anecdotes about almost any telework situation, and be a quick study on the details of company policies and procedures. That is, the trainer should be able to make the training very company-specific.

You might also wish to use an outside expert simply to train your trainers. In this case, after the train-the-trainers session(s), your own trainers would conduct the employee sessions, possibly with the outside trainer monitoring the first few sessions.

➤ Training Sessions

Training is most effective when there is active participation by *all* of the people present in a session. In practical terms, this means that each session should have from 15 to 25 trainees. If there are too few, cross-fertilization of ideas is more difficult. If there are too many, the session can too easily wander off track.

We usually set up three sessions for each training set (as outlined in Chapter 9): one only for telemanagers, one only for teleworkers, and a joint session where they mutually formalize their working agreements. The first two of these sessions last about a half-day each, both done the same day. The joint session is often shorter and can be scheduled either the next day or a few days later, in order to give time for all the advice to sink in.

Emphasis in the sessions should be on interactivity. Although the sessions may be held in a classroom-like setting, they should not turn into canned lectures by the trainer, with passive listeners. The focus should be on personalizing the training so that each participant comes away with a feeling that he/she *owns* teleworking.

Formal teleworking/telecommuting for each participant should start within one month after the formal training is completed. A start within a few days is even more desirable. Remember, the trickle-away theory works here as with most other learning experiences.

➤ Reinforcements

Despite the incredible excellence of the trainers and the limitless intelligence and attention spans of the trainees, some aspects of telework management are likely to fall in the cracks during a single half-day session. This calls for one or more follow-up sessions, both to reinforce the training and to help you fix problems with technology and operating procedures. We usually conduct these sessions as focus group meetings (without the one-way glass in the background). These sessions are more informal—and shorter than the first training sessions, and can have somewhat larger attendance.

We have experimented with teleworkers-only and telemanagers-only sessions and come to the conclusion that mixed groups produce better results. Further, even better results come when the mixture includes people from different organizational units ("You mean that *they* have the same problems that *we* do?"). The session moderator has two jobs (beside keeping the discussion on track): flagging problems for later investigation; and disseminating fixes, either from prior experience or as told by attendees within the group.

Each of these sessions should result in a list of action items. Each action item statement should include a description of the problem, a list of potential remedies (and their costs, as appropriate), the name and address of the person responsible for fixing it, and a schedule. Naturally, some of this may require a little negotiation.

The number and timing of these follow-on sessions depends on the number of problems raised and the frequency at which they occur. As a rule of thumb we start with a session one month after teleworking begins, followed by one or more additional sessions at growing intervals.

■ REVIEW AND EVALUATION

One of the most frequent complaints I get from telework demonstration project participants is that they feel evaluated to death. We certainly do our share toward contributing to that feeling. The reason for that is that we try to make the project evaluation as "bullet-proof" as we know how. This usually involves administering several types of questionnaires—some of them several times—to the teleworkers, the telemanagers and, wherever possible, to the teleworkers co-workers. These are covered in Chapter 7. Yet, most of the participants realize that the future of telework in the company depends on their completion of these tests.

➤ Questionnaires

I suggest, as a minimum, that you construct (or otherwise acquire) a formal evaluation questionnaire that covers all of the topics in your critical success criteria list. Actually two different questionnaires are needed: one for the teleworkers, another for the telemanagers. If possible, assemble a set of the teleworkers' non-teleworking co-workers to also complete the teleworker questionnaire. This questionnaire should be administered at least three times: once before—or just when—formal teleworking begins; once at the project midpoint; and once at the formal conclusion of the measurement period. This procedure gives you data for both a time series analysis and a teleworker-non-teleworker comparison.

Other questionnaires may also be necessary. For example, if one of the program objectives is to estimate the impact of telework on automobile use, you might need to have the teleworkers (and their family members) complete weeklong travel logs. You might also wish to interview the teleworkers' customers, whether internal of external to the company, to get another view of effectiveness changes. If you are willing to cope with a horde of graduate students, you might volunteer to distribute one of more of their questionnaires (after changing your office and email addresses).

➤ Costs and Benefits

The questionnaires can provide a quite detailed view of both the quantitative and qualitative impacts of telework in your company. But to nail down the results you need to have a comprehensive cost-benefit analysis and forecast. The elements are outlined in Chapter 7. Be sure to remember that it is the *marginal* costs and benefits with which you should be concerned; only those changes that are specifically attributable to teleworking should be contained in the summary analysis. However, it may be important in your project report(s) to point out the difference between total and marginal cost/benefit in some key categories, such as technology and effectiveness changes.

➤ Job Analysis and Design

The demonstration project is generally not all-inclusive by design. That is, some types of workers or organizational units may not be included because of size, manager reluctance, or budget restrictions. Consequently, one of the tasks in the project evaluation is to estimate the ultimate number of your company's teleworkers.

You can do this by careful analysis of the content of each of the company's job descriptions. An experienced person, such as you, should read each description and estimate how much of that job is potentially location independent (see Chapter 2). As necessary, augment that analysis with some interviews of the appropriate incumbents. You should be able to get a reasonably accurate estimate of how teleworkable, if at all, each of your company's jobs is. This estimate, coupled with salary information and the effectiveness results derived from the questionnaires, will allow you to forecast the bottom-line impacts of telework for the company.

Further, some of the focus group results and questionnaire data may point to some job redesign options. Test arranging task allocations so as to increase the level of teleworking either by better clumping of in-office tasks or near-elimination of them altogether for some individuals.

➤ What Needs Changing?

Not every problem discovered or issue raised during the demonstration will be resolved, possibly. The project is quite likely to have produced a number of requests for changes in any one or all of the components of the design. The final task of the demonstration project is to produce a report that lists its accomplishments, the bottom-line consequences, and the changes needed for further growth of telework in the company.

■ ROLLOUT STRATEGY

Either as part of the final demonstration project report, or as a separate document (compiled after the CEO approves the final report) you need to develop a rollout plan. It's easy! Just start again at the beginning of this chapter, add your intervening experience and data, mix thoroughly, expand the numbers, and go! The goal of the rollout is to quickly reach a critical mass of teleworkers. By that I mean sufficient teleworkers so that organizational leadership changes, such as a new CEO or your being promoted to another spot won't derail the progress of the rollout. That critical mass tends to be somewhere above 10% of the potential teleworkers in your company.

Chapter

11

Organization Design Impacts

Telework, in addition to providing increased locational flexibility, also allows greater organizational flexibility. Because of technological advances over the past few decades, several other forms of organization are now possible that could not exist in previous times. Here are the main types.

■ THE INDUSTRIAL REVOLUTION TRADITION

As was noted at the beginning of this book, the hallmark of an industrial economy is the emphasis on physical centralization of the means of production: factories. This is a direct consequence of the development of various systems of mass production that required many workers to attend large machines that necessarily were located in or near transportation centers. The central locations were also needed to more efficiently concentrate raw materials and ship manufactured products. These were dominant requirements throughout the heyday of the industrial revolution—from the late eighteenth century until the last third of this century. They are still principal requirements of large manufacturing organizations.

The industrial centralization model was applied to the information sector as well. The only difference was that, instead of big machines pounding out car bodies or bolts of cloth, mainframe

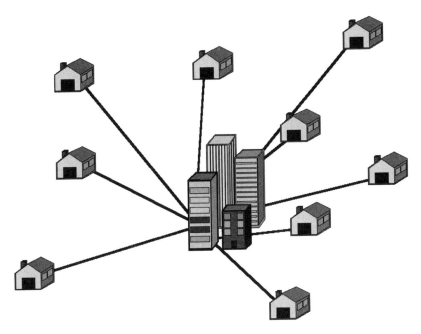

Figure 11.1   Centralization.

computers were the dei ex machinae of the industry, pounding out data and reports. The big machine in its air-conditioned temple, surrounded by its acolytes, the programmers and computer operators, was a perfect analog of the production line in the factory down the street. Like the factory workers, the information workers were required to come in from their homes every day to attend the machines, as shown in Figure 11.1.

■ FRAGMENTATION

But, sometime in the late fifties, a few large employers felt that concentrating their administrative (or research, or development, etc.) operations downtown was not productive. Because of the traffic congestion problems (induced by the near-universal centralization assumption), employees were arriving late to work or, worse, were increasingly hard to employ. Turnover rates were increasing and worker replacement costs, not to mention the escalating costs of downtown office space, were rising.

Several of these employers attempted to solve this problem by opening new facilities, usually in the suburbs, to which their

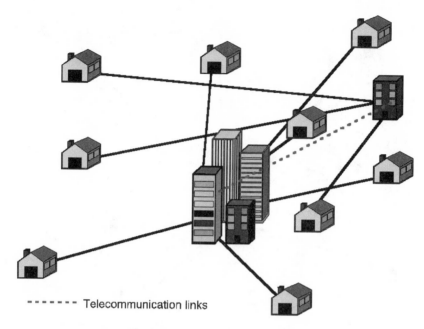

- - - - - - - Telecommunication links

Figure 11.2 Fragmentation.

employees could report. This, in itself, was a fairly neutral, even laudable strategy except for one problem: the moves continued the centralization assumption. Employees were not assigned to the new centers on the basis of their residence location but because of the organizational unit in which they worked. That is, the company fragmented itself, breaking off chunks of its hierarchy to work at the new sites. Thus, the design department, for example, moved *in toto* from downtown to the new facility.

The residence location patterns of the employees of centralized organizations tend to follow a circular normal distribution (a bell-shaped curve) over time. A large number of employees live within three miles of the central facility, a smaller number live from four to seven miles away, a still smaller number commute from eight to fifteen miles, and so on.[1] This pattern tends to develop over a period of years when the company stays in its central location. Employees

---

[1] This is modified somewhat by rank in the organization. The entry-level employees tend to concentrate in the lower income sections of town while the executives come from the wealthier areas. In the U.S., this means that the entry-level people live nearby while the executives are in the distant suburbs. The reverse tends to be the case in Europe.

changing jobs want to work for the closest employer, all other things being equal.

When an organization fragments (see Figure 11.2), this pattern is disrupted. On average, the employees who are assigned to the new facility (unless it is quite close to the older one) have longer commutes and, consequently, higher traffic stress. In some cases, where the new facility is fairly distant from the older one, the company is forced to pay relocation expenses for highly prized employees. Even in those cases the "lucky" employees often face resistance from their families. Stress increases. Morale drops. Productivity suffers. Some employees, particularly those with highly marketable skills, switch to other employers rather than move their residences.

Fragmentation, risky since the sixties, is even riskier now with many two-earner families that are dependent on employers in opposite directions or, together with single parents, rely on local support structures for their children—quality child care is not a universally available commodity.

■ DISPERSION

Dispersion is similar to fragmentation in that it involves the use of dispersed office sites. However, there are two major differences:

1. Company site locations (telework centers) are selected so that they are in areas close to the residences of current (or prospective) employees
2. Employees are assigned to work at the site closest to their residence, regardless of their job function; much of their intra-work-unit communications are done via telecommunications rather than by face-to-face interaction.

The dispersion mode (shown in Figure 11.3) was characteristic of the first telecommuting programs in the mid-1970s. At that time, employees who worked with computers had to use "dumb" terminals connected to distant mainframe computers. If all of these terminals were to be located in employees' homes, the costs of telephone service would have been prohibitive. Hence, the satellite office or regional telework center was more attractive because the centers could contain concentrator computers attached to dedicated, high-speed phone lines going to the central office.

A dispersed organization is similar to one with branch offices or separate divisions in that it comprises a "main" or headquarters

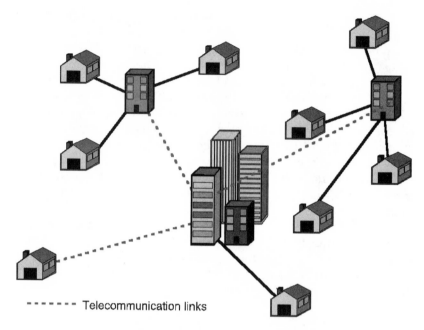

------- Telecommunication links

Figure 11.3 Dispersion.

office and a series of other offices in various locations around an urban region. Today, telework centers are examples of dispersed designs, whether employees from single or from multiple organizations occupy them. Some companies have hybrid versions of this where part of the staff is there in the traditional centralized mode; others simply use office space because it is close to their home, even though they work for different organizational units than the "locals."

■ DIFFUSION

In diffusion, the power of current information technology is a key factor. Here, the work site is the individual employee's home or a telework center that is close to the employee's home but quite far from the organization's headquarters. The home-based telecommuting that is the dominant form in the U.S. today is a version of diffusion. In most of these cases today, the telecommuters live within typical commuting distance of their principal office, to which they do commute two or more days per week. The rest of the time they are telecommuting from home or, in the case of sales or field service personnel, from their clients' facilities.

The central characteristic of diffusion is that an organization can have components that are broadly scattered geographically— even down to the one worker, one location level—*while retaining logical connectivity among all of its components.* The extent to which diffusion is practical depends on a number of factors, but information technology is one of the most important—after management style. Figure 11.4 shows the arrangement.

The style of management that is most successful for a diffused organization is one where authority and responsibility are extended as far as possible; up to the "edges" of the organization where the employees interact with the extra-organizational world. For this to happen successfully, the business rules and key aspects of the corporate culture must also be diffused to these edges. In the ultimate example, each employee acts like a hologram of the corporate culture, behaving like someone in the main office regardless of his/her actual location. However, at less ethereal levels, the rule is that if an employee produces results according to the corporate objectives and strategies, then the employee is effective. This rule is independent of the employee's location.

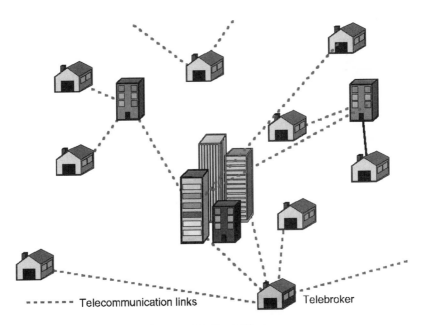

- - - - - - - Telecommunication links   Telebroker

Figure 11.4 Diffusion.

This idea of location independence is central to teleworking and telecommuting and to the existence of diffuse organizations. While mostly an element of more traditional organizations that have adopted some form of teleworking, the concept of location independence gives rise to some other organizational forms.

■ NETWORK ORGANIZATIONS

A network organization is one that interconnects far-flung components, each of which may have a well-defined centralized role, into a coherent whole. Obvious examples of network organizations are the telecommunications networks themselves: telephone companies and broadcast networks. A major characteristic of a network organization is that the separate nodes in the network operate relatively autonomously, although governed by the overall policies, business rules, and procedures of the network as a whole.

Although many network organizations retain some of the characteristics of the traditional form (a central "head office," some form of hierarchical command structure), this is not always necessary. The Internet itself is a network organization in which no one entity is "in charge" and there is no central control. Its growth is at the edges and it works because all of the disparate components adhere to a few rules and protocols of operation. (Critics of the Internet will say that it *fails* to work because of its lack of central control, yet it was deliberately designed to be highly diffuse in order to survive destruction of any central facility. Despite its growing pains, it has proven to be remarkably resilient.)

Just as a networked franchise, such as Benetton or McDonald's can comprise many autonomous units, so can a network organization consist of separate companies or government agencies that routinely interact for a common purpose. This purpose may be the only one that the participating units have in common; each unit also has its own set of other goals.

Although traditional network organizations do not necessarily have to be dependent on the latest in information technology, those that rely on swift adaptation to a rapidly changing market environment—or a widely dispersed array of their means of production—require it. One widely dispersed array of the means of production could be the set of experts in a particular subject. For example, JALA International is part of a consortium of organizations forming the European Community Telework/Telematics Forum (ECTF). The Management Group of the ECTF includes a representative from each of the countries of the European Union, plus one each from the U.S. and other countries. The purpose of the ECTF is to educate European organizations about telework. The primary means of this is to produce a series of workshops and conferences in Europe. The primary means of interaction within the Management Group is via fax and e-mail, with face-to-face meetings once or twice annually.

■ EVANESCENT ORGANIZATIONS

Evanescent organizations are like network organizations except that the interacting components typically combine on an ad hoc basis. When the particular project of mutual interest is completed, the organization dissolves, possibly to reform later with a slightly (or almost entirely) different set of contributors. For example, JALA International was part of a research team exploring the impacts on the environment of advanced communications technologies. Other participants were from Austria, Denmark, France, Italy, and Spain. The project coordinator was in Rome and most interactions were over the Internet, with semiannual meetings in Europe. Although this is a fairly common scenario in modern research programs, it is likely to also become much more common in everyday business activities.

An interesting example of an evanescent organization is one in which the core of the organization is, in effect, an information broker. The function of the broker is to make the connection between the buyers and sellers of information. The buyer needs a particular piece of research done, for example. The broker spends a substantial amount of time monitoring activity on the Internet in the areas of research of interest to the buyer. She knows, from watching the activity, who the prominent researchers are in the relevant areas and arranges with them to supply the needed information, negotiating the price—and her fee—with the buyer. When the next research request comes in the process is repeated, although possibly with an entirely different set of researchers.

The concept of evanescent organizations is a venerable one even if the name is recent. For example, most movie production teams are evanescent groups, bringing together the stars, supporting cast, the director, writer, etc., for one product. What makes the concept more important is the much greater ease of formation of such groups because of information technology.

This form of organization is growing in numbers for some basic economic reasons:

1. The transaction costs of physically diffused workgroups continue to drop as it becomes easier to communicate with and learn about other workers; that is, the participants need not often transport themselves (expensive if the distances are great) and can concentrate on transporting just the inputs and outputs of their work (increasingly inexpensive as telecommunications deregulation expands)

2. A premium is being placed on innovation; if the required skills are not available locally—at a desirable price—they may be acquired at a distance

3. Aside from the innovation issue, shifts in the nature and composition of organizations' markets force changes in the number, types—and locations—of specialists required to effectively react to them.

Clearly, standard manufacturing production work, where both the production and market processes are well understood, does not need (nor particularly want) evanescent teams. However, such mature market situations are dwindling in number. Hence, the (temporary but high value) process of fast and flexible innovation may often require the use of evanescent teams, whether it be in car design or marketing work.

■ UP-, DOWN-, UNDER-, AND RIGHT-SIZING

➤ The Flattening of Organizations

One of the consequences of the information revolution is the reduction in the number of levels in organizational hierarchies. The primary reason for this has been the continuing and increasing pressure of competition on decreasing operating costs as a means of increasing (or attaining) profitability. The headlines of business journals continually refer to the actions of Corporation X or Government Agency Y in eliminating so many thousands of jobs as part of their downsizing (or some similar euphemism for sloughing off personnel) efforts.

The motivation for these moves is cost reduction. The reason that they are possible is that senior managers have discovered that:

➤ Middle management can effectively increase its span of control from four or five subordinates to dozens or more, and

➤ A number of services that once were considered "musts" for internal use only can now be safely subcontracted.

Much of this change in perceptions is also a result of the growth of information technology. Business rules can be embodied in software—such as spreadsheets and databases—included in desktop and laptop computers. This reduces the need for some forms of supervision (the boss doesn't have to check; it's built into the program). Some software packages automate functions that may be relatively complex, so that they can be operated by people lacking special expertise.[2]

Managers have found that some types of expertise are only needed occasionally, such as at tax time. They ask: "Why pay a full-time employee when we can subcontract that service?" Computers and software also give individuals more productivity-increasing power. In an industry that is static or declining in size, that means that fewer people can do the required work. These remaining people, while needing computer skills, do not necessarily need to be experts in all of the topics with which they regularly work.

The consequence of this is that once huge organizations are now merely big (until they merge with other big organizations and become huge again). Big organizations are becoming middle-sized insofar as the number of their employees is a measure of size.

Mergers also cause some structural unemployment (which is what the above is). As organizations merge, they usually find that there is some apparent, if not real, duplication of effort. As with downsizing, part of the motivation for merging is to make more efficient use of resources, including human resources. Hence, if each of two mergees had three people to do the work of 2.5 people (since people tend to be indivisible), then the merged organization only needs five, not six, to do the job.

The publicity given to downsizing over the past few years understandably has produced jitters in many classes of workers, not just information workers. Recent stories in the popular media to

---

[2] This causes some concern about "the dumbing of America" although the demand for highly skilled workers has never been higher.

the effect that even white-collar workers are not immune to being laid off are symptomatic of the issue. In fact, white-collar (that is, information) workers, since they are now the majority component of the workforce, may be more susceptible to these fears.

Implicit in the discussion above is the idea that computers and loss of jobs are connected in some sort of cause and effect. Yet, in 1976, Marc Porat (now the President of General Magic, a Silicon Valley software company) wrote a Ph.D. dissertation on the information economy that was the result of a detailed and exhaustive analysis of the economic trends in the U.S. One of his findings was that the net effect of each new computer was to increase the number of jobs.[3] It is not certain that this is still the case in 1998. However, job growth in the U.S. has kept up with population (much better than in the less computerized countries of Europe, for example) to the point where 1998 saw record low levels of unemployment.

One problem is that it is fairly easy to see what jobs have been eliminated as a result of technological progress (particularly if yours is one of them) but difficult to see what new jobs are being created. It is not particularly encouraging to the newly un- or under-employed person to hear that most of the jobs of the year 2020 have not yet been invented. What about this year?

➤ The Rise of Micro- and Mini-Businesses

Two converging trends promote an increase in the number of small and very small businesses. One is the downsizing movement discussed previously; the other is the growth of information technology. The former, by setting skilled individuals adrift, forces them to search for new ways of earning their livelihoods. The latter, by strengthening the power and reach of their intellectual arms, can enable them to successfully run a business without a large (or any) support staff. Quite often, the company that laid off a particular information worker, for any of the reasons in the previous section, finds that it still needs those skills some of the time and is willing to hire the ex-employee as a consultant. In fact, many companies have learned to regret their indiscriminate downsizing, having learned too late that the most able employees

---

[3] Marc Uri Porat. *The Information Economy: Definition and Measurement.* Washington: US Department of Commerce Office of Telecommunications, Special Publication 77-2, vol. 1, Chapter 9, 1977.

are often the ones who first jump at the offer of a lucrative "early retirement" package.

Although the term "consultant" is often considered to be a pejorative one ("a consultant is someone who is between 'real' jobs"), many information workers are learning that the status has some advantages. While apparent job stability is lower ("you don't have a full-time job with any of your clients"), real job stability may be higher ("you don't depend on the whims and vicissitudes of a sole boss"). Once restricted to clients within easy driving or flying range, many information workers are finding that they and their clients are location independent for much of their interaction time.

Further, as family pressures increase (such as childcare needs), together with the number of two-earner households, the attractiveness of telework for at least one earner also increases. While a spur to the rise of such micro-businesses, this is a fear of some organizations employing teleworkers: "They'll become so proficient at working on their own that they'll quit and start their own businesses."

Similarly, Table 11.1 depicts the growth of various forms of home-based work in the U.S.

➤ Get It Where You Can: The Global Economy

So far, I have focused on relatively local trends. But the same principles apply on a global basis. If X is the product in demand, then its cost to the buyer is simply the cost of production, plus the cost of transportation/distribution, plus profit to the supplier. In an information economy, a principal means of distribution will be telecommunications. As competition increases in the telecommunications sector, the likelihood increases that large amounts of

Table 11.1 Home-Based Work Trends

	Americans Working at Home, 1988-1993, Millions					
Year	1988	1989	1990	1991	1992	1993
Primary Job	9.7	9.9	11.3	11.8	12.2	11.3
Part-time Job	7.4	7.6	9.2	10.6	11.5	12
Corporate Job	4.9	5.6	10.1	10.4	8.8	9.3
Telecommuting	2.5	3	4.2	5.8	6.7	7.8
TOTAL	24.5	26.1	34.8	38.6	39.2	40.4

time-bandwidth will be sold at a flat rate, rather than by usage.[4] In this situation, the cost of information transportation can be quite low, even negligible in many cases. Then, the relative locations of the buyer and seller are not a factor in the transaction. In short, the seller of information could just as well be halfway around the world as down the street, as far as the price is concerned.

Well, almost. Clearly, the cost of transmission is not the only factor. Another is the ability of the seller to produce the information at the required cost, timeliness, and level of quality. The economic needs and skills of the seller influence this, in turn. The good news is that a highly skilled teleworker in Southern California can think about having clients anywhere (provided that they use languages with which the teleworker is familiar). The bad news is that an equally skilled teleworker in a country with a lower standard of living may offer equivalent services for a lower price. Chapter 13 delves into the possibilities.

---

[4]For a discussion of this see the special section on telecommunications in *The Economist,* vol. 336, no. 7934, September 30–October 6, 1995.

12

Marketing
Telework Centers[1]

When our research team first explored the realities of teleworking in the early 1970s, our focus was on a telework center oriented model, primarily because of the technology limitations of the era. Telework-appropriate technology has changed dramatically since those days but the fundamental business considerations have not. Over the past decade a number of attempts have been made to establish independent telework centers that cater to a variety of types of clients. My perception has been that most of those attempts, both in the U.S. and elsewhere, have failed, largely because they neglected the business fundamentals. Typically, these centers started as the result of some form of short-term government subsidy—usually, in the U.S., as part of a traffic reduction program;[2] when the subsidy disappeared, so did the telework center.[3]

---

[1] Much of the material in this chapter was developed as part of a project sponsored by the State of California and the U.S. Department of Transportation. Much of the credit for the basic content and organization of the chapter goes to Kristen Kirkpatrick for elaborating on the implementation details.

[2] In Europe the more frequent reason is economic development, specifically to reduce unemployment.

[3] In the California project mentioned above, the sponsoring agency failed to implement some of our key marketing recommendations. The fact that most of the telecenters in the project closed after the subsidies disappeared may not be coincidental.

This chapter covers the fundamentals of marketing a telework center, from the point of view of the prospective center entrepreneur. It assumes[4] that there is also a competent business plan to go with the marketing plan to be developed from the material covered here. Many of the steps described below are iterative. That is, they may be repeated in sequence in (hopefully) an ever-converging process of filling the center and honing both its physical attributes and its operational procedures.

Furthermore, the emphasis here is on the use of telework centers to house telecommuters; that is, people who live near the center and would otherwise commute to an employer in the region. Although some of these may be long distance teleworkers, in the near term most will be telecommuters. *If you're not interested in running your own multi-client telework center, then feel free to skip this chapter.*

Please note that marketing and sales are different and distinct activities. *Marketing* is the process of finding the customer and persuading him/her to be receptive to your ideas. *Sales* is the process of closing the deal; getting the customer to plunk down cash to use your services or buy your goods. This chapter focuses on **marketing.** Also note that some of the details of the marketing process discussed here are specific to the United States; the data sources and relevant implementation regulations may be different in other countries.

The following is not intended as a fixed recipe; deviation from the details of some of the steps discussed here is not likely to be fatal. On the other hand, omission of one or more steps may be. We assume that your long term objective is to make the center a viable business, not dependent on the vagaries of public or private subsidy. If so, then it is very important to get the center on a sound economic footing as soon as possible. This overview is written with that overriding objective in mind.

■ GOALS

Throughout this discussion keep in mind the overall goals of your telework center. Typical goals are the following:

➤ Stimulate the local economy
➤ Become self-sustaining

---

[4] If for no other reason than size limitations for this chapter.

➤ Reduce traffic congestion by eliminating (or greatly shortening) vehicle commute trips

➤ Reduce air pollution by eliminating (or at least greatly reducing) commuting via cars

➤ Improve the profitability of your tenant organizations

➤ Re-humanize the local community[5]

➤ Offer a greatly needed service where none currently exists

■ THE TARGET MARKETS

Given these goals, a central question remains: Just who or what constitutes the market(s)? Let's start by defining a major, if not the only, purpose of your center, as follows:

> To serve as an effective office environment for tenants who live in the locality, who otherwise would work somewhere else at a greater distance, whose work can be done in traditional *or* non-traditional locations.

Neighborhood telework centers further focus on the traffic reduction purpose: tenants who ordinarily will walk, skate, bicycle, use transit systems, or otherwise eschew driving their cars to get to your center.

➤ In General

First, *office environment* implies that your tenants are information workers. That is, their work consists of creating information,

---

[5] One of the principal benefits of telecommuting comes from the increased time telecommuters spend in their communities. That time bonus goes toward more involvement in family affairs, civic activities, sports and cultural pursuits, among others. Bedroom communities can become full-time communities. But the economic constraints must be met first.

manipulating or transforming it, rearranging it, or running an information machine, such as a computer or typewriter. They are not chefs, household domestics, farm workers, truck drivers, or other individuals whose job *always* requires them to be in some particular location other than your center. That distinction eliminates about 40 percent of the workforce as prospective tenants. Of the remaining 60 percent, some probably will also not be good candidates for your center. That leaves possibly 40 to 50 percent of the workforce as prospects.

Second, the key word is *locality*. A regional center, will likely have some mix of drive- and walk-in teleworkers. A neighborhood telecenter will have a target area within a circle of one- to three-mile radius around your center *plus* a similar, but narrower, swath around any transit operation that comes very close to your center. Each of these types has its own set of requirements for location and size. A regional center can attract teleworkers living in several nearby communities, while a neighborhood center, as the title implies will be very focused on a single community, with a proportionally smaller pool of potential telecommuters. Further, while most of this discussion concentrates on teleworkers who are full-time employees of a single employer, there will be a growing population of multi-client teleworkers as well.

Third, that group may be further diminished in size by the requirement that they be commuters. Local people who already work locally may not be candidates, unless there is a large group of home-based teleworkers in the area who might use the center. However, in today's world that restriction probably does not take a big bite out of your collection of prospects. Further, there are two types of people who work locally: people who have local employers and home-based telecommuters. The latter group may still be candidates for your center part of the time.

That generally describes the types of people who could work in your center, but that is only a partial description of your market. The remainder of your market comprises the employers of those individuals, as well as their families and other key decision influences, such as regional air quality management authorities.

➤ Narrowing the Focus

Given the general characteristics of your market, as just described, it is important to set some priorities as to how you go about approaching the market. Here are some practical rules, generally in order of decreasing priority for a newly developing center:

Concentrate on the Employers

Finding willing telecommuters is rarely a problem. They, after all, are the ones who have to put up with the long commutes to work. The employer usually views this daily commute grind as the employee's problem, not the employer's. That is why it is important to show how the problem really does affect the employer. Use of your printed materials is important here.

Go for the Easy Ones First

Developing a telework center should not be an exercise in discovering how much pain you can stand. Some employers are more receptive than others to telecommuting, especially if they must operate under some form of air quality mandate. Try them first. If they already have effective home-based telecommuting in operation, so much the better. They probably already realize that some employees will do better in a center than at home. Some organizations may already have family friendly policies, which telecommuting could augment.[6] Some are growing out of their quarters, facing expiration of leases, or trying to cope with air quality regulations. All of these are naturals for telecommuting.

If you find employers who already have successful telecommuting (or more general telework) programs, see if you can get their CEOs to help you recruit their peers. A recommendation by a

---

[6] A major case in point is the federal government. On July 11, 1994, President Clinton signed a memo exhorting Executive Branch heads to adopt family-friendly policies including "telecommuting and satellite work locations."

fellow CEO usually carries substantial weight even if it is a "To Whom It May Concern" letter.

This rule works within the organization as well as among organizations. Some supervisors are more receptive to telecommuting than others (as is covered extensively elsewhere in this book). It may be a good strategy to try to find the lowest ranking (and proactive) executive who can make a decision for a good part of the organization as the person on whom to concentrate your efforts—as is also the case for home-based teleworking programs. That is, find one or more champions as you would for your own internal telework program.

Also work on discovering which jobs/individuals are most likely to be accepted by management as telecommutable. This will vary, depending on the culture of the organization. In some cases, routine jobs, such as clerical or data entry workers, will be most accepted. In other cases, seasoned professionals will be the most likely candidates.

But Don't Ignore the Prospective Telecommuters

They can serve key roles in your marketing effort. First, they are motivated to reduce their commute; they are on your side. Second, they know better than you who the key decision-makers are. They can materially shorten the path to those desks. Also, they can make sure your message gets heard around their company. Finally, they may have good ideas as to the relative acceptability for telecommuting of different types of jobs in their organization.

Or the Community

Although "the bottom line" is the primary consideration of most viable organizations, their standing in the community may also be an important factor both in the first decision to begin telecommuting and in later decisions to continue it. Establish good relations with the community leaders and help them deliver the message to employers with employees in your area.

And Go for the Long Haul

Every one of these groups is likely to have a decision-making cycle that is longer than yours. Big organizations, especially, can take

more than a year to make a decision about telecommuting. For each group you contact, try to get an accurate idea about how long it will take to get through the approval system and what additional information you can provide to help them. This lag is one of the reasons why you should try to get to the key decision-makers as soon as possible. Persistence (as long as it doesn't become annoying to the client) is a virtue.

All of these techniques will help you concentrate your efforts. Each provides information for the others, so expect to use all of them. As telecommuting proves itself to be successful for your client employers, you will see that the "hard cases" will start to show greater interest in telecommuting. But don't expect that to happen overnight, it can take years. This is why it is important to continue marketing long after the center has first become occupied.

■ SITE SELECTION

After—or in conjunction with—the selection of your target market, you need to address a crucial question, namely:

Where, exactly, should your site be?

Site selection is not a trivial problem, particularly for neighborhood telework centers, where the emphasis is on serving the very local community. The question is, which comes first, the actual center, or the set of telecommuters who are to occupy it. In Chapter 3, the assumption was that an existing company site might be used for a center. In the more general, multi-client case covered here some further site selection effort is required.

As the old real estate saw goes, there are only three key requirements to meet:

1. Location
2. Location, and
3. Location.

This rule has to be interpreted very carefully. Much experience has shown that picking the center location first (say, because it's a nice building and it's available), then hoping that the telecommuters show up is an excellent way to send large quantities of money down the drain. There is more to it than that.

The trick, then, is finding that ideal spot. This requires some research. Three primary factors have to be balanced against each other:

1. The density of prospective telecommuters
2. The availability of willing employers
3. The availability of buildings suitable for housing the center

A fourth factor may also be very important: the availability of some form of mass transit close to the potential location. The most effective way to merge and evaluate all of these factors is with a computer-based Geographic Information System (GIS). A GIS will allow you to make maps of the candidate areas, showing the necessary statistical information and the road and highway system. The statistical information is provided to the GIS in the form of one or more geographically indexed databases.[7]

Versatile, PC-based GIS software packages generally start at about $1,000. In case the idea of learning yet another set of PC skills is too daunting, many GIS producers will give you the names of companies that perform these operations routinely.

➤ The Potential Telecommuters

The primary targets in the search for site location are areas where there is a high density of information workers. This can be derived from census data files.

The second search criterion is commute time. The 1990 U.S. census did not ask commute distances, but time is usually a better indicator of commute stress than distance (taking a long time to go a short distance is especially stressful). Look for commuters

that take at least 30 minutes (or at least the average commute time for the region) to get to work.

For both of these question sets, divide the number of people in each census block by the area (in square-miles) of the block. This gives you the population density (people per square mile) for the block. This is what you

---

[7]More details on the market data development process are given beginning on p. 256.

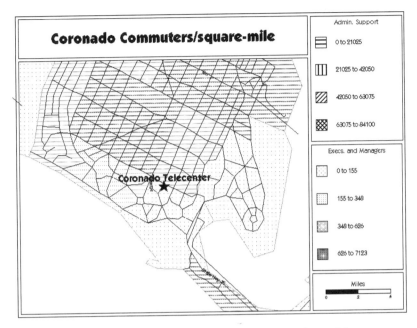

Figure 12.1 Demographic map of Coronado, California.

want displayed on the map for locating a neighborhood center. If there is a quality transit network in an area, you may want to extend your analysis to include areas adjacent to the transit routes.

The maps won't necessarily give you the final answers, if only because the data are aging. New developments may have been built since the last census, or the neighborhoods may have changed in character. Transit routes may have changed, etc. The long duration commuters may not be information workers after all.[8] But the information is probably good enough to get you very close to an ideal site location. Figure 12.1 gives an example of such a map.

➤ Their Employers

Census or other data sources generally are not available that provide the link between resident and employer. If there are such data

---

[8] Naturally, some of them won't be information workers, but there is no reason to believe that information workers generally have shorter commutes than non-information workers. On the contrary, there is evidence that information workers tend to live farther from work than do non-information workers.

available to you, that will help in your marketing efforts. More likely, you will need to resort to local knowledge about the existence of good prospects, as discussed elsewhere. In any case, you do not need to map the locations of employers, since they are all likely to be outside the region of attraction of your site.

On the other hand, if you *know* from your own experience or collateral information that one or two likely-candidate employers have many potential-telecommuter employees in your general area, you may wish to use those employee residence locations as the first guide to locating your center.

➤ Available Buildings

The hardest temptation to resist is an available building at "attractive terms." Many telework centers have foundered on this particular rock. The iron-clad rule should be: FIRST find the telecommuters, THEN look for a building. Yet, even here, rules are meant to be bent. There is no ideal telecommuting building. What you need is a building that is, or can be made, suitable for telecommuting without major (expensive) renovation. It should have office space and one or more conference spaces. It should have a receptionist area if the building is to be visited by non-telecommuters. It should be attractive enough so that prospective telecommuters don't look upon working there as a form of banishment.

➤ The Tradeoffs

Ideally, your site should be located right in the middle of a residential area filled with eager-to-begin telecommuters who work for benevolent and progressive employers. In reality, this is rarely the case. Given the zoning laws that are common in U.S. communities that were developed since the 1950s, it is more likely that your site must be near the outer edge of a residential section. That may reduce your area of attractiveness (unless there is a comparable residential section on the other side of your site) or increase the likelihood that the more distant telecommuters will drive to your center. The fundamental tradeoff is this:

The harder it is, or the longer it takes, to get to your center from home, the lower the likelihood that it will attract the telecommuter, and vice versa.

Still, there are other factors that influence this decision. For example, if your center is located very near other attractions, such as a child care center, restaurants, shopping, business or personal services, recreational, or medical facilities, then its attractiveness is increased. The effect of these secondary attractions will depend on the desires of your prospective telecommuters. Think about using local schools after classroom hours, or vacant retail or office space in the most desirable locations.

■ THE MARKETING PLAN

As is the case with the other aspects of telework covered in this book, it is best to have a reasonably formal plan for marketing your telework center. One of the primary benefits of developing a marketing plan is that it helps establish clear objectives and priorities. These, in turn, aid in selecting the specific marketing tactics that are vital in the long term success of the center.

➤ Defining Marketing Objectives

The first task is to define your marketing objectives. What is the marketing effort supposed to accomplish? The simple—or simplistic—answer is: fill the center right away and keep it filled forever. That is a start, but it's not enough. There are some important other considerations. Here are some of them.

You may only need to develop the marketing materials once, or once every few years. Designed properly, they may be useful for at least a year, and possibly for many years. But, assuming that your center is successful, this marketing effort, once begun, must be *continuous.* The reason is that you will likely have a continuing series of changes over the years in both the employees working at your center and in the employers for whom they work. Your objectives may change as well, as your program progresses. Therefore, it is important to realize that this plan should be in place for the long run, not just the startup of your operations.

The Influence of the Business Plan

First, your business plan should have the objective of filling the center. Ideally, it should be working at 100 percent capacity all of the time. Realistically, that is not likely to happen. Something less than 100 percent should be your realistic goal. How much less? That depends on the economics of the center. At some level of average capacity you will be just breaking even. Clearly you need a higher number than that in order to make a long term profit. Of course, you need not attain that level of support right away if you have some sort of start-up support, from whatever source. Nevertheless, at some point your start-up funding will have been spent and the center must be self supporting to be successful. Your business plan should have that date as an integral part. Therefore, some of the objectives of your marketing plan are set by your business plan. Of course, they are interactive; as you implement your marketing plan, your business plan may change and vice versa.

Requirements for the Objectives

The objectives must meet four requirements. They must be:

➤ *Attainable.* You have a finite set of resources at your disposal. You have a finite time in which to attain your goals. What do you think you can do with those resources in that time?

➤ *Time Specific.* You won't achieve all of your objectives at once. Which one comes first? Which next? And so on. They all have to be started and completed (except the eternal ones) by some certain date and each will take some time to accomplish, within the limits of the resources available.

➤ *Measurable.* How are you going to know if an objective has been achieved? It should be couched in terms that can be measured somehow.

➤ *Both Quantitative and Qualitative.* If at all possible, that measurement should be quantitative, such as the number of responses to a survey, or the number of clients signed up for the center. But there can be qualitative aspects as well, such as the likelihood that the signed-up clients will be at the center a year from now, or the general satisfaction of the telecommuters with your center.

Each objective you list should meet these requirements.

Sample Objectives

Here are some examples of the marketing objectives for a telework center, together with approaches to be taken to realize them. You should particularize these for your own center—and add others, as you see fit. *For all of these, though, it is crucial to realize that there are always two major market components: the teleworkers and their employers.* Although there are common elements to each component there are also significant differences in the techniques needed to reach them.

Know Thy Market Objective 1: Review Available Market Data. The ultimate goal of the marketing effort[9] is to connect you with employers of the potential telecommuters who live in your target area, since the employers make the final decisions to allow telework. In the interest of major commute reduction, the emphasis in many telework centers is on commuters with at least half-hour one-way commutes and, therefore, non-local employers. (The assumption here is that local residents with local employers—and short commutes—may be less inclined to become telecommuters.) Ideally, there would be an available list of the employers of the individuals living in the target area. You could then concentrate on the tasks of developing and delivering the appropriate messages to the employers.

It may take one or several weeks to find whatever market data are available—or to find what isn't available. You should not take much more than that to find the information before going to the next step.

If you can get it, market data needs to be fairly quantitative. For a neighborhood center you need to know how many homes are within walking or bicycling distance, how many of these homes

---

[9] As contrasted to the ultimate goals of your telework center, listed earlier.

house potential telecommuters,[10] who their employers are, etc. For a regional center you need to determine the maximum attraction radius—that is, what is the greatest distance the center can be from a teleworker's home before he/she will decide that getting to the principal office is not much more difficult than going to the center. Qualitative information from traditional sources is not much good at this stage.

Know Thy Market Objective 2: Collect Local Market Data. If an adequate supply of market data is not readily available, you must collect it. The most gratifying objective would be to get suitable data on every household in your region. The most direct way to get that would be to canvass the area repeatedly until all of the households had responded to your questions. It is unlikely that you have either the time or the money to do that job. It is more likely that you will have to work out some form of statistical sampling technique to achieve the desired goal: a *large* list of the names of potential telecommuters and their employers. You will want to get the information by one, or some combination, of telephone interview, mail survey questionnaires, door hanger questionnaire, local newspaper clipouts or similar direct techniques.

The first question is: how large is *large* in the sentence above? That depends on the size of your center. Suppose that you have N seats to fill. Suppose further that your telecommuters are only going to telecommute one day per week. Then you will need a group of $5 \times N$ telecommuters to completely fill your center. If your marketing is quite successful, you will be able to convince about 10% of the employers you contact to have employees working at your center. Suppose that the average employer of residents in your area has only one employee living there who is a potential telecommuter. Then you will need to locate $50 \times N$ employers in order to convince $5 \times N$ of them to sign up! Clearly, the more eligible employees there are in your area who work for a given—and receptive—employer, the better off you are. Similarly, the more often you can get individual employees to telecommute, the better off you are.

---

[10] Potential telecommuters typically are individuals who are information workers; that is the fundamental filter. Others include those with long commutes, who have a suitable proportion of their work that does not need face-to-face interaction, etc. For initial search purposes, use the first two criteria: information workers with long commutes.

This brings up another issue. If your center is too large, that is, it has too many work spaces, it may be impossible to fill it with local telecommuters. You will have to escalate to a regional marketing plan. If your center is too small, then you will be much more vulnerable to random fluctuations in the number of telecommuters unless you have other ways of leveling the load. The optimum center size depends on the *density* of telecommuters (that is, telecommuters per square mile) in your area.

One example of a variant on this are the Kinko's centers in the U.S. Originally developed as copy centers, many have expanded in recent years to include rental of computer time and even videoconferencing facilities. Here, support of teleworkers is a sideline rather than a primary business objective. However, if you are developing a center with telework as the primary objective, then the idea of providing more general business services as well should be very seriously considered. This has the added advantage of being more generally appealing while the idea of local telecommuting is taking root. In any case, your survey should cover the demand for these services in the area (as well as the extent to which that demand is already satisfied elsewhere).

Thus, that attainability question for the market survey depends on the survey techniques used, the size of your center, and your budget.

Surveys can take significant amounts of time—and cash. First the survey instrument(s) must be developed (questionnaire, interview script, mailer, etc.). Next the survey process will typically take several weeks. For example, a mail survey may take two rounds to be effective: a tickler to get people to watch for the actual survey (instead of throwing it out as so much junk mail) and the survey itself. Even then, your response rate may only be 2% to 3% of the number of questionnaires mailed. A telephone survey may similarly take repeated calls to get people at home—and in a mood to answer your questions. Door hangers may come somewhere in between.

Don't neglect to use local, low cost resources, if possible. Since your telework center provides a benefit to the general community you may be able to enlist the aid of school children (literature to their parents), scout troops (door hanger delivery), and other civic organizations in your distribution efforts. Here are some low-cost strategies from one telework center manager:

➤ "Distribute info via school children's take-home packs. I made a small donation to a local soccer team to get them to distribute 3500 door hangers.

➤ "Contact the closest day care centers and ask them to hand out literature to their commuting parents. Set up a booth at the local farmers' market or other community affair.

➤ "Ask the PTA for five minutes to speak at the next meeting, as the benefit to families (and teachers trying to get together with parents) is obvious.

➤ "Meet the van pools as they arrive at the Park and Ride lots."

Ingenuity pays off.

Know Thy Market Objective 3: The Serendipity Effect. Satisfaction of all of the preceding objectives involves some sort of active testing or communication with the community outside your center.

 Another aspect of your marketing should not be ignored, and can even be more important than the other activities: *keeping a close eye on what is going on in the area.* This is easily accomplished by reading the local newspapers and other news media, listening to local electronic news, networking with colleagues and business associates, even watching activities on such exotica as the Internet. The idea, as with all of the others, is to discover employers who may need your center.

A fine example of this is the discovery by a telework center operator—as a result of his regularly reading the local newspaper—that a local employer was moving to a new facility out of town. This sort of move always causes disruptions and discontent among the employees because, on average, they either must quit their jobs and find other local employment or face a significantly longer commute to work. Diverting them to the local telework center provides a solution acceptable to all sides. Although you may not find an opportunity as ideal as this, stories about employer moves that affect local people will often provide similar options.

This is an objective that begins on Day One and continues as long as the center is in operation. It should be part of your routine.

It is easy to measure whether you are performing this task. More difficult is the assessment of the payoff of this activity. Let's just say that the effort required is not that high and the payoff can be considerable.

Inform the Market Objective 1: Develop Direct Contacts and Provide Focused Information for Employers and Employees. The primary objective of this component of marketing is to develop a set of printed materials to be delivered to the key decision maker(s)— the contacts—of the employers of your prospective telecommuters and, through those decision makers, to the telecommuters themselves. It is important, given the large quantities of junk mail that most employers receive, that the materials be eye-catching, brief, and to the point.

It is also important to keep in mind the fact that many, if not most, employers have never heard of telecommuting or, if they have heard of it, have major misconceptions about it. Therefore, you may have a significant task of education to perform through the written materials and through subsequent face-to-face contacts. The materials should be developed with this end in mind.

The primary elements of this aspect of your marketing program are multicolored, printed brochures— one for the employers, another for the prospective teleworkers. Each brochure should contain a definition of telecommuting/teleworking, an explanation as to why it is important for the employer/employee to adopt telecommuting, and a description of your site as an ideal place for this to occur. Telecommuters want to telecommute in order to reduce commuting stresses and increase their freedom of action. Employers are generally unmotivated by employees' commuting problems but are clearly interested in bottom-line impacts.

If your market surveys indicate that some employers have numerous potential telecommuters in your "capture" area, then it might be advisable to have additional materials that specifically address their interests.

If the materials are not already available, it can take several weeks to develop them. Since the primary means of first exposure of your prospective employers is through mailed brochures, quality and professionalism of the brochures are crucial. If you don't have them on your staff, hire a designer and marketing writer. Your message must be presented in a high quality, professional manner if you are to be perceived as professional business operator.

There are three measures of success for this component:

➤ Did the materials get to the right people?

➤ Did they get the message?

➤ Were they the "right" messages for employers and employees?

The materials need to get to the people who can make the decision to adopt teleworking at your center. Throughout the market research process, the focus should be on finding out who those key decision makers are. Second, you should find out what their most pressing business problems are—and determine how having telecommuters at your center will help them (as is covered throughout the rest of this book). That message is what should be in the written materials. If you have time and budget, test your written materials with one or more focus groups prior to committing them to the printer. Alternatively, print your materials in batches, the first of which can be used to test their effectiveness. Both of those alternatives take time and money.

It is harder for the measures of this objective to be entirely quantitative. It is easy to test (with a few phone calls) to see that the people you sent the brochures to actually received—and read—them. It is harder to determine whether they were the right people and whether your message resonated with their goals. Certainly, if they agree to a subsequent telephone or face-to-face conversation, you have at least partially fulfilled this objective. The final assessment generally comes during, or as a result of, your subsequent conversations with them.

Inform the Market Objective 2: Develop Indirect Contacts with Employers/Employees. This is part of a belt and suspenders strategy of marketing: get to the prospective employer decision makers by as many means as are feasible; do not rely solely on the direct contacts developed as a result of satisfaction of the previous objectives.

Although it may appear to be less efficient than the tightly targeted approach, a selective public relations campaign can be even more effective and have high rewards. Part of the problem with the targeted component of your marketing is that you can't always easily find the target by direct means. Even after all the market research you can afford, there may be employers of potential telecommuters in your area that you have not identified or whose key decision makers you can't pinpoint. Further, because of the fairly general ignorance of telecommuting, you probably need to increase the general awareness of your presence and contributions in the community.

The trick is to discover the combination of public relations efforts that will provide the most bang for your buck. As an example, you may very effectively get the attention of commuters by buying radio spot commercials over your local station(s) during peak commute periods. Most stations will also throw in some non-peak air time at no cost to you as part of their PSA (Public Service Announcement) activities *IF* you are a non-profit corporation.[11] Lunch time speeches at local service clubs (such as Rotary and Kiwanis) may get the message to local employers but may miss the more distant ones who might be more motivated to participate in your program.

As another example, we have found that a general brochure or information kit is useful. It explains teleworking as well as the services offered by your center, as a means of getting your message to the press, the service groups, and to employers who may have employees in your target region. Other "gimmicks," such as a balloon filled with clean air (and so labeled) or a cardboard "briefcase" explaining telework and the center's attractions have also been effective in catching employers' attention.

Events related to your center's activities make good occasions for public relations. Your opening ceremonies, anniversaries,

---

[11] You may need to show the station a letter of determination from the IRS certifying that you are a non-profit under section 501 (c) 3—or equivalent—of the internal revenue code to get the PSAs.

expansions and similar events all help reinforce your value to the community and encourage employers to use your services.

This objective may have several sub-objectives as you develop parts of the program. You should estimate milestones for each of the components. Like the directed component of your outreach activities, this broader marketing should be a continuing process.

The same three questions have to be answered for this goal as for the previous one. If your efforts are successful, people will contact you about your services. Ask them how they found out about you—and keep records of their responses. Even where you have made the initial contacts through your targeted marketing, your general marketing may play a part in the decision to have telecommuters at your facility. Ask your contacts about those influences. As in the previous general objective, the measure may be more qualitative than quantitative.

➤ Market Research Resources

You needn't depend solely on your own resources to implement your marketing plan. Here are some that you can use to help you along.

Demographic Data

The first pass at developing the market data should be an analysis of census data. This information is readily available from the Census Bureau (or its equivalent in other countries) either in the form of paper-based reports or computer-readable media such as CD-ROMs. Census data may be available at the census block level. Although census blocks vary greatly in size, they are always smaller than postal code areas, the other means of aggregating demographic data.

The bad news is that the CD-ROM data are revised only after each decennial census, and then generally two or more years after the surveys are made. This is not a problem if you are in a community with a stable population. But, if you have some recent residential development in your area, the data may be obsolete. The error magnitude is in proportion to the elapsed time since the last national census (not a good bet in 2001 before the results of the year 2000 census have been released). The Census Bureau maintains service centers in a few large cities, where there are personnel who may be able to help you find the proper data. Your Community Planning or Building Department may be able to provide statistical data for newer subdivisions.

➤ Other Resources

Air Quality Management Organizations

Most urban regions in the U.S. now have quasi-governmental organizations with responsibility to make and enforce regulations to improve air quality, including changes in commuting patterns as one of the desired options. Often called the Air Quality Management (or Air Pollution Control) District, the agencies have databases of employers who are required to comply with their regulations. In large districts these databases are updated regularly and provide information on the larger employers in the region as well as the number of employees (by postal code of residence) and the names of key contacts for each employer. The down side to this is that the data usually are confined to employers with at least 100 employees per site, thus missing the large number of smaller organizations.

Chambers of Commerce

Look to your local Chamber of Commerce as a source of information about employers in your region. Chambers ordinarily keep lists of their members and the key officers in their organizations. These are usually indexed by the name of the business and by their classification (insurance—with several subcategories, health care, etc.). The local chamber may also have special committees that would be receptive to hearing about your center.

Since many, if not most, of your ultimate telecommuters may work in other communities, you will also want to canvass the Chambers in those areas where you know—or suspect—the telecommuters work.

Advisory Board

Just as in the case of setting up an internal telework program, a very good source of local information, contacts, influence, and enthusiasm is an advisory board for your center. This is not a requirement for successful operation, but an advisory board can be a major help.

If you can, recruit influential members of your community and representatives of some of your key employers to serve on the board. Their advice can save you much time that might otherwise be wasted in tracking down unpromising leads. They may also become direct marketers for your center. Since the board members usually are all volunteers (if your center is not-for-profit), and probably have many demands on their time, be sure that you *often* let them know how much you appreciate their advice.

Economic Development Offices

If your city or region has an Economic Development Office, you may find it a good source of information about local/regional employers as well as a direct supporter of some of your marketing efforts.

Transportation Management Associations (TMAs)

Your local TMA, if there is one, keeps a list of its participating employers. The TMAs provide a number of services to their employers, particularly advice on reducing employee automobile use. One or more of these employers may be a good prospect for your center. In fact, the TMA may help market your center, since telecommuting is clearly a traffic management activity. By helping you they help themselves.

Unfortunately, not all employers belong to a TMA, since air quality regulations currently tend to emphasize membership by employers with at least 100 employees at a given facility. Thus, small companies in the region—as well as some larger ones—may not belong to a TMA. Further, you may want to concentrate on more distant TMAs: those in cities where your neighborhood residents may work.

In any case, your task is to ask the TMA-member-employers if they have employees living in your neighborhood. Then proceed with the rest of the marketing efforts for those who answer in the affirmative.

Rideshare Agencies

Most large urban areas in the U.S. have a rideshare agency that is supported by the government. Often, but not always, called [fill in the community name] Rideshare, these agencies have databases of employers with rideshare programs. As in the case of TMAs, their coverage is not complete. The agencies generally have a variety of available data on commuters and commuting patterns in their areas. However, their data are confined to people who request information about joining rideshare programs—less than forty percent of the workforce. Further, the rideshare agencies are forbidden by law to reveal employer-employee relationships so that they can't tell you which employers have employees living in your neighborhood, although they may have origin/destination maps to help you locate target areas. Hence, their situation vis-à-vis your program is similar to that of the TMAs.

However, many rideshare agencies have publications, such as a monthly newsletter, that are distributed to a wide range of employers. These can be useful means of getting the news of your center to prospective employers and employees. Also as in the case of the TMAs, the rideshare agencies may help you with a variety of marketing support and/or services as part of their outreach programs—and you may wish to contact the agencies in more than one metropolitan area near you.

Other Telework Centers

Both regional and other neighborhood telework center managers can be excellent sources of information, both about prospective leads in your area and about techniques that they have found to be particularly successful. It is not only desirable but imperative to include these centers as arrows in your quiver of resources.

One prime reason for cooperation is the need to present an unambiguous picture of telecommuting to prospective employers. Confusion at employer X is sure to result if representatives for several different centers approach the employer, each with different and uncoordinated stories. The most likely result in that situation is that no one wins.

➤ Strategy Development

The object of the marketing effort is to provide qualified leads to the employers of potential telecommuters. Your strategy should be to mount a multifaceted, integrated approach to achieving that goal. Each element of the marketing effort should be designed to dovetail with the others so that a comprehensive array of information sources and marketing materials is available for the subsequent sales effort. The desired situation is that the employers of those living in the targeted areas will be *surrounded* by quality information about your center.

In developing your strategy it is important to know beforehand what your strengths and weaknesses are. With this knowledge you can more easily play to your strengths and work around your weaknesses in order to build the most robust approach to the market.

➤ Challenges

This is the place to list your weaknesses. Be frank about them. It will help you prioritize your self-improvement and your needs for assistance from others. The list of categories below is simply a reminder; you may wish to add to it or eliminate entries. The key question to ask yourself is: "What could prevent me from attaining my objectives?"

Knowledge of Telecommuting

In general, employers and, to a lesser extent, telecommuters have to be convinced that adoption of telecommuting is advantageous enough for them to alter their current ways of operation. Our experience over the last two decades tells us that employers, employees and the local communities all have to be given some level of education on the nature of telework center telecommuting as a necessary condition for their adoption of it. You are the most likely provider of that education.

Therefore, your own level of knowledge about telecommuting is an important factor in this process. If telecommuting is new to you, it is imperative that you educate yourself as quickly as possible. In the U.S. one that you might particularly wish to investigate is your local or regional chapter of the (ITAC),[12] the International Telework Association and Council. In Europe, try the European Community Telework/Telematics Forum.

---

[12] ITACs Web site is: http://www.telecommute org., and the ECTF Web site is: http://www.telework-forum.org.

Knowledge of Business Practices

Since one of the key positive impacts of telecommuting is its positive effect on the bottom line, your discussions with prospective employers will have more force if you speak from experience. If you know, or can clearly visualize, how telecommuting can affect business operations of each individual company you contact, this is a strength. To the extent that you are unsure about the impacts, you need to heighten your awareness. Chapter 7, for example, provides some of that methodology.

Similarly, your center will need to be tightly operated if it is to be a long term success. Competitors to the center include home-based telecommuting and executive suites, among others. Although cost advantages over these options may not be a complete necessity, it will be important to show some form of cost competitiveness as part of your marketing—and sales—approaches.

Knowledge of Employers' "Hot Buttons"

"Hot Buttons" are the factors that really get the attention of the employers who prospectively will use your center. The more you know about them, the better off you are in showing how the center will address their business problems.

Local Environment

Is the center attractive in appearance? Is it easy to get to? Are there physical security problems (such as isolation, poor external lighting at night, etc.)? Are the surroundings quiet? Check carefully for problems that might detract from its attractiveness.

Characteristics of the Center

Your center has to be attractive to the telecommuters or it will not be successful in the long run. There are several issues to consider here, since a description of your center is part of the marketing package. They include:

Layout of the Center. The prospective telecommuters may put up with an office that is less attractive than the one they have in their principal facility, but too much of a downgrade may alienate them. (Of course, an upgrade certainly will do no harm.) Here it's important to get a feel for the kinds of facilities that your prospective telecommuters are used to. You may not get this entirely right at first, actual experience will help you fine-tune it. But, if you have a good idea about what already is the norm for likely telecommuters in your area you will be able to come close at the outset.

Equipment and Services Availability. This issue can pose a dilemma. Some employers will want you to supply personal computers for their telecommuter, while others will insist on bringing their own. Similarly, some will be satisfied with POTS (Plain Old Telephone Service) while others will insist on ISDN lines or other high tech communications capability. Most will insist on having photocopy and fax machines in the facility, although some will balk at extra charges for use of the machines. Marketing the center as a complete, high tech facility may materially aid in winning over some employers and have little, or even negative (if they feel that it raises the price) effect on others. On the other hand, a premature investment in technology may saddle you with costs that may never be recovered if most of your tenants are self-sufficient types. To resolve this dilemma it is important to add this to your hot button investigation list.

Fee Schedule. How are you charging for services? The more flexible you are, the more attractive you are to employers. On the other hand, you have to be sure that you can cover your operating costs on a monthly basis as well as plan for future operations. In some cases you can attract an employer with an annual (or longer) lease arrangement. In other cases, you may need to provide some space that is rented on a daily or even hourly basis, using some sort of sliding scale of charges that is graded according to the length of the employer's commitment. The bigger the commitment, the better the price.

➤ Opportunities

Here we get to the reverse of the set of issues just presented. The key to the long-term success of your center is that it is somehow better than the competition in your area. Here the question to ask yourself is: "What is it that we offer that is unique and appealing?" Reviewing the list above, you might add some of the following possibilities—or others.

Local Environment

In addition to satisfying the general attractiveness criteria, you may be near a shopping center, restaurants, medical facilities, child care, business, banking, or other services that your telecommuters could walk to during lunch breaks.

Characteristics of the Center

Layout of the Center. If your center has a flexible floor plan, you will probably have an advantage. For example, a layout with modular walls that provide acoustic and visual isolation, and can be moved to suit the needs of the telecommuters without major impacts on costs, will be more attractive to mid-level managers and professionals than will an open, "bull pen" environment. But don't forget that, unless your prospective employer has many telecommuters—and therefore can reduce office space at the principal office building—your space charges may be viewed as additional rent in the employer's cost-benefit analysis.

Equipment and Services Availability. Aside from the dilemma of what standard equipment and services to offer, you may have some special attractions. For example, in earthquake- and brushfire-riven California, it is imperative that mission-critical backup data be stored in a location (or locations) other than the principal facility. Is your center a viable option for this service? Do you have a link to the Internet that your telecommuters can use? Do you have special training available? Do/can you have special telecommunications access or services such as ISDN, ATM, and/or videoconferencing to the employer's facility and/or to other telework centers? Make sure to point out any special "standard" features. Be sure that you offer adequate data/file security.

Hours of Operation. One of the benefits of telecommuting to home-based telecommuters is that they can often work during the hours of their choosing rather than during standard business hours. Is this option available at your center? With suitable security provisions for both center users and their data?

➤ Strategies

After you have assessed your strengths and weaknesses, you should decide how you want to position yourself in the market. What is the best, or most cost-effective, way to deliver the necessary information to your prospective clients?

Competitive Strategies

Your overall marketing strategy has to do with the way in which you will place yourself relative to the competition. The obvious first question in this strategy development is: Who is the competition?

The most likely answer to that is fourfold:

1. *Executive Suites.* Office buildings that rent or lease space on a monthly or longer basis. They usually provide conference facilities, a receptionist, photocopy and fax services. Prices will vary according to location, the number of other services available, whether furniture is included, etc.

2. *Telecommuting from Home.* This option often appears to be less expensive to the employer, since the telecommuter usually absorbs both the rent and most equipment costs. But some potential telecommuters can't or won't work from home and some employers may prefer your centers to home-based telecommuting.

3. *Copy Centers.* Kinko's is a prime example. Some centers rent space, computers, and all the equipment and services necessary for many business purposes, on a per-use, hourly, daily, or even longer basis. Pricing is usually high, though, compared to operations where longer-term use is the norm.

4. *Change Denial.* The employer can decide that nothing other than business-as-usual is suitable. Telecommuting won't be adopted until it's a pre-bankruptcy stratagem.

Each of the first three options has its positive and negative attributes. The first thing to do is check on which ones exist in your area. Home telecommuting is almost always one of the competitive options, but one or both of the others may not be in your area.

Assuming that they are, then you have two primary means of competing: through *price* or through *product differentiation*. One of your primary strategic decisions is on which of these two strategies to use.

Price Competition

Price competition simply means that you can offer facilities and services at a lower price than the competition. You can achieve the lower price either by having costs that are less than the competitors' or by being more efficient at running your operation.

One common strategy in telework center start-ups is to persuade someone to subsidize the operations for some period of time, typically a year. This allows you to price your facilities and services at a point below the market. In effect, your prospective tenants are getting something for free, a tasty opportunity for them. The problem comes when the subsidy ends and/or when your competitors begin complaining to your subsidizer about unfair competition. Here are some options:

➤ *Mount* campaigns to counter the adverse publicity

➤ *Find* new or continuing sources of subsidy

➤ *Reduce* your costs so that you do become price competitive without the subsidy

➤ *Increase* your utilization rate (assuming that you're not 100% booked and still losing money) through some combination of more paid advertising, word-of-mouth advertising and/or exercising your network of contacts

➤ *Diversify* to provide new/other business services (see *Product differentiation* below)

➤ *Offer* graduated or tiered lease agreements by quarter (1st quarter is free, 2nd is at 25% of nominal, 3rd at 50%, etc.). The hope is that, once there, they will stay in the center.

Product Differentiation

In a product differentiation strategy you develop a product that is palpably different from that of the competition. You offer facilities and/or services that they don't have, at a price that still is attractive but possibly is higher than the competition. Here it may be important to target your market carefully (back to the "hot buttons"). If you can develop your facilities and services to very specifically address the needs of your clients—in a way that your competition doesn't match—then you have a competitive advantage. In general, it is better to have your strategy rely on product differentiation than price competition. You have a better product than they do.

Marketing Strategies

Having decided how you are going to compete generally, the next decision is on how to position yourself in the marketplace; how to present the right image to your prospective clients.

Advertising/Media. Advertising and media strategies involve an evaluation of the media mix (magazines, direct mail, print or broadcast), a description of how each medium is to be used, costs of each, and a schedule for when each media element will run. This is at the heart of the media strategy, because the most successful strategy will be a combination of different media and schedules throughout your project.

Branding/Image. Image strategies focus on the qualitative elements of your marketing program. Educating the general public on the merits of teleworking—or showing happy telecommuters at work—or reporting their increased productivity to their happy boss—might be examples of image marketing.

Direct Response. Direct response, on the other hand, is more quantitative in nature. Direct response strategies include some kind of consumer call to action, such as directions to call an "800" number, return the enclosed card, and so on. In marketing telework centers, the direct response strategy will be most effective in providing you with a database from which to convert prospects into tenants.

What to Use and Why

Having reviewed the options presented above, you must decide what single strategy, or what combination of strategies to use. For each one, write out a description of the strategy and the reasons why you are using it and why you think that it will be effective.

■ MAKING IT HAPPEN— IMPLEMENTATION TACTICS

Once you have identified the marketing strategies, it is time to consider implementation tactics. Now we get down to the details of what, who, when, and how for each approach to use. Try to work these out in chronological order. You can segregate the implementation activities into three major groups:

➤ Marketing programs
➤ Media activities
➤ Non-media activities/promotions

Some of these must happen sequentially, others can work in parallel. As you develop them, keep revisiting the who, when, and how of them to make sure you can accomplish the steps with the resources you have available.

Also keep very firmly in mind the fact that, in a marketing program, not everything is in your control. You can control the application of your own resources. You have some control over the schedule and outcome of subcontractors, such as printers, but *you have little or no control over the reaction times of your prospective clients.* It is very important to realize that many organizations have decision cycles that run on an annual basis. Whatever the cycle time, you must try to synchronize your efforts with their decision processes.

For each of the tactics you decide to employ, there is a standard list of questions to be satisfied:

1. Who/what is the audience?
2. Is this a short- or long-term/duration tactic (when does it begin; how long does it last)?
3. Is it cost-effective?
4. Does it reach my primary market(s)?
5. Who is responsible for making it happen?

Following are some examples.

■ MARKETING PROGRAMS
➤ Market Research
The Audience

The obvious first step is the market research and analysis component of your objectives, as described earlier. Unless you have a fairly good idea as to who your center will serve, you can waste enormous, even fatal, quantities of resources in misdirected marketing activities. So make a list of all the methods you will use to find out who your telecommuters will be and who their employers are. Possible steps include:

➤ *Review of census data* for pertinent characteristics
➤ *Gathering equivalent data* from local real estate agencies, the local newspapers, city hall or other resources. Some of it may be better than census data, but don't count on it.
➤ *Surveying the neighborhood.*

Give free rein to your ingenuity.

Timing

CAN I HAVE THE ABBREVIATED VERSION?

This has to be done at the outset of your program. If you can rely on census data alone (doubtful), the main part can be completed in a few days. Surveys take longer, typically several weeks for a mail or door hanger survey (that requires a response from the residents), less for telephone or supermarket-interview surveys. Surveys should be kept short and, except for address information, should consist of multiple-choice questions. People will toss long surveys and ones with open-ended questions.

After the start-up survey you should keep trying to refine your database on the neighborhood, so that, as telecommuters leave the center, they can be more easily replaced. *Keep your survey data to the minimum required to identify who works for whom.* Basically, all you need is the respondent's name, daytime phone number, job title (a telecommutability indicator), self-categorization of job (for example, manager, professional, sales, secretarial, clerical, and other), employer, work address, whether the employer has telecommuting or related programs, and whether or not you can use the respondent's name in contacting the employer.

Cost-Effectiveness

Assuming that you have a personal computer with a CD-ROM drive, the 1990 (or 2000) census summaries can be had from the

Census Bureau for $150 for your area ($300 for the entire state of California). Examination of census tables at the local library or college may be much less expensive. But you don't get household-specific data, so census figures are best used just to determine whether you are in the right general location in your community. You will probably need to do some sort of house-to-house or other sample survey to get more specific information.

Surveys can be expensive, either in material costs (printing and postage) or personnel time, or both. Plan the survey techniques so as to use as many free resources as possible (such as inserts for utility bills in the neighborhood). Yet, surveys definitely do get to your primary targets: the potential users of your center.

Validity

Surveys particularly get to your primary market. However, surveys have to include the right questions, appropriately phrased to eliminate bias. Further, they have to be fairly short or you won't get people to answer them, even if they are paid a nominal fee (which further raises the cost). If they are well prepared and accepted by your target audience, they can be invaluable. Census data cover the market but (again, because of the questionnaire length limitations) lack both specificity and detail.

The Implementer

If you, or your staff, are sufficiently well versed in statistical sampling techniques and survey design, you can probably handle this yourself. Otherwise, you may need to hire a survey professional to do the job. The trick is to see if you can get, say, 70% of your key information from less than 10 questions. It might be possible to get local school children or organizations such as the boy or girl scouts to distribute the surveys, since you are providing a service to the community. It might also be possible to enlist the aid of your local "Commuter Computer" organization, or your local utility company, to mail questionnaires to clients/residents.

➤ Marketing Materials Design and Production

The Audiences

The primary audience for your marketing materials comprises the target employers and their employees who live in your neighborhood. Secondary audiences are residents and organizations in your community. The message you want to convey to each of these groups is:

> Telecommuting works
> Telecommuting benefits you (the audience member)
> Here's where it should happen (your center)

To do this, you probably need slightly different forms of media for each of the three groups. For the employers you want materials, such as a brochure, that focus on the hot buttons that you have discovered, the famous "bottom line" always being one of them. For employees, the more important issues tend to be concerns about work rules, lifestyles, stress reduction, trust, and promotability. You can verify the key issues by talking to a few prospective—or active—telecommuters. Here are the most common ones:

> How often can I telecommute? (Attitudes range from: CAN I do it all the time? to Do I HAVE to do it all the time?)
> How will this affect my promotability?
> Do I have to work standard hours?
> What happens if (something breaks; I finish my work early; I need to change my schedule; I need to get in touch with _____ ; etc.)
> Who pays for what?

For the general community—and for employers who may have employees in other areas who could work at centers there—you may want materials similar to the employers' brochure but less focused on the specifics of your center. To the extent that your budget allows it, you may want to add posters, bumper stickers and other items to distribute in your neighborhood.

Timing

As in the case of the market research phase, you want to make a large effort as soon as you have satisfactorily identified and defined the market. You may wish to produce a small quantity of the designed materials at first as a market test. The test results should be used to refine the designs.

Even better, first use a focus group to test prototypes of the materials. The materials should be very focused on the target markets, hence it is important to test them before committing to large print quantities (small quantities are expensive on a per-piece basis) or media buys.

Also consider using the technology that many of the teleworkers will use on a daily basis: the World Wide Web. Set up a Web site for your center using HTML versions of the promotional materials.[13]

Once the center is at least sixty percent occupied, you will still want to provide—and possibly modify—your materials for your continuing marketing process.

Cost Effectiveness

This is a critical issue for this component of your strategy. The design and production of marketing materials are likely to be one of the most expensive parts of your marketing effort. Whatever your overall strategy is, you have to convey a professional image to your target markets. In many cases, the marketing materials constitute the customers' first encounter with your center. First impressions are important, especially since poor first impressions can preclude the possibility of a second.

Consequently, you must devote serious consideration to the tradeoffs between materials cost and their impact on your potential clients. There are no guaranteed rules here, which is why materials testing is useful if you have the time and resources to do it. If not, then it is important to have as experienced a design and production team as possible; experienced not only in marketing but in telecommuting as well. If you don't have one in-house, then this is the place for subcontracted, *experienced* help.

As you go through the list of potential marketing materials, keep thinking of your audience for each possibility. How likely is this item to get the attention of the audience? How likely is it to convey the message you want? How likely is it to motivate them to contact you instead of waiting for you to contact them, turning them from passive to active participants in the process?

The Implementer

Unless you have extensive expertise in marketing, you had better use the services of a professional marketing organization. You, or

---

[13] HyperText Markup Language, more Internetese.

staff member X, need to know enough about your target markets to clearly define them, but not necessarily enough to design the campaign from scratch. It is important to keep in mind the fact that telecommuting is an unknown quantity to many members of your target market. Consequently, you have to make sure that your materials effectively get past that barrier. For example, although most of the occupants of your center will be telecommuters, by my definition, we have found that the more generic term, tele*work,* is more effective in getting employers' attention.

➤ Media Activities

Because the media can be one of the most effective ways of reaching the general public, their importance to the success of any marketing program cannot be ignored. Media activities can be paid or unpaid; or a combination of each might be considered if you are a nonprofit organization.

Press Releases

The Media.   Your first decision concerns selection of the publications to target. Should you concentrate on the general media, business journals, high tech media, local weeklies, regional monthlies, or some combination?

The Audiences.   Your first audience for the news release is the person(s) making the decision whether or not to run the story. Get a name, not just "Assignment Editor" or similar title. The first paragraph of the release must grab the attention of the assignment editor and at the same time summarize what is contained in the rest of the release. Once that hurdle has been passed, the balance of your release must tell the story summarized in the first paragraph so that your second audience—the general public—will understand and respond appropriately.

Timing.   As the mantra for comedians goes: "timing is everything." That is particularly true with news stories. You should plan to send your release during a week ahead of when you want the story to run so that reporters have time to do some background work but not so much time that they forget about your story. Do NOT send your release around major holiday weekends or at times when other news is breaking (such as around election time). Weekends tend to be lighter news days, so the likelihood of seeing your story in print might be stronger then—and more likely to be read by busy workers.

Cost Effectiveness. This is a fairly inexpensive way to contact the media particularly if a wire service is used for the distribution. We recommend phone follow-ups and re-faxing of the release to those papers and stations which you want to be sure run the story.

Validity. If the headline and first paragraph grab the attention of the editor, this can be an excellent way of communicating with the public. However, if an unexpected crisis occurs in the world, your story might be pre-empted. Releases that are regionalized to the target media will also have a higher likelihood of placement. For example, a story on a Chicago conference on telecommuting will hold interest to the Waukegan paper only if commute patterns of Waukegan residents are included in the story.

Implementer. There is a science to placing a story in the media, and a logical form for news releases to follow. Professionals might be better for this task, although anyone who writes well could learn to write a release. Successful placement of the story can also be improved if professionals who know the assignment editors personally are listed as the contact person.

Radio Spots

The Audiences. In most cases the target audience for a radio spot is the commuter. Commuters are generally the employees, but can include the employer/decision maker, as well.

Timing. Air times during the morning and afternoon drives are optimal, particularly if they are placed on a program just before or just after regular traffic reports. "Metro Traffic" is a service most news-talk stations subscribe to, and offers an ideal air time schedule for telework center advertising.

Cost Effectiveness. Urban radio is much more expensive than rural, so a Metro Traffic buy in Megalopolis will cost substantially more than in Crabtree Corners. If most of your potential teleworkers live in Megalopolis, then you're faced with the higher expense. More likely, the target audience will be commuting from a suburb to another suburb or to Megalopolis; since they have longer commute times, by definition, you might better concentrate your attention to the morning pre- or evening post-peak hours in the suburbs. The number of potential customers reached by this kind of targeted radio makes this tactic very cost-effective. Buys on local stations are very inexpensive, but may have limited broadcast range. Nonprofit organizations can usually negotiate additional air time at no cost to run (Public Service Announcements).

Validity. Again, the ability of radio to target the primary markets of the telework centers makes this a very effective tactic. The Grass Valley Telecenter in California, which has used radio to reach potential telecommuters, found this to be an effective way to get people to call for more information.

Implementer. Professional advertising agencies, which can produce either a recorded spot or a recorded spot with a DJ live script, are the best to implement radio. Most agencies also offer competitive buying ability and can frequently negotiate the best price or paid/unpaid contracts.

➤ Non-Media Activities

There are a number of community relations/general publicity activities which can be effective tools in marketing the telework centers.

Meetings, Conferences, and Workshops

The Audiences. For the most part, your audience will be prospective telecommuters who are eager to learn how telecommuting might benefit them individually, but who are also gathering information that can be used to "sell" the concept to their corporate management. If properly designed and publicized, these events will also attract corporate transportation managers, human resources directors, and possibly a very few innovative CEOs.

Timing. Check with other organizations in your area (Rideshare, Chambers of Commerce, Air Quality Management [AQMD] or Air Pollution Control District [APCD]) to make sure similar events are not already on the calendar. Avoid any dates that already are set for a large community event, even if the audience is not the same. Better yet, co-sponsor the events with them. Cover more information, involve more people, and save money.

Cost Effectiveness. Smaller events, such as meetings for prospective telecommuters, can be done in small rooms at little or no cost, with only coffee and a few handouts required. Larger events, such as an all-day telecommuting conference, generally cost more because of banquet room charges, speaker fees, food and beverages, and publicity/invitation distribution. Some of these costs can be covered with a nominal charge and/or sponsorships.

Much of the reason why teleworking has seen such limited success is that there are still large segments of the population who don't know what it is. Or, worse yet, who THINK they know what it is and really don't. While these events may not result in obtaining tenants right away, the long-term benefit can be significant, since you are building a pool of potential clients to combat turnover and/or fulfill expansion plans.

As a site developer, you are undoubtedly quite capable of planning and implementing small group meetings and workshops. We recommend that professional event planners or large committees with committed members who are willing to work (large events can be very labor-intensive) be used to manage all the details of a large conference. Here, too, a good strategy may be to co-sponsor the events with organizations that may have different goals than yours but common objectives.

Grand Opening

The Audiences. Grand opening events should be attended by local government and business leaders, leadership from organizations like the chamber or rideshare, prospective telecommuters and their supervisors, the media, residents of the neighborhood in which the center is located, and representatives of your sponsoring organizations.

Timing. In order to start your official operations on a positive note, it is important to have the center fairly well occupied with busy telecommuters. Nothing is more off-putting to a potential client than to see a mostly vacant building. Therefore, you should try to "seed" the center with telecommuters from those first "easy" clients before you have your official grand opening celebration.

Other considerations include time of day (before noon is best if you want television coverage that night), day of the week (check the local business calendar), and idiosyncrasies of your audience. For example, we recommended that one telework center (which occupied a building on the grounds of a local school) tie its grand opening into a major school event such as an open house because they could offer tours of the center as part of the school event.

Cost Effectiveness. Grand openings can generate a lot of publicity at a very low cost, particularly if some community "movers and shakers" are part of the program.

Validity. Ribbon cutting ceremonies offer an official start to what we hope will be a long-term establishment in the community. To simply open the doors for business without the fanfare of a grand opening would cause you to miss a great PR opportunity.

Implementer. These should be done entirely by site developers, with support from a local event planner or marketer (if needed). Resources which might offer assistance could come from local government (if your congressperson is speaking, his or her staff will be eager to make sure this is done right!), the Chamber of Commerce (they host ribbon-cuttings all the time) or your local TMA.

■ SCHEDULE

The next task is to schedule all of these activities in such a way that you can perform all of them within the necessary time limits and with the resources you have available. For a better view of your activities, expand the table to include events by week—or even by days. Fill in each marketing activity, its time line, and annotate it with a description of the resources required. Alternatively, you may want to make use of some sort of computer-based project planning software (such as Microsoft Project) to help you do this. Such software will usually also include the resources for establishing your budget.

■ BUDGET

In this section we are referring to the marketing budget, not your total budget. Clearly, your business plan addresses the total budget for the center. Yet the market plan may cause you to reevaluate your business plan. As you develop the budget, try to picture exactly what will happen in each step, who does what, and what it will cost in time and cash outlays. Here are the main factors.

➤ Personnel Costs

Staff Time

These are the allocated salaries and benefits for every one of the center's employees. That includes the center manager, clerical staff, and any professionals that work on the marketing aspects of the center's activities. It does not cover the time of any specialists that you may hire to accomplish some aspect of the marketing plan; those costs are accounted separately.

Outside Help

However, you may want to hire some consulting help in developing your plan and strengthening your identified weaknesses, if any. This cost should be included here as a separate category.

➤ Production Costs

Even if you have your own staff of advertising or marketing specialists, the production costs should be specified separately. Here are typical cost categories.

Design

Someone has to design and write the details of your marketing campaign. That includes defining the content—the messages to be delivered and the wording, layout of graphical/printed materials, scripting of videos, etc. If you are trying to rifle your marketing efforts to very selected audiences, this can require several variations of a main theme.

Design is a critical part of your marketing. A well designed set of materials generally doesn't cost much more to manufacture—and may even cost less—than a poorly designed set, but the impact difference can be tremendous. For example, if the materials look pretty much like all the other solicitations that cross a manager's desk, there is high probability that they won't even be read. If the materials stand out—in an attractive, not gross way—and are succinct and to the point, they will be read and understood. Your goal: maximum impact—positive interest in your center—per dollar spent.

There are creative ways to stretch your budget. For example, print generic text on one side of a handout, with industry-specific content on the other; or size the pieces to gang more than one on the press, thereby eliminating one setup charge.

Camera-Ready Art

The end product of much of the design process is camera-ready art; the stuff that goes to the printer or film/video maker for reproduction and manufacturing. In the computer age most print-destined materials are delivered on magnetic or optical media. Video materials are on one-inch tape, audio feeds are on cassette, and all can be on CD-ROMs. In fact, a CD-ROM- (or DVD-) based multimedia presentation would be a very appropriate addition to the marketing mix.

Each of these items costs something, whether it is produced originally or culled from files or records. The end uses of these materials include:

Letterheads

Brochures

Flyers and direct mailers

Door hangers

Posters

Press kits

Video tapes

CD-ROMs

Audio tapes for commercials

Press release forms

Web pages

All of these items need some form of design and production management and should be consistent in appearance.

Materials

A key question for each marketing item produced is: "How many?" Door hangers and survey questionnaires can go to thousands of residences. Posters may number in the tens or hundreds. How many brochures are needed to reach your prospective employers, their employees? And so on.

There usually is a tradeoff between quality and quantity. Printed media using flimsy, clearly inexpensive stock can tarnish the image you are trying to build. Using only the finest materials may be overkill; less expensive materials may do just as well. If it's a brochure, what stock should you use for the covers, and what for the insides?

One of the key design decisions for printed materials is the number of colors to use. Colored stock with one, two, or three colors of ink? White stock with four colors? CMYK[14] versus spot colors, ultraviolet coating, matte or gloss, spot or flood, all have cost implications. Don't forget, each color requires another print run and setup charge. One trick for a campaign that requires some specialized messages is to keep all the common materials in the core pages and all the specialized information in the outside pages. With this technique, you can make a single print run for all the core materials, adding smaller runs for the specialized outsides. If you're not versed in all these approaches, use a professional. It will save you time and money.

Press Media

Although printed materials distributed by you are likely to be a major component of your marketing, the press media should also be used. Here, the idea is to get as much free publicity as possible (assuming it's positive). But you probably will have to pay for

---

[14] Cyan, magenta, yellow, and black: the ink colors used for color halftone processing.

some of your exposure to your target groups. In most cases, your best results will be had from some combination of the following.

The primary media are broadcast (radio and TV) and print. Your exposure possibilities via these media are the free ones (interviews, news stories, and magazine articles) and the paid ones (advertisements). The press release is the main means of getting the "free" exposure, while media prepared by you or your advertising staff/subcontractor are the basis for the paid exposure.

"Free" exposure can still have costs. Preparation of press releases, buying space on the wire services, making and keeping key contacts in the media all cost something. Generally, though, these costs are far less than the others. Further, you are likely to have little control over the outcome of your efforts; the reporters' and editors' own priorities—and biases—take precedence.

So you may also want to buy some time and/or space in the media to ensure that *your* message, not the reporters', is delivered in the manner you wish. As much as you can, you want to have your message focused on your target group: your prospective tele-employers, telecommuters, and community influentials. If you're using the print media, try to focus on the media most likely to be read by your targets—such as the local[15] Business Journal—rather than a more general medium that might not be read carefully.

Among the broadcast media, radio is definitely lower cost and quite likely more effective than TV for your advertising purposes. Go for the local radio station that most of your commuters listen to as they drive to or from work. Buy spot announcements during rush hour periods. They are more expensive than non-rush times (rush hours are prime time for radio) but they have your captive target audience. Usually, you can work a deal with the radio stations so that they will also broadcast your ad free (as PSAs—Public Service Announcements) during non-prime hours. The ratio is often two paid prime- for each free non-prime-announcement.

The remaining option for radio is whether to have your announcements in the form of DJ scripts or recorded spots. Scripts involve fewer production costs, but may have higher air-time costs, as well as less control over how your message gets delivered. Recorded spots can get complicated—depending on how acoustically complex they are—and expensive, but may be significantly more effective.

---

[15] Local to your prospective employers, that is.

➤ Other Cost Factors

Then there are all of the other costs of running a marketing campaign. Each instance of these items is small, but lots of repetition builds the total. This category includes:

➤ Postage

➤ Office supplies (paper, pencils, toner cartridges, etc.)

➤ General telephone and fax charges

➤ Distribution costs for new releases—fax, postage, and/or news wire

➤ Photocopying and other duplication services

➤ Transportation (such as, how you get to those meetings and conferences)

➤ Shipping

Unfortunately, there is no rule of thumb for estimating these costs. For one thing, they depend closely on the types of contacts you develop as part of your campaign. As with the other factors, try to specify the following factors for each of your marketing efforts as a first step to cost estimating:

➤ What message are you trying to convey?

➤ To whom?

➤ With what result?

➤ What is the value of the result?

■ EVALUATION

Regardless of how masterful your planning is, chances are that not every marketing tactic will work perfectly, or even as well as you had hoped. If a particular tactic is not working, you will want to quit using it. If another tactic is working beyond your wildest dreams, maybe you should put more resources into it.

But how will you know how well each tactic (or strategy) is working? Evaluation is required. You have to test the results.

In order to do that, you must go back to the original marketing objectives and decide what measurable factor is an indicator of success for each of them. There are several feedback factors that will give you this information. Ideally, you would like to know the contribution, if any, that each of your marketing tactics made to the success of each of the factors. Some key effectiveness factors are:

➤ Rate of responses to your outreach efforts

➤ The number of interviews with prospective employers

➤ The number of tours of your facility

➤ The level of (free) media coverage (column inches of articles, minutes of broadcast coverage, etc.) in your target market area.

➤ The number of new telecommuters

As responses start to come in, try to determine what prompted the inquiry. You might want to make a simple spreadsheet as a means of keeping track. In each blank block put either the count (such as number of responses) or other measure of success.

As this tracking system progresses, you can begin to see how effective each method is. Don't rely too closely on the numerical results, however. Some of your tactics may not show up directly as the chief motivator for the responses you get but, in the long run, they might be important nevertheless. The only way to get an estimate of these more subtle responses is with a longer interview with some of your respondents. Try the straightforward approach: "We're trying to keep our costs down and still get to the right people. Would you mind telling me what the key things were that prompted you to contact (or respond) to us?"

Now, go back to step one and do it again.

Chapter

13

Telework around the Globe: A Peek into the Future

Now that we've covered the fundamentals, let's take some time to see where all of this is taking us (or, more positively, where we are taking it). As an applied futurist I am well aware of our inability to *predict* the future, at least in the same sense that we forecast tomorrow's weather. Since human beings, as well as many other types of organisms, seem to have the ability to alter their behavior—and consequently their environments—and since there are billions of individuals doing just that, it is not feasible to make detailed predictions for other than very short periods. However, it is possible to derive an estimate that is close enough to help you estimate climate change and build strategies for coping with the future.

■ THE FLOW

The first thing to remember is that the future is irrevocably tied to the present and, to a lesser extent, to the past. The future begins *now*. Having read this, you are now a tiny distance into what was the future a few moments ago. The *real* future begins *Now*. Not much different is it?

Well, possibly it is. You have taken a breath or two, someone has just died somewhere, about 2.7 someone else's have been born, some ancient, fossilized ferns have been converted to carbon and nitrogen oxides and water vapor via automobile engines, some telephone calls have been made, a few trillion computer processor cycles have been completed, and so on. All of these things have been happening at about the same *rates* as they were when you started reading this chapter. Incremental changes have occurred.

The most important fact about the future is, first, that it depends on a series of changes in almost everything and, second, that it is impossible to know what all of those changes are or will be. That is, the future is the result of the growth/decline of a vast number of trends, each of which comprises an infinite number of events, a few of which are (or seem to be) discontinuous.

Discouraging as that sounds, there is still hope. We can still do a reasonably good job of estimating quite a number of these changes, while many of the others may not be of concern to us in the short term. So, when it comes to assessing the possibilities of the future for oneself or one's own organization, a relatively manageable set of examinations may suffice to give a fairly accurate picture.

Another important fact is that **the past has inertia;** the near future tends to be pretty much like the past—huge, abrupt changes are rare.[1] Further, barring comets and other such astrophysical anomalies, *homo sapiens* is probably the greatest change agent there is, at least in the short term (a few decades or centuries).

Therefore, one key to understanding the possibilities of the future lies in understanding what people are doing to change the present. There are three primary things that people are doing to shape the future:

1. They are reproducing faster than they are dying; therefore, their relative impact on the global allocation of resources is increasing.

2. They are inventing and using ever more powerful tools; therefore, the per capita leverage on resource use is also increasing.

3. A growing proportion of these tools primarily are information manipulators rather than physical resource extractors/manipulators; therefore, the interaction range of

---

[1] But not impossible. When they happen, the consequences tend to be spectacular.

individuals is increasing. To the extent that the information tools enable more efficient design of the other tools, they act to reduce resource impacts of those tools.

Each of these aspects of the future can be characterized in terms of *critical trends* and *pivotal events*. So, the process of assessing the future boils down to:

1. Identifying the key trends (that might affect you and/or your organization).
2. Identifying the pivotal events that may act to alter those trends.
3. Identifying the interactions between the various events and trends.

Simple, isn't it? Just follow the easy, step-by-step instructions. The gory details of that process, and forecasting options, are given in Appendix E. Suffice it to say that we have developed a wide variety of scenarios about the future as it is related to telework. At the country level we rely on mathematical forecasting models, while at the corporate level we may place more effort on statistical models and cross-impact analyses (as described in the Appendix).

■ TELECOMMUTING IN THE UNITED STATES

After that introduction, it's time to look at the possibilities for telework around the globe. The following are preliminary results of some of my analyses of the world situation. Part of the problem in these analyses is that the input data vary widely (and wildly) in quality from country to country and source to source. As you might expect, the less-developed world presents the most problems in this regard. All of the forecasts in the rest of this chapter are *nominal forecasts*. That is, they represent the *most likely future*, given what we know today about the underlying factors.

First, let's look at the United States. In earlier chapters we saw how the distribution of the workforce has changed over time—the historical trend—and how it is most likely to continue for the next decade or three. Over the years I have developed and honed a mathematical forecasting model (a multivariate version of the logistic curve design mentioned earlier) of telecommuting in the U.S. The 1997 version of the results is shown as Figure 13.1

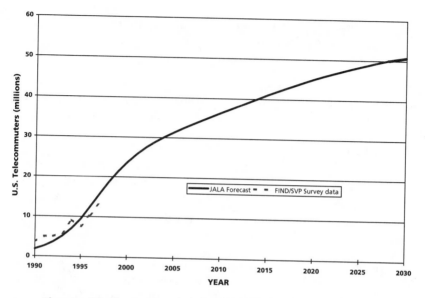

Figure 13.1 Projected growth of telecommuting in the U.S.

The solid curve in the figure is the result of the nominal fore-casting model. The dashed curve shows the results of a series of surveys conducted by FIND/SVP under the direction of Tom Miller. These surveys involve queries of about 2,000 U.S. households. Note that the survey curve wanders around both sides of the results of the nominal case—a common occurrence for long-range models since reality never seems to strictly obey mathematical models thereof. The dip in the survey curve seems to correlate with the peak of the downsizing fad in the U.S.; an indication that prospective telecommuters were nervous about staying out of sight too long. Since then, the reality trend appears to be tracking the model, although at a slightly lower value. The survey results are reality, at least within the limits of the survey techniques used. Other scenarios you might develop would depict other possible realities about the nominal curve.

■ TELECOMMUTING VERSUS TELEWORKING: SURVEY PROBLEMS

Also note that Figure 13.1 just shows telecommuters. The number of *potential teleworkers* (including *current* telecommuters) in the

U.S. was higher by about a factor of four in 1997. Unfortunately, no one seems to be surveying teleworkers in general. This is due partially because the definition of teleworker gets fuzzy at the edges; almost everyone in business does some form of teleworking—in that she phones people who are somewhere else—but is that *real* teleworking? My rule is that telework must involve a change in "normal" behavior. That is, if you can accomplish something via telecommunications and/or other information technology that *normally* would require that you travel to somewhere else, then you are teleworking. Since what's normal changes with time, this is a moving target.

Let me give an example. A few years ago I was talking with a mid-level manager in a major multinational corporation. This manager was responsible for the activities of several groups that were physically scattered about the U.S. Ordinarily (that is, pre-email) he would make monthly trips around the country to review the activities of each group. Each meeting would occupy at least an entire day because of the time spent in finalizing the agenda, exchanging background information, chasing down some of the intended meeting participants, etc. After everyone in the groups became linked by email, most of the time-wasting preliminaries were accomplished before the manager ever left his office in California—they were teleworking. The manager still made trips to these groups, but they were fewer in number and each trip was better organized than before, allowing him to accomplish the same results in just an hour or two.[2] Videoconferencing is expected to further increase the amount of teleworking and decrease the number of coordination trips (notice that I didn't promise a decrease in the total number of trips). Still, this aspect of telework is very difficult to measure in a general survey.

■ THE FUTURE AROUND THE WORLD

With those caveats as background, my preliminary forecasts of the global growth of telework are based on the assumption that other countries will evolve telework along the same lines as happened in the U.S. That is, they will follow certain historical, technological, and economic patterns similar to those of the U.S. As the earlier parts of this chapter showed, this approach has certain perils. For example, population, economic, education, and technology

---

[2] This presented a new problem: what to do with the rest of the day.

growth patterns may be quite different in other countries, as may government regulations, trade barriers, food supply, and cultural acceptance patterns. The 1998 version of my model does not explicitly take into account all of these influences on the future. Therefore, in each of the following sections, I will try to indicate why the model may be too high or too low in its results.

➤ The OECD Countries

The member countries of the Organization for Economic Cooperation and Development (OECD) are generally considered to constitute the so-called developed world. The list includes Australia, Canada, most of the countries of Western Europe, Japan, and the U.S. There are some interesting differences among the OECD countries. For example, Australia and the Western European countries are ahead of the U.S. in the extent of ISDN availability. Sweden and Finland have the world's highest penetration of digital cellular phone services, thereby allowing them to deliver quality telecommunications services to sparsely populated areas. Yet European companies and governments tend to be far more conservative in their rates of acceptance of teleworking, even though the European Commission has been seriously promoting telework since the early 1990s. Therefore, I think that the forecast shown in Figure 13.2 may be too high for the next few years. In fact, my initial estimates for teleworking in the European Union countries had to be revised downward to match 1994 survey data.

Clearly, the U.S. has by far the largest number of teleworkers at present (and this graph only includes U.S. telecommuters), but it may be overtaken in numbers by the rest of the OECD countries around the year 2008, provided that these countries live up to their potential.

➤ Latin America and the Caribbean

This group includes most of the non-European Spanish- and Portuguese-speaking countries. Long saddled with the stereotype of "banana" dictatorships and general backwardness, the trend toward market-oriented democracy has been strong in all but one of these countries in recent years. Aided by capital inflows from the OECD countries, this group is beginning to develop the level of infrastructure necessary for widespread availability of telework. However, serious economic problems and deficiencies in the educational systems of several countries—exacerbated by high population

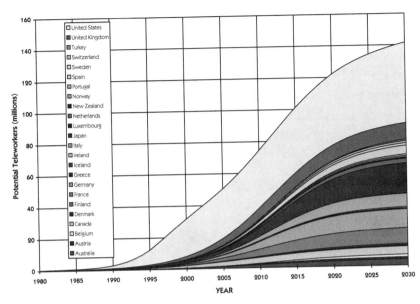

Figure 13.2 Projected growth of telework in the OECD countries.

growth rates—may be significant deterrents. Still, even a small, well-educated fraction of a very large population, such as Brazil's, can constitute a major force in the global labor market. Figure 13.3 shows my projections for the region.

➤ Eastern Europe

This group includes all of the countries within the former Soviet Union, as well as the so-called middle-European countries. The dominant country in the future of telework in this region is Russia, as one might expect.

A conventional way of looking at the prospects might point out that the Eastern European group actually includes most of northern Asia, with its huge expanses of sparsely settled land. Yet, with the implementation of global satellite data networks in the next few years, low population densities (and therefore low likelihood of wired interconnection) in those areas may not be a very strong deterrent to telework.

Furthermore, the former Soviet bloc countries generally have well-educated populations. This will allow them to be major competitors in the telework markets of the future, always assuming

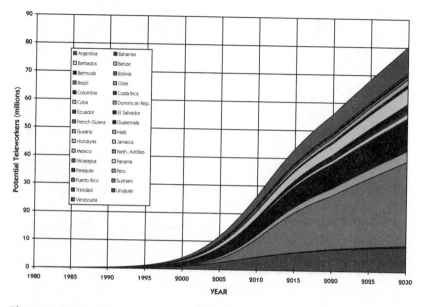

Figure 13.3 Projected growth of telework in Latin American and Caribbean countries.

that the economic and political systems of the region support such activities. My estimate of the growth of telework in this group is shown in Figure 13.4.

➤ Asia Pacific Region

This set includes South Korea, Thailand and most of the non-continental pacific countries except Japan. It also includes Hong Kong since, although now a part of the Peoples Republic of China, Hong Kong is a major economic power in its own right. These countries for the most part are rapidly making the transition from less-developed to developed economies even though, in 1998, some are experiencing serious economic setbacks.

The Philippines, for example, is already a source of programming and data entry services for the rest of the world. Singapore is already a major telecommunications hub in Southeast Asia and, together with Malaysia and Indonesia, forms a major economic force in that part of the world. Indonesia, with a projected population of nearly 240 million by 2010, is rapidly urbanizing. All of these countries have major traffic congestion problems but only

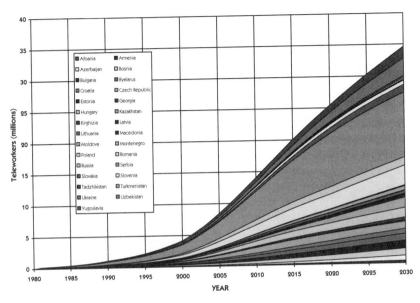

Figure 13.4 Projected growth of telework in Eastern Europe.

just now are most developing the telecommunications infrastructures—and organizational attitudes necessary for adopting telework, with Singapore, Johore Bahru, and Kuala Lumpur leading the way. Although many of these countries have authoritarian political systems, that has not appeared to impede economic progress significantly.[3] Further, each of these countries has a growing middle class. My estimate of the growth of telework in this part of the world is shown in Figure 13.5. By 2030, Indonesia, the Philippines, South Korea and Taiwan should be the primary players, with just over 30 million teleworkers for the entire region, if this forecast proves accurate.

➤ South Asia

This region comprises the Indian subcontinent plus Afghanistan. Just from population considerations alone, India is likely to be the

---

[3]The political unrest in Indonesia in 1998 offers some interesting contrasts. Although Indonesia has a low GDP per capita, it has two communication satellites, and with potential Internet access from all of its 13,000+ islands. An important factor in the overthrow of the Suharto regime was the use of the Internet by the students to organize their activities.

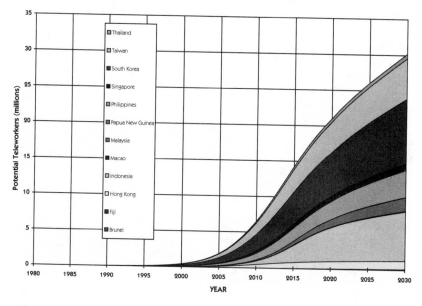

Figure 13.5 Projected growth of telework in the Asia Pacific region.

leader in the growth of telework in this region. Further, since English is a first or second language for most educated people in the region, and English is by far the most common language of Internet commerce, the inclusion of India in global information trade should be relatively painless. Already, Indian software developers are routinely teleworking for firms in the U.S. and Europe. As with the other countries with large populations, it is not necessary for all the population to be literate and numerate. If even 10% of the population of a country of 1 billion inhabitants are information workers at an educational level that approximates that of developed countries, then there is also the potential for at least 50 million teleworkers added to the world supply. These sorts of considerations are included in the calculations behind Figure 13.6.

➤ Asia Planned Economies

The socialist, central-government-ruled economies form the next group, comprising Asian countries entirely. These countries historically have been low achievers in a technological development sense, and are among the poorest in the world on a per capita

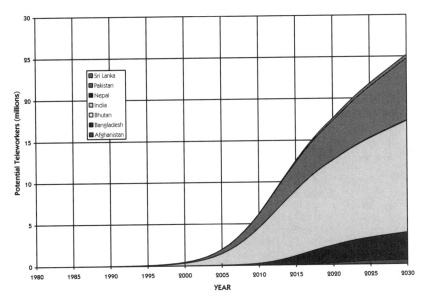

Figure 13.6 Projected growth of telework in the South Asia region.

basis.[4] Nevertheless, at least some of these countries, particularly China, are beginning to modernize at a rapid pace. China is also exerting considerable pressure on reducing population growth as a means of ensuring that expanding population does not negate the effects of economic development. Even so, China, with its largely agricultural workforce, may face a serious crisis in food supply as industrialization swallows up farmland. If per capita grain consumption rises along with the standard of living, as is most likely, then China's shortfall in grain production could reach the equivalent of "the world's entire 1994 grain exports," according to the World Watch Institute.[5]

What does this have to do with teleworking? Extrapolation of historical trends does not work if there are great intervening discrepancies, such as famines, earthquakes, and other such disasters, natural or otherwise. Figure 13.7 shows the forecast assuming that

---

[4] The Peoples Republic of China, with the highest gross domestic product per capita of the group, ranks 123rd of 146.

[5] Lester Brown. *Averting A Global Food Crisis.* Technology Review, vol. 98, No. 8, p. 50.

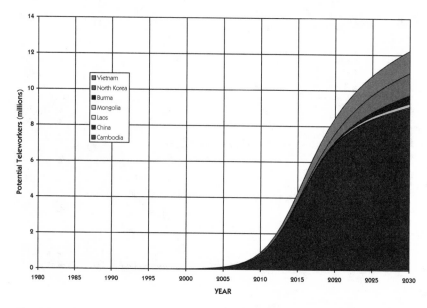

Figure 13.7 Projected growth of telework among the Asian planned economies.

no such crisis occurs. (The South Asia forecast also assumes that there is no nuclear war starting between India and Pakistan.)

➤ Africa and the Mid-East

This final sector includes all of Africa and the Middle Eastern countries. The region is characterized by very low economic situations in much of central and northern Africa and a great variety of types—and levels of stability—of governments. The anticipated leaders in technological growth and number of teleworkers (according to the model) are Algeria, Egypt, Israel, Nigeria, Syria, and South Africa, although the total number of teleworkers in the region is not expected to reach 1997 U.S. levels until after 2017. A possible exception is Angola, which, because of its oil and mineral wealth, may experience faster growth than is forecast in the current model. The composite results of the model (not broken down by country this time because of printing difficulties) are shown in Figure 13.8.

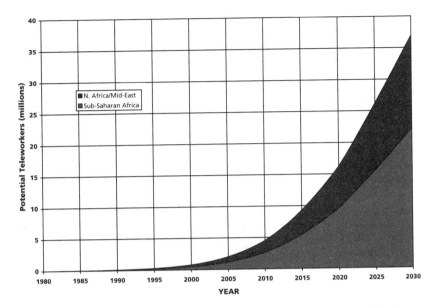

Figure 13.8 Projected growth of telework in Africa and the Mid-East.

■ CONSEQUENCES

So what does all this global carryings-on mean to you as any sort of manager? As the saying goes, where you stand depends on where you sit. If you are the Chief Executive Officer or the CIO of a multinational organization involved in the information sector of the global economy, then the preceding sections should give you some thoughts for your long-range strategies, both for market and resource development. If you are mid-level manager and/or professional exploring potential job opportunities, then start to think globally. If you are a budding tele-entrepreneur, thinking about new ways of doing business, use this material to help explore the options for the future.

➤ The Growth Trends

All of the results from the available data and my models of the future point to one conclusion: telework will steadily increase as a work mode over the next few decades, possibly to the point where it will become invisible; it won't even be distinguished from more

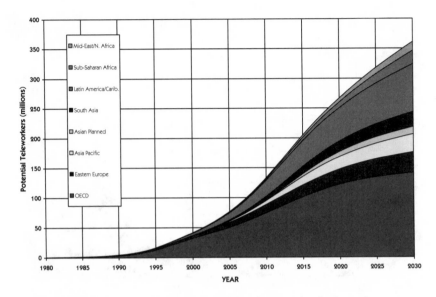

Figure 13.9 Projected worldwide growth of telework.

traditional forms of work. The rates of growth will vary considerably in different parts of the world, but the composite picture is shown in Figure 13.9. The OECD countries will still have the majority of teleworkers until after 2012, according to this nominal forecast. After that time Eastern Europe and the Latin American countries will be the dominant non-OECD players (unless they become OECD members by that time).

The Telecommunications Industry

A fundamental requirement for the rapid growth of telework is low telecommunications prices. The global telecommunications industry, historically comprising monopolistic, mostly government operated, organizations concentrating on voice telecommunications, is about to be transformed by deregulation[6] and competition. Although voice traffic will still constitute a major part of message traffic, data communications will grow to be the dominant component.

---

[6] Actually, *de*regulation is somewhat of a misnomer. The idea is to eliminate regulations that support monopolistic practices while retaining or enabling regulation that promotes free competition.

For years the telephone monopolies have set their prices to provide high profit margins on business, long-distance and international calls, partly to subsidize local residential and rural traffic. Yet the cost of carrying business and long-distance calls has dropped to little more—and often less—than that of residential service. Tariffs on international calls are far beyond the cost of making them. All this is to change, as a consequence of the 1997 World Trade Organization agreement, beginning in 1998. Also, the explosion of the Internet is transforming telecommunications rate structures, further reducing costs.

Although the traditional telephone monopolies will attempt to slow the liberalization process and impede the inroads of smaller, younger competitors, they will not prevail. Competition will grow at every level of service and for every scope of coverage, driving down prices and increasing the options for businesses and consumers. Large organizations that own their own telecom networks may lease spare capacity to resellers, just as they leased spare computer capacity in prior years. If the technology of using the electrical power system for Internet access becomes a practical reality, then an entirely new set of competitors will enter the telecommunications market. As the various global low altitude satellite systems come on line by 2002 (or so) yet another option will be available. The idea of location independence will change from speculation to reality.

At least that's the theory. In practice the road may not be quite that smooth. The 1996 Telecommunications Act in the U.S., designed to foster competition in the telecommunications market, has had mixed results so far, with fewer not more, competitors as a consequence of the merger of some of the "Baby Bells." Similar mergers and partnerships on a global scale (such as MCI and WorldCom) further cloud the competitive horizon.

But the Internet has opened Pandora's box: because there's no there there, the Internet continually escapes capture by any one organization. It keeps offering alternative, low cost telecommunications to all comers, whatever their location. As voice and video technologies become perfected over the 'Net they will help force competition on even the most reluctant monopolies.

Telecommuting

As countries develop, and individual incomes grow, one of the first major purchases of the wealthier families is some form of motorized personal transportation; from scooters to cars. Consequently, like the U.S., much of the early development of telework in most of these countries will be triggered by urban traffic problems. That is most of it will be telecommuting. No large city in the world is devoid of traffic congestion, with many cities in each of these sectors experiencing daily gridlock. As countries become more environmentally aware, the air pollution resulting from the rapid expansion of traffic will also cause pressure for faster adoption of telecommuting. Those companies that are first adopters of telecommuting will reap the benefits described in previous chapters.

International Trade

The more general forms of telework will expand alongside, or even ahead of telecommuting in many countries. Singapore, for example, has long had more jobs than workers, very stringent automobile use laws, and has developed telework connections as a result. The software production capabilities in India, Taiwan, and the Philippines, will grow and be emulated by other countries. At the same time, the demand for information products developed elsewhere will also grow in these countries.

Telework trade will be a particularly critical area in global economics. Whether telework is seen as a threat or an opportunity depends on where you stand. The chief factor to keep in mind is that labor costs tend to be the dominant costs in information work, with information services (particularly telecommunications) and computer-related expenses a close second. The primary differences between countries are likely to be labor skills and costs, and telecommunications prices. Here are some simple rules for the future.

Rule 1: Low Skill Levels Imply Low Demand and Income, High Levels of Competition. This may be a primary option in developing countries that have large populations of unskilled workers who can compete globally only by undercutting wage demands of workers in more developed countries. This is the dominant model in shifting manufacturing production from high-wage to low-wage countries, provided that the new workers can be trained easily and economically for whatever level of automation is available to them. However, the usual scenario is that the workers in the low-cost country increase their skills to the point where wage demands increase. Often this results in transferal of the production to a new country with lower wages and less skilled people. The business model for this form of trade is: find acceptable skills at the lowest total cost. In telework, this usually is applied to routine data entry operations.

Rule 2: High Skill Levels Imply High Demand and Income, Low(er) Levels of Competition. While Rule 1 applies largely to the work flow from less developed to more developed countries, Rule 2 is two-way. The so-called services trade (mostly information work) is a growing part of U.S. international trade. Expertise in any field of reasonable complexity is usually fairly rare and commands a higher price than lesser expertise. Countries lacking local/national expertise must find it elsewhere. As developing countries begin to expand their economies, they will need tele-expertise from the developed world. Similarly, as developing countries produce their own expertise, as India has done in abundance, they will be able to export telework at prices that may be more competitive with the internal prices in developed countries. Unfortunately, our work on modeling those telework flow scenarios is as yet incomplete.

Rule 3: Technology Will Give Low Cost Global Access to Most Skills. This rule simply emphasizes the main point of telework: distance is no object. The growth of telecommunications technology, especially ground and satellite wireless communications, coupled with the Internet is making the distance between participants in a communication a matter of indifference, except as the transaction is distorted by government regulation. That is, the price of communication will be a small part of the total cost of most telework transactions. English has become the de facto language of commerce worldwide so that, even though there are occasional bizarre misunderstandings, language barriers will continue to fall.

Rule 4: Skills Must Be Continually Upgraded for the Survivors. As location independence becomes a reality for more of the world's inhabitants, so will the need for continuing upgrading of one's personal skills. In a world of truly open markets, telework brokers will have global catalogs of available expertise, include language-specific skills, all of which will be accessible on the Internet. Although it will take some time—decades—before global telework trade stabilizes, eventually the point will be reached where fees commanded are primarily a function of the skills of the teleworker.

Rule 5: The Demand for Authentication Will Increase. As employers begin increasingly to go beyond their immediate localities to hire workers they will have the same uncertainties as the first tele-managers: how do I know I'll get what I bargained for? This uncertainty is exacerbated as the employer ventures into areas where employees have different cultures and native languages. Hence, the demand for honest brokers will increase. These individuals/agencies will provide some level of certification and support to their clients; to the employers that the teleworkers are competent, and to the teleworkers that they will get paid.[7]

■ THE BOTTOM LINE

The increased flexibility of the new work arrangements—together with decreasing telecommunications prices—will spur the development of the new organizational forms described in Chapter 11. The net result will be a rapidly expanding global information marketplace; multilingual, multicultural, and ripe with possibilities.

For those who wish to preserve the status quo, this is likely to be seen as an expanding threat. For those who seek adventure, remember that the future starts today.

---

[7] For some months I have been watching the interchanges on the European Tele-work Forum *(http://www.eto.org.uk/)* where the discussion—usually among independent teleworkers—often began with the need for such brokers and ended with various attempts to set up the rudiments of such services in Europe.

Appendix A
Supervisor's Telecommuting Check List

To ensure that your telecommuting employee is properly acclimated to the Company Telecommuting Demonstration Project,
the following checklist has been provided to you to follow during
the orientation process. Employees who work only from telework
center offices need not comply with items 4 and 6:

Subject	Date Reviewed
1. The employee has read and understood the explanatory materials in the TeleGuide.	_____
2. The employee has reviewed and signed the Telecommuter's Agreement form prior to actual participation in the project.	_____
3. The employee has been provided with a schedule of his or her work hours or guidelines for work hours. Consistent with Division rules and bargaining union contracts, all requests for overtime to be worked or use of sick leave, vacation, compensatory time off, or any other type of leave, must be approved in advance by the supervisor.	_____
4. Employee has been issued equipment as listed in the attached Exhibit A.[1] (Note: To be included as appropriate.)	_____

---

[1] Exhibit A is simply a list of the company's equipment and/or software that is the
employee's responsibility to protect and care for in his or her tele-office.

5. Performance expectations were reviewed and jointly agreed upon. _____

6. The employee is familiar with minimum re-quirements for safe and adequate office space at home and asserts that they have been met. _____

I have reviewed the above listed items with _____
Please Print

prior to his or her participation in the Telecommuting Demon-stration Project.

_____   _____
Date   *Supervisor*

Appendix B
Telecommuter's Agreement

In order to determine where and how telecommuting is a viable work alternative for the Company it is critical that specific data be collected from the participants in the Company Telecommuting Demonstration Project.

I understand that as a condition of my participating in the Company Telecommuting Demonstration Project I am responsible for providing the project leader with certain information discussed below. I further understand that my failure to provide this data within the specified time frames could result in my being removed from the project and returned to my former working status.

I also understand that I am required to adhere to the guidelines set forth in the *TeleGuide* and specifically to the following requirements. If I fail to do this my participation in the project will be withdrawn.

1. If I telecommute from home I am expected to keep my home telecommuting office as clean and free from obstructions as if it were my primary Company office. If I have a work-related accident at home, I am expected to report it promptly as if the accident had occurred in my primary Company office. If a third party is injured at my home in connection with my telecommuting work, I will report the accident and/or injury promptly to my supervisor.

2. It is my responsibility to ensure that any Company equipment and software used in my job are used in businesslike conditions, whether at home or in a telework center. This includes protecting the Company equipment and software against abuse or other violation of existing Company rules concerning protection of its property. I may *not* use

Company equipment or software for purposes in contradiction to Company, city, state, or federal laws, rules and/or regulations, or copyrights, nor may I or my family or friends use Company equipment or software to perform work for other employers.

3. Upon the receipt of authorization, I may use my own equipment and/or software to telecommute. Company assumes no responsibility for the maintenance or repair of my own equipment or software.

4. If there are any equipment or software failures while I am working at home, I am responsible for immediately informing my supervisor. I also understand that I may be asked to return to the primary office until repairs are completed or a substitute has been provided. I further understand that any repairs made by the Company will be performed at a location designated by the Company.

5. I will protect Company information and data against loss or misuse in accordance with all applicable Company rules and regulations, and with at least the same level of care as is used in the primary office.

6. I understand that I will not get travel expenses for the times when I have to come in to my primary Company office for meetings. Mileage and per diem for work-related travel will be calculated from the primary Company office, home telecommuting office, or telework telecommuting office, as determined under existing guidelines.

7. I must *average* at least one *full* day per week telecommuting over a six-month period to remain in the project.

8. My specific telecommuting work periods will be arranged with my supervisor and may be revised at intervals throughout the project. All other work rules and approvals are as already established and remain in effect.

9. At times during the course of the project I will be asked to complete a questionnaire covering work and telecommuting-related activities. These times will be: once near or just prior to the beginning of telecommuting; once near the midpoint of the project; and once near the end of the formal part of the project.

Only the research team consisting of the Project Leader and those individuals conducting the project evaluation will have access to the detailed individual telecommuters' questionnaire and survey results. Company management participating in the project will have access to the statistical results and will, of course, be the ultimate decision makers for individual changes during the course of the project. All sensitive information will be kept strictly confidential; only aggregate results of the demonstration project will be released to anyone.

[The following paragraphs are for cases where the company wants to get detailed information on the effects of the telecommuting.]

10. I will participate in a one-week logging session of my, and my family's, daily car use. [This provision is for cases where the company needs to demonstrate reductions in car use.]

11. I will keep a monthly log of my utility bills (gas, telephone, and electricity) if I telecommute from home. [This provision is for cases where the company wishes to identify the energy costs of telecommuting.]

12. I am to report any problems I may be having with—or because of—telecommuting to my supervisor (such as relatives or friends always popping in and causing distractions from work, feeling isolated and needing more interaction with my co-workers, etc.). I will also participate in occasional discussion group sessions for resolving these or other telecommuting-related problems.

13. If I have any questions regarding any of the above or regarding telecommuting, I will check with my supervisor.

I have read the TeleGuide and this document. I understand and accept the responsibility of adhering to the conditions set out above and in the TeleGuide and to providing the above listed information as a condition of participation in the Company Telecommuting Demonstration Project. I further understand that if I fail to adhere to these conditions my participation in the project may be withdrawn. I understand that changes in assignment may cause my removal from the project. I understand that I may be removed from the project at any time at the discretion of my supervisor.

_____   _____
Employee Signature   *Date*

_____   _____
Supervisor Signature   *Date*

Appendix C
Department Telecommuting Policies

The following items governing telecommuting are to be filled in by your own department.

■ EQUIPMENT

In this section should be a list of the specific equipment normally provided either by the employee or by the Company in order for the employee to telecommute from home. The list should include, but not be limited to, personal computers, computer terminals, modems, printers, facsimile machines, typewriters, photocopy machines, and furniture. (Note that Exhibit A of the supervisor's telecommuting checklist [see Appendix A] may also include special equipment and/or software.)

■ EMPLOYEE RESPONSIBILITIES

This covers any general, department-specific responsibilities of telecommuters for care and handling of equipment, including any requirements for insurance coverage.

■ EQUIPMENT AND/OR SOFTWARE INSTALLATION

The Company is willing to install equipment in telecommuters' homes, or to subcontract such services. The costs will be billed to the user department. Each department should decide whether to use these services, provide its own, or leave any equipment installation to the ingenuity of the telecommuters. A similar situation prevails with software and the information services department.

■ EQUIPMENT MAINTENANCE AND REPAIR

In general, departments are expected to maintain and repair their own equipment and software, regardless of its location. However, policies may differ as to who should provide maintenance and repair of telecommuter-owned software and equipment that is used for Company business. The department's policy should be stated here.

■ WORK RULES

This includes any department-specific rules on work hours and/or availability periods, meeting attendance, reporting schedules, and the like. It does *not* include the details of the employee's job requirements. That is covered in the *Detailed Work Agreement*.

■ RETURNING TO WORK

This covers any department-specific rules for termination of telecommuting.

Appendix D
Detailed Work Agreement

This is to include any detailed agreements arrived at by you as the supervisor and your telecommuting employees during, or subsequent to, the joint telecommuting training session. The period covered, to be filled in above, is whatever is comfortable for both of you. It can range from a day or two to several months, depending on the level of autonomy to be assigned to the telecommuter. The form should be completed for each telecommuter assigned to you.

■ PERFORMANCE EVALUATION CRITERIA

What objective[1] criteria are there, such as number and quality of reports completed, documents reviewed, audits performed, contacts made, lines of bug-free computer code produced, transactions processed, etc. In this section just list what they are. Don't get hung up on numerical criteria if they are not appropriate to the job.

➤ Specific Work Objectives and Milestones

For example, in developing a plan the objectives might be: contacting or meeting with the key people affected by the plan; outlining its contents; developing agreement on the issues; suggesting and selecting approaches; developing consensus on the optimal approaches; drafting the plan; coordinating review of the draft; developing the final plan.

---

[1] The difficulty, of course, is in deciding what's objective and what's subjective, particularly where issues of quality are concerned. What is most important at this point is that both supervisor and supervisee agree on whatever the criteria are.

Milestones might be: meetings concluded; outline produced; first draft completed; final plan produced; each with an associated date.

➤ Activities to Be Performed

This is a list of the specific activities that must be performed to meet the objectives above. It can be as terse or as prolix as you and your employee wish.

➤ Anticipated Results

What are the end products of all this? In the example above, it's a plan plus a state of mind (consensus, motivation) of the participants.

Appendix E
Tools for Assessing the Future

Chapter 13 provides an overview of the nominal possibilities for the global future of telework. This appendix provides some more details about how you can design your own analysis. The future comprises an infinite number of trends, each of which is in turn composed of an infinite sequence of connected events. The ability to forecast the future weather, your own life, or that of your company, depends on how well you can estimate the events and their associated trends that are most important.

■ CATEGORIES OF TRENDS AND EVENTS

However, before jumping into a full-fledged attempt on the future, let's examine some of the types of trends and events with which we have to be concerned. These groupings are admittedly somewhat arbitrary, but they are selected partially to point toward sources of information about the nature of the past and present from which the future evolves.

➤ Society

Some of this category is easily assessable. It includes such factors as world/national/regional/local demographics, size of the work-force, education (years of schooling), and the like. Most of this is available from various government sources, at least for the U.S. The data tend to be less easily available and/or reliable in some other countries.

Other factors may be less accessible. For example, group or individual attitudes toward X, customs, consumer demand, educational attainment of various sorts (particularly education outside the formal system), and communication patterns.

➤ Technology

This group is by far the easiest to forecast, at least for a decade or so. The reason for this is that most of the technologies that will be in common use ten to twenty years from now already exist in a lab somewhere. The trick is in estimating the adoption rates of the technologies, which often depend more on the human equation than the physics. Information technologies (including many bio-technologies) have the highest sustained growth rates and are the dominant force in influencing other trends and events.

➤ Economy

The economy, whatever that is, is usually a perfect example of the need for better chaos theory. The one-handed economist is an oxymoron. Nevertheless, trends in the general economic climate, and many of the economic details are powerful influences on almost everything else. Failure to acknowledge or take account of economic trends and events has led to disaster for many companies and governments.

Key economic trends include the composition of the workforce and employment demand, GNP and GDP, stock and bond prices, etc. Here, as is the case for societal trends, substantial amounts of data are fairly accessible.

➤ Laws and Regulation

The legal and regulatory environments can place constraints on the growth of trends or on the occurrence of events. They can also accelerate the growth of trends and increase the likelihood of events. For example, air quality laws and regulations in the U.S. act to inhibit the use of private automobiles for commuting to work. At the same time, they act to increase the rate of adoption of telecommuting, shifting the "market share" from one set of technologies to another. Similarly, telecommunications regulations can act to enhance or impede other trends.

While information on the existence of various laws and regulations tends to be readily available, information on their influences on other events and trends often is more problematic.

➤ Marketplace and Competition

This category covers the actual composition, growth, and decay of various markets and products and the competitive influences thereon. Data on markets and competition, while available from numerous sources, are often of questionable quality and reliability. Hence, one of the main challenges in this important category is finding trustworthy sources.

➤ Organization Structure and Operations

This category deals with the questions of how organizations work: how they are structured, how work is accomplished, how organizational units interact among themselves, with suppliers, and with customers. "Downsizing" and "outsourcing" are organizational trends that have been growing for at least a decade. Also in this category are such things as trends in the size and geographical distribution of organizations, the formation of new types, such as network organizations, or modes such as hoteling and other forms of teleworking.

■ SCENARIOS AND ALTERNATIVE FUTURES

A natural response at this point is: Why do I have to know all this? After all, my job is to make next week's payroll; why should I worry about things that may not happen for years? The answer to that depends on your planning horizon. If your job consists solely of getting through the day you probably wouldn't be reading this in the first place. If your present or anticipated job has to do with plotting a course for your company in today's turbulent times—and you also want to be doing so ten or twenty years from now—then this is important. Successful strategy formulation requires accurate assessments of the possibilities of the future.

➤ Future Funnels

As those first few statements about the future implied, our uncertainty about the future[1] increases with distance. We know pretty well how last week turned out, we may know how today will finish, next week is a little more iffy, next month even more so. As to next year, or ten years from now, who knows?

The bad news is that the future is a collection of funnels, with today at the spout and the distant future out at the wide end. Inside each funnel are all the possible paths that a particular series of events—a trend—may take. The width of the funnel at the

---

[1] Or with the past, for that matter.

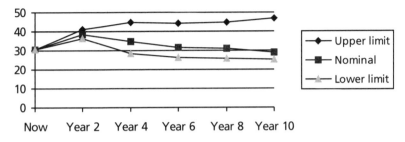

Figure E.1 The "future funnel."

distant end is a measure of our uncertainty in estimating those paths.

However, the good news also is that the future is a collection of funnels. It is not completely indeterminate; it is not a hemisphere starting with the present. Some things just won't happen in a given time horizon, others are certain to happen. Our task is to see how tightly we can specify the outlines of the funnels. Figure E.1 illustrates the idea in two dimensions.

Further, we need to realize that the future comprises two components:

1. Things we can't do anything about, like the weather and earthquakes.
2. Things whose outcome we can influence, like investment decisions.

We need to know about both of these, either to realize how they might influence our personal futures regardless of what we do, or to estimate how we can alter the course of the future to increase the likelihood that it will evolve the way we want it to.

Several things are illustrated in Figure E.1:

➤ First, future trends rarely unfold as straight lines; as linear (or exponential) extrapolations from the past.

➤ Second, there usually is a "nominal" or most likely future, somewhat like a strange attractor in chaos theory parlance.

➤ Third, there tend to be upper and lower bounds to the future, beyond which it is extremely[2] unlikely that a particular trend will go.

---

[2] Sometimes a number can be associated with "extremely" that indicates the non-zero probability that the trend will go beyond it. This recalls the lines from Gilbert and Sullivan's *Mikado:* "What never? No, never! What never? Well . . . hardly ever."

➤ Fourth, the upper and lower bounds need not be symmetrical about the nominal case.

➤ Fifth, pivotal events act to alter the course of trends. That's why they're called pivotal. Such an event is anticipated in Year 2 of the trend in Figure E.1.

Usually a first step in assessing your future is to identify the trends, in all of the categories above, that are relevant to that future. Next, estimate the course of the trends over a sufficiently long term; that is, until it no longer matters or it becomes completely unguessable. Then, estimate what events could occur to alter the course of the trends. Having accomplished these exercises, you are ready to begin some serious crystal ball gazing.

➤ Cross-Impacts

Another important fact about the future, as well as the present, is that **everything seems to be connected to everything else,** although the strength of the ties between any two events/trends may be imperceptible. Thus, as your next step in divining the future, it is necessary to estimate the impact of the occurrence of event A upon the likelihood of occurrence of event B in trend C. Then if event B occurs, partiality as a result of the prior occurrence of event A's occurrence, what is the effect on the likelihood of occurrence of events D and E? What if the anticipated event B (or A) doesn't occur, or occurs later than expected? What then?

In short, what are the key cross-impacts in your future?

Events and trends don't ordinarily just happen at random, although it may seem like it at times. Usually any important trend is accompanied by a series of pivotal underlying events and trends. Computers are important today partially because some labor problems in 18th century France (a growing trend) prompted Basile Bouchon and, later, Joseph Marie Jacquard to develop punched-card-controlled looms in their textile factories (pivotal events). Much of the contemporary information industry owes some part of its existence to a laboratory curiosity assembled by John Bardeen, Walter Brattain and William Schockley at Bell Telephone Laboratories (a pivotal event). Because it was neither a conventional conductor or a resistor, but somewhere in between, they called it a *trans*istor. The consequent development of microelectronics (a major trend) has made possible lunar landings, Star Trek, the Global Positioning System, the

Internet, declining population growth in developed countries, and Mutant Teenage Ninja Turtles.

Detailed cross-impact analysis involves setting up a matrix (or successive series of matrices depicting successive times in the future) of events and trends. Each row of the matrix starts with an event heading. The column headings indicate the probability of occurrence of the event and the names of other events and trends. Each intersection in the matrix indicates the probability of occurrence of the impacted event—or the nominal change in slope of the impacted trend, given that the originating event has occurred. This provides a better feel for these often complex interrelationships.

➤ Scenario Development

All of the preceding is a buildup for creating scenarios: descriptions of alternative futures. A scenario, as the title implies, is simply a play-by-play description of the future. Starting with today, the future is described at several regular (or reasonable) intervals up to the end date, some days, weeks, months, years, or decades hence. The description derives from an interval-by-interval analysis of what has just "happened" as you venture into the future. The scenario—or the latter portions of it—is the most common way of presenting future possibilities to more general audiences.

The usual quantitative scenario recipe goes like this. (Figure E.2 gives an example.)

1. Start with today. Describe the principal characteristics of today that are important to you.
2. Now, jump to the first stop in the future; say, next year. What is the range in status of the important trends?
3. What pivotal events have "occurred?"

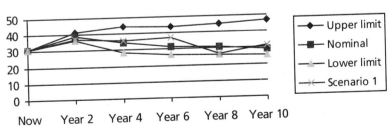

Figure E.2 The future funnel plus a scenario.

4. What has been the effect of those on the trends and on the likelihood of other events?

5. The answer to step 4 gives you a reason to pick the "actual" value of each trend for the end of that interval. So, now you have a new description of the status of your world at that point in the future.

6. Repeat steps 2 through 5 for the subsequent intervals to develop the complete scenario.

This particular method gives you one specific path through the future. Its utility is that it demonstrates that the future never exactly follows the original trend lines, but tends to wander about them. If you want to get a more global view of the possibilities, it is necessary to repeat the recipe many times—several thousand in the case of scenarios involving many trends and/or events. Known as Monte Carlo scenario development, this task is best left to computers.[3]

■ TOOLS FOR FUTURE CLIMBING

Throughout this discussion there has been the implicit assumption that somehow you already know the shape of the trends and the occurrence and impact statistics for the pivotal events. In real life this is rarely the case, except for problems that are so well defined as not to be interesting. If you wish to come to grips with the future it is usually advisable to use some formal tools to help shape your understanding.[4]

➤ Formal Mathematical Models

Every strategically useful description of the future involves some quantitative descriptions. We need the numbers to help assess the relative merits of the alternatives presented to us. Formal mathematical models can help in this process. They are used to generate

---

[3] Usually, this is done with a customized computer program. However, an add-on to Microsoft's Excel for Windows, called (what else?) Crystal Ball, can do this task to some extent. In conjunction with Strategic Futures International, we have developed a program, called Serious Scenarios, that does Monte Carlo scenario computations.

[4] For a much more detailed overview of these tools, see *Technological Forecasting for Decision Making* by Joseph P. Martino (North Holland: Amsterdam, 1983).

specific trend lines and can be used in a piecewise manner,[5] thanks to computers, to account for the impacts of pivotal events.

Formal mathematical models are equations that describe a particular type of future behavior. An example is the so-called logistic (or epidemic) curve that fairly well describes a huge variety of real phenomena from inception to growth to maturity to decay. Exponential curves may be good for relatively short term forecasting (nothing grows exponentially forever). Even straight lines may work in some situations. Formal models are most useful where the trends are fairly well constrained; that is, not subject to many random-appearing alterations in course.

➤ Statistical Methods

For more complicated trends, statistical tools may be the choice. An entire sub-industry uses statistical methods to anticipate the moods of the stock market (program trading being one of the fruits of these efforts). Generally, the objective is to curve-fit; that is, identify some sort of formal mathematical model that matches the sequence of means of a statistical analysis of a train of past events. Like the case of the other formal mathematical models, the hope is that the nature of the events won't change during the post-data forecasting interval.

➤ Delphi

Statistical methods and formal mathematical models are fine when you have quality historical data and/or an accurate idea about how a trend will unfold.[6] But what about those cases where there are no data—the trend hasn't begun yet—and you don't have a clue as to its likely course of development? In these situations, the Delphi method is often the principal tool.

The fundamental principle of Delphi is: Ask the experts what they think. The process is a little more complicated than that. First, it is important that you ask certified experts; people with established track records of guessing right in their chosen fields. Second, to minimize the danger of one expert unduly influencing the others, do *not* bring them together, either in a face-to-face meeting or in a teleconference version thereof; ask your questions via some

---

[5] That is, with the parameters of the model changing from interval to interval.
[6] For example, the trend in question may be expected to be very similar in shape to a previous, well-defined trend. This is often the case for technological trends.

form of private correspondence (a questionnaire) and keep their answers anonymous. Third, ask multiple experts for each set of events and trends, compile the results and send them to your panel, asking for further comments. If there are any large discrepancies and/or differences of opinion, ask for clarification (sometimes you have to reformulate the questions). Keep doing this until you have reached general agreement about the shape of the trends (including upper and lower limits) and the numbers for the pivotal events.[7] Once you have the events and trends nailed down, do the same for the cross-impacts.

■ BUILDING STRATEGIES

All of the above is simply preparation for the real purpose of futures research: developing strategy and tactics for your organization. Consider the term **strategy:** a plan for realizing a specific goal; putting yourself in a position where you can take best advantage of the opportunities that arise. Adapting yourself to the future.

This brings us to another important rule: **There is no THE future.** A particular scenario is not a description of what WILL happen; it is a view of one particular train of events (among an infinity of possibilities) that is almost guaranteed not to happen in detail.

Does this mean that developing scenarios is a waste of time, since they never really turn out that way? Not at all. Scenario development, particularly repetitive scenario development, is extremely useful in testing your strengths and weaknesses, your ability to adjust to the REAL future as it unfolds.

The reason for all this modeling and scenario development activity is so that you can develop a map of all the rocks, shoals, and currents of the part of the future that will affect you. Particularly important is the use of these techniques to detect surprises.

This results in the mention of another rule: **When you are formulating events for your scenario development, make sure you include as many as you can think of that, while they may be very unlikely, have high impact.** Earthquakes may not happen all that often but, if you're in one it's nice to be prepared to cope with it. Ditto for opportunities of a lifetime. The Gulf War strategy (ours, not Saddam Hussein's) was based on a huge series of prior

---

[7]The numbers are: What is the likelihood of the event having occurred by $time_1$, $time_2$, $time_3$, etc.

"games" such as those outlined here. Intel apparently didn't bother with this sort of exercise prior to reacting to the Pentium floating point unit problem.

The description above of scenario development needs another step. Call it 5a:

5a.   After reviewing the result of the scenario increment, ask yourself: What can we do to change things so that the next step is more in line with our goals? What will it cost? What are the risks/benefits? Therefore, what should we do now?

This is where you can formulate strategic options and test the possible impacts of your strategic decisions. In principle, it's the same as an arcade game; you are training yourself to use the tools you have to avoid dangers and arrive safely at your (possibly mobile) objective. The future holds an infinite number of possibilities. Unfortunately, your resources to cope with them are probably very finite. Therefore, they have to be allocated wisely. Gaming the future, by this sort of repetitive scenario generation and analysis can give you a tremendously heightened awareness of how your decisions can affect the outcomes.

Index